Mystery, Beauty, and Danger

"Mille D'Angeville on Mont Blanc." From Gribble, *The Early Mountaineers.*

Mystery, Beauty, and Danger

The Literature of the Mountains and
Mountain Climbing Published in English
Before 1946

Robert H. Bates, Ph.D.

Peter E. Randall Publisher
Portsmouth, New Hampshire
2000

Design: Peter E. Randall

Many of the early books about mountains and mountaineering are beautifully illustrated and produced. Because many of these volumes are now quite rare and unavailable except in specialized libraries, the author has selected representative illustrations to show the reader how the 19th and early 20th century writers and publishers enhanced their books with drawings, and in some cases, photographs. Added to the list of illustrations are three rare photographs of Everest taken by T. Howard Somervell on the same route where just three days later Mallory and Irvine disappeared in 1924. The author recently acquired these photographs from Somervell's son, Dr. D.H. Somervell, and added them to the book not only because Mallory's writting is discussed in the text but also because his body was found in 1999 not far from where these photographs were made over 75 years ago.

Peter E. Randall Publisher
Box 4726, Portsmouth, NH 03802

Distributed by
        University Press of New England
        Hanover and London

Library of Congress Cataloging-in-Publiction Data
Bates, Robert H. (Robert Hicks) 1911-
    Mystery, beauty, and danger : the literature of the mountains and mountain climbing published in English before 1946 / Robert H. Bates.
        p. cm.
    Includes bibliographical references and index.
    ISBN 0-914339-91-5 (alk. paper)
    1. English literature--History and criticism. 2. Mountains in literature.
    3. American literature--History and criticism. 4 Mountaineering in literature.
    5. Mountain life in literature. I. Title.
    PR408.M68 B38 2001
    820.9'32143--dc21

                                                                        00-059252

To Jane and George F. Russell Jr.,
close friends for half a century.

Books by Robert H. Bates

Five Miles High, with others, Editor, 1939

K2, The Savage Mountain, with Charles S. Houston, M. D., 1954

Mountain Man, The Story of Belmore Brown, 1988

The Love of Mountains is Best, 1994

Foreword

Here is the recovery of a lost thesis. I'd heard the rumours that this work existed, but it was not until Bob Bates came to England with Charlie Houston in 1999 to take by storm the 13th International Festival of Mountaineering Literature (receiving the first standing ovation in the Festival's history) that I was able to urge belated publication. Now we can all see what an important and timeless work this is.

There is still, after nearly half a century since it was written, not another book like it. It remains the most thorough and readable introduction to the literature of our sport before 1946 that has been written. Indeed, it works like a guide through an anthology of judiciously chosen extracts from books that are old friends, books we've always wanted to read, and books we have now got to read. The charm and wit of Bob Bates himself provides the perfect guide through this vibrant storehouse of the epic and the ecstatic, tragedy and triumph, mystery and misery, There is a rigorous literary evaluation being conducted through this book, but with the gentle elegance of style and generosity of spirit that is the essence of the ever-smiling Bob Bates. Now that this important book is at last published we can all climb on its shoulders and enrich our own experience of groping between mystery, beauty, and danger.

Terry Gifford, Director, International Festival of Mountaineering Literature
Reader in Literature and Environment,
Bretton Hall, University of Leeds, UK

Contents

Acknowledgments   xi

Preface   xiii

Introduction   xvii

Are They Sacred, Beautiful, or Horrible?   1

The Magic Attraction of Mont Blanc   23

Watchers From Afar   79

Climbing and Writing   125

Conclusion   191

Endnotes   19

Bibliography   207

Index   217

About the Author   229

Acknowledgments

My thanks to Professor Alfred Harbage, who in 1945, suggested that the literature of the mountains would be a fine subject for my Ph.D. thesis.

Special thanks to Faith Chase, who retyped the changed manuscript, and to Doris Troy for professional editing. Thanks to Nick Clinch, Kurt Diemberger, Terry Gifford, and Charles Houston for comments on the work, and especially to David Robertson for his very careful reading of the text and various suggestions. Bradford Washburn not only read the text but also contributed the photograph of Belmore Browne. Also thanks to Michael Chessler who suggested that I republish my thesis in book form.

Many thanks also to Dr. D. H. Somervell for providing three of his father's photographs, taken on June 24, 1924, at the highest point he reached on the north side of Mount Everest. These photographs were made just three days before Mallory and Irvine disappeared during their final attempt to reach the summit. These pictures were at the time the highest photographs ever made.

Finally, the author points out that the basic text of this book was written before 1946, and therefore some of the statements are dated and are no longer true. For instance, the statement about Mallory: "Why he and Irvine disappeared no one knows," was true when written in 1946, but not now.

Preface

IN SEPTEMBER 1941, on my return from an expedition to the St. Elias Mountains in Alaska and the Yukon Territory, during which we had tested a tent, a packboard-sled and survival rations for the U.S. Army, I received a letter from Lieutenant Colonel L.O. Grice of the Quartermaster General's Office in Washington, asking me to have dinner with him a few days later at the Essex Hotel in Boston to discuss U.S. Army needs for cold-weather or mountain operations. I accepted at once, and at the appointed time went to the hotel.

As I entered, so did a fellow of about my age, who apparently was there on the same mission. With an engaging smile and easygoing manner, he introduced himself as Paul Siple, a name I already knew. Paul was the former Boy Scout who had been selected by the Boy Scouts of America to go with Admiral Byrd on his first Antarctic expedition. Since then he had been with Byrd on all three of his expeditions, and had become a well-known expert on Antarctic exploration.

Colonel Grice greeted us warmly. He turned out to be a no-nonsense, old-time Army officer, who had worked his way up to become head of the Standardization Branch of the Quartermaster General's Office, in charge of all changes in Army clothing and equipment except for special items used by Ordnance or the Signal Corps. He already knew something about our backgrounds, at least about Siple's career in the Antarctic and my recent testing in the St. Elias Range.

When he asked us about our plans, we each said that short term we hoped to complete our theses to receive our Ph.D.'s.

Paul had an unusual thesis, for which he had already collected material in the Antarctic. He told us that during Antarctic expeditions, the part of his forehead not covered by his hat or his snow glasses frequently froze, especially on windy days, although on calm days, even when the temperature was colder, it did not. His idea was to chart the cooling effect of different combinations of cold and wind: Using a stopwatch, he had carefully recorded how quickly a cubic centimeter of water would film over with ice under variable conditions. When Grice asked Paul what he was going to call his chart, he replied that privately he simply called it "wind chill," a term widely known and understood today.

For my thesis I had done summer work in the Bodleian Library at Oxford University concerning John Aubrey, an eccentric but creative English antiquarian and theorist, who lived in the seventeenth century and was sometimes referred to by his contemporaries as "maggoty headed." He was a fascinating man and I was intrigued by him, his ideas, and a mass of largely unsorted papers, but I knew that to do justice to him would take considerable time.

Our answers to the questions Grice asked apparently satisfied him, for he said that there was great need for our experience in his office and that we soon would hear from the Quartermaster General. At that moment I did not realize that Paul and I would start working for the U.S. Army in the same office, and would be there off and on for the next four and a half years. Aubrey had to be forgotten.

In October, when I arrived at the Standardization Branch, one of my first duties was to go as an observer to the Second Infantry Division, which was undergoing winter training in northern New York State. There the commanding general asked me to stand with him as the whole division passed. All the troops were wearing standard infantry gear: long woolen overcoats and floppy, open galoshes. To me our troops looked more like soldiers of the Russian army in 1916 than what I had expected. I couldn't imagine modern infantry charging forward with flopping galoshes and long overcoats that once wet could never be dried under field conditions. Colonel Grice was right. Much change was needed to prepare the U.S. Army for potential involvement in World War II.

By the end of World War II Paul Siple and I, who had worked to improve army clothing and equipment, had become lieutenant colonels and had been honored with Legion of Merit medals. I also had a Bronze Star for work at Anzio, Italy. Neither of us was looking for an Army career, however, and so we parted in different directions. Paul's main interest was cold-weather operations, either in the Arctic or the Antarctic. He had received his doctorate and gradually became well known for his work in both areas of the world. Later, the

Siple Station at the South Pole was named for him. His death in middle age was a personal loss to me and a great loss to the country.

The war had given me fascinating experiences. Several jobs were open to me after it ended, but I decided to return to teaching and my love of what I had been doing at Exeter. Accordingly, the next step seemed to be finishing my work for the Ph.D.

While I had been in the Army, others had been working on the Aubrey material and now books on it were coming out. Also, I had become less interested in carrying out a long-term project overseas. Professor Harbage, chairman of the English department at the University of Pennsylvania, was a friend, and I spoke to him of my Ph.D. problem. He quickly asked, "What would be fun to do, something that won't take years? You've lost too much time already." That did it. "Mountains," was my answer.

The next weeks were delightful, as I began work in the comfortable library of the American Alpine Club, then situated in an old firehouse at 113 E. 90th Street in New York. In those days there was no climbing wall, but there were other attractions for armchair mountaineers: big, open stacks, good reading lights, and big, roomy lounges. I loved it all. I read through books that I had wanted to read for years but never had the time and skimmed others. Now I did have time, and I absorbed it all. In fact, the diversity of the books on my subject and the variety of their writers was fascinating. To look up references not found in the library, I also went to the New York Public Library, and before I was finished even checked a few references in the great Congressional Library in Washington and the Harvard College Library in Cambridge, Massachusetts.

What made my work in the American Alpine Club doubly pleasant was an invitation to stay with Oscar and Nellie Houston, parents of my old companion Charles Houston, at their house in Great Neck. When Professor Harbage said to do something that would be fun to do, I doubt that he realized how much fun I would have working on the thesis. When I had finished, I turned in a typed copy to the University of Pennsylvania to meet my requirements, but did not get the book printed. I had no idea that the subject would be of interest to so many people. This error is being corrected now.

"The Literature of the Mountains and of Mountain Climbers before World War II" became my thesis and this, with a minor change or two, is what I wrote. You have it here.

A DRAGON IN THE ALPS.

Some Alpine dragons were described as breathing fire, inhaling birds, and throwing off sparks "as from a red-hot horseshoe." From Gribble, *The Early Mountaineers.*

Introduction

> Old travellers saw a mountain and called it simply a hideous excrescence; but then they peopled it with monsters and demons; gnomes wriggled through its subterranean recesses; mysterious voices spoke in its avalanches; dragons winged their way across its gorges; the devil hailed the ghosts of old sinners to its lakes to be tormented; the wild huntsman issued from its deep ravines; and possibly some enchanted king sat waiting for better days in a mysterious hall beneath its rocks. Was not this merely expressing in another way the same sense of awe which we describe by calling the mountain itself sublime and beautiful[1]
>
> — Leslie Stephen

SINCE THE DAYS of Homer and Moses, mountains have stimulated men in various ways. During medieval times mountains were places of terror and mystery to avoid, and although a few daring men like Leonardo da Vinci, impelled by curiosity, visited them in the sixteenth century, it was not until two hundred years later that mountains began to attract people to see and write about them.

The first writers in English were travelers, generally young men of wealth who visited mountainous areas while on the grand tour. The writings of these men reflect general distaste and fear and are not noteworthy. At about the same time, literary figures such as Horace Walpole and Thomas Gray, and others began to travel in Switzerland, but their comments, too, reflect the general feelings of their period about natural beauties.

During the nineteenth century, attitudes changed. Writers about the mountains became far more numerous, including large numbers of amateurs and a considerable number of the better-known poets and prose writers of the day. Examining the works of both types of writers, one soon finds that the professional writers describe imaginatively and subjectively what they see, but show ignorance of what mountain areas beyond their reach are really like. Shelley, Wordsworth, Byron, Tennyson, and many other literary figures describe what they see from the valleys, but fail to understand what exists above the tree line.

About 1830, English mountain climbers began to write of their exploits in the Alps. This was the beginning of a literature of mountain climbing produced by mountain climbers, not by those who did not climb and saw the mountains only from below. The best literary work by the climbers came about the middle of the nineteenth century, when Leslie Stephen, author and mountain climber, produced delightful essays. This was the "golden age" of exploration in the Alps when Tyndall, Whymper, Wills, and others were making first ascents and writing with considerable skill about them. *Peaks, Passes and Glaciers,* a compilation of many of the outstanding stories by mountain climbers of the day, represents some of the best work of the real climbers of this period.

Among non-climbers who were influenced by the mountains in this century, Ruskin stands out, partly perhaps because he had done some mountaineering in his younger days. Other literary men who at one time or another wrote well about mountains include such diverse characters as George Meredith, Lafcadio Hearn, Robert Louis Stevenson, Hilaire Belloc, and Mark Twain.

Since the turn of the century, mountain climbers as a whole have been less subjective and more technical in their writings. Exceptions include A.F. Mummery and Geoffrey Winthrop Young and such literary figures as A.E.W. Mason, C.E. Montague, and John Buchan. Most books on recent mountain expeditions lack the charm of the *Peaks, Passes and Glaciers* days, though the *Alpine Journal* has continued to publish a high level of nontechnical prose.

It is clear that mountains, one of the great sources of inspiration, affect the climber and the non-climber very differently. They have caused each to produce accomplished work; and under their influence large numbers of amateurs have produced writing that, for brief intervals at least, shows they are moved by strong bursts of inspiration.

Are They Sacred, Beautiful, or Horrible?

Who knows no toyle can never skill of rest
Who always walks on carpet soft and gay
All silent as the emerald gulfs below,
Knows not hard hill nor likes the mountaine way
—Thomas Churchyard

B ENOIT MARTI OF BERNE, who climbed the Niesen in 1558, was surprised to find that some earlier climber had carved in Greek on the rock at the summit: the love of mountains is best.[2] Marti was overjoyed. Not only did he approve the sincere feelings so deliberately incised, but he also believed they were inscribed on the right mountain, a place of great charm and loveliness.

The assumption that your mountain of the moment is the most delightful spot in the world is one that has been shared by many climbers in wide-spread lands during the centuries since Marti's well-recorded climb, and must have been experienced by countless others before him, most of whom unfortunately never left their thoughts for posterity.

Mountains have always meant different things to different people, and for more reasons than the obvious diversity of the human intellect and emotions. For instance, the Niesen, which Marti found "charmante," probably would have appeared to him anything but delightful in another season, or in the same season during stormy weather, although it is true that with some men the mountains in winter are preferred to the mountains in summer, for both mountains and mountaineers in their moods as in their aspects have infinite

1

variety. The pages of mountain literature reflect the varying thoughts and feelings of climbers and the multiple reasons why they climb: the search for beauty, scientific curiosity, love of the unknown, the thrill of pitting one's strength against nature, the joys of companionship in testing physical and mental struggle, and often religious devotion.

Marti, for instance, goes on to say:

> Who would not admire and love places of this sort? Who would not delight to contemplate them, to visit them, to climb them?
>
> Of a truth, those who are not moved by things so beautiful deserve, in my judgment, no better names than imbeciles, fools, boobies, fishes, and slow tortoises. I am indeed powerless to describe the enchantment and instinctive love which drew me to the mountains, and which make the hours I spend upon the ridges of the Alps the happiest of my life. No walks can give greater pleasure than those I take among mountains. Even if it is novelty you seek, mountains will show it to you in abundance; for instance, plants of every kind, wonderful and brilliant in astonishing variety, wild birds found nowhere except in mountains, and besides, shady glens, softly murmuring streams, wide and distant views over the plains, lakes, rivers, cities, castles, and finally air that gives new life. And all these things can bring enchantment by their novelty to those who are unfamiliar with such scenes and pleasures. If you want to see what is old, you will find there monuments that go back into the dawn of history, precipices, rocks, overhanging cliffs, bottomless gorges, fearsome chasms, hidden caves, ice which never softens in the heat of summer; but what need to say more? This is the realm of the Lord.[3]

Whether Hebrews or ancient Greeks climbed mountains for pleasure, we do not know, but it is certain that both these peoples, like Marti, though with different emphasis, felt a strong religious significance in high places. It was on Mount Moriah that the Lord tested Abraham, on Sinai that he gave the tablets to Moses, and on Carmel that Elijah threw into confusion the prophets of Baal. The sanctity of high places is impressed on the reader of both the Old and New Testament, as shown for instance by the 121st Psalm,

I will lift up mine eyes unto the hills,
from whence cometh my help.
My help cometh from the Lord, which made
Heaven and earth.

The beauty of hills and mountains is never stressed in the Bible, but Homer, who lived long before the Biblical writers, pictures with rare emotion the rocky hillsides of the Greek islands with their ever-changing chiaroscuro as clouds drift across the sea and the mountains. In general, however, the Greeks, though they loved their mountains, viewed them from afar. To them, Olympus was the abode of the eternal Gods, Parnassus the home of poetry, and the rocky crags of Delphi the source of the greatest oracle. Little wonder that the Greeks regarded mountains from a distance and built up legends about them (as the Tibetans do today), while the sea, that rival source of inspiration, became more familiar to them and absorbed their natural energies for travel. As Wordsworth says,

Two voices are there; one is of the sea,
One of the mountains; each a mighty Voice,[4]

and the mighty voice of the mountains was heard by many of the ancients, though few have written about their feelings. For instance, Philip of Macedon climbed Mount Haemus four hundred years before Christ; and Empedocles the philosopher, Emperor Hadrian, and others climbed Etna during Roman times, but nothing of literary value has come down to us concerning these ancient ascents or indeed any climbs during most of the Middle Ages. Roman coins have been found at the top of the Théodule Pass, to be sure, but medieval people generally were too busy existing and protecting themselves to think of mountainous regions other than as places of refuge or strongholds to be fortified against predatory men. Most men in medieval times probably agreed with the bishop who postulated that mountains did not exist until the fall of man, when the devil was allowed to put them in for man's punishment.[5]

Awe, disgust, and terror seem to be the emotions mountains generally aroused in medieval men, and few apparently went to them as did Master John de Bremble, a monk of Christ Church, Canterbury, who reached the top of the Great St. Bernard Pass in 1188. Master John's reactions were definite as he promptly showed in a letter to his sub-prior Geoffrey:

"Lord," I said, "restore me to my brethren, that I may tell them that they come not to this place of torment." Place of torment indeed, where the marble pavement of the stony ground is ice alone, and you cannot set your foot safely; where, strange to say, although it is so slippery that you cannot stand, the death into which there is every facility for a fall is certain death. I put my hand in my scrip that I might scratch out a syllable or two to your sincerity; lo, I found my ink bottle filled with a dry mass of ice; my fingers, too, refused to write; my beard was stiff with frost, and my breath congealed into a long icicle. I could not write the news I wished.[6]

Master John probably expressed the normal sentiments of his time, but he lacked the poetic spirit of Petrarch, who, a century and a half later, with his brother completed a plan of many years and climbed Mont Ventoux in Provence. Despite the toil and dangers of the adventure, the poet delighted in the ascent and in his feelings at the summit:

At first I was so affected by the unaccustomed spirit of the air, and by the free prospect, that I stood as one stupefied. I looked back; clouds were beneath my feet. I began to understand Athos and Olympus, since I found that what I heard and read of them was true of a mountain of far less celebrity. I turned my eyes to that Italian region to which my soul most inclines, and the great rugged Alps (through which, we are told, that the greatest enemy of Rome made his way with vinegar) seemed quite close to me, though they really were at a great distance. I confess that I sighed for that Italian air, more sensible to the soul than to the eyes, and an intense longing came upon me to behold my friends and my country once more.[7]

Then he took a small volume of Augustine's *Confessions*, which opened by chance, so he tells us, to the passage, "There are men who go to admire the high places of mountains, the great waves of the sea, the wide currents of rivers, the circuit of the ocean, and the orbits of the stars—and who neglect themselves." The passage must have startled him, for he goes on, "I confess that I was amazed; I begged my brother, who was anxious to hear more, not to interrupt me, and I shut the book half angry with myself, that I, who was even now admiring terrestrial things, ought already to have learnt from the philosophers that nothing is truly great except the soul."[8]

What finer example of observations and reflections on a mountain summit or testimony against the fetters that bound the human spirit in medieval times? Petrarch had so far forgotten himself as to enjoy the beautiful world he lived in and to want to see more of it, when all the time he should have been turning his eyes inward and examining his immortal soul. No wonder there were few who wrote about the mountains in the days when the mildest instincts to enjoy God's natural beauties were crushed by the church.

Yet some men in these black ages did yield to their natural instincts, and sought new experiences in the mountains. For instance, in the thirteenth century King Peter III of Aragon, who fought the king of France and the Pope at the same time, also used his energy to climb Pic Canigou in the Pyrenees, where he allegedly found a "horrible dragon of enormous size."[9] More convincing is the story of the ascent in 1492 of Mont Aiguille, near Grenoble, by Dompjulian de Beaupré, Chamberlain of France, on orders from his king, Charles VIII. This well-certified ascent was most remarkable, for the peak, then called Mont Inaccessible, is not an easy one and was not ascended again until 1834. Preparations for the climb were made with all the care of modern expeditions setting out to attempt Mount Everest; Mass was celebrated and attack begun. After careful siege and by use of "subtle means and engines," the ascent was completed by Dompjulian and seven of his men. They built a "house" and spent the better part of a week on the meadow at the top, making sure that their ascent was officially recorded, and then, after setting up their crosses, made their descent, which was declared to be "still more terrible than the ascent."[10]

As the ascent of Mont Aiguille is the most remarkable recorded in the Middle Ages, there is little wonder that Rabelais uses the event as an incident in *Pantagruel*, and so becomes the first French writer concerned with mountain climbing;[11] but the official accounts of the Dompjulian climb are comparatively brief, and Dompjulian, though a man of courage and enterprise, did not have an interest in mountains for themselves. A few other medieval men did, however, such as Leonardo da Vinci, who, apparently impelled by scientific curiosity, climbed one of the spurs of Monte Rosa late in the fifteenth century; and Conrad Gesner, professor of physics at the University of Zurich, a friend and contemporary of Marti. In 1541, at the age of twenty-seven, Gesner wrote as follows:

> Most learned Avienus, I have resolved for the future, so long as God suffers me to live, to climb mountains, or at all events to climb one mountain every year, at the season when vegetation is at its best, partly for the sake of studying botany, and partly for the delight of the mind and the proper exercise of the body. For what, think you, is the pleasure, what the joy of a mind, affected as it should be, to marvel at the spectacle of the mighty passes of the mountains, and lift up one's head, as it were, among the clouds. The mind is strangely excited by the amazing altitude, and carried away to the contemplation of the Great Architect of the Universe ———- Cultivators of philosophy will proceed to contemplate the great spectacles of this earthly paradise; and by no means the least of these are the steep and broken mountain-tops, the unscalable precipices, the vast slopes stretching towards the sky, the dark and shady forests.[12]

Whether this great naturalist and philosopher kept his fine resolutions we do not know, but twelve years later he published an account of his ascent of Mount Pilatus, near Lucerne. This account is all the more remarkable because of its rejection of the medieval bondage that restrained Petrarch and its almost modern approach to the mountains themselves. Pilatus, it should be observed, was no ordinary mountain in the Middle Ages, for as we learn from the Bishop of Genoa, writing about 1290, the lake near the top of Pilatus was supposed to hold the body of Pontius Pilate. The legend held that after Pilate's death, his body caused terrible storms and disturbances in Rome and was successively transported to Vienne and other places, bringing calamity with it, until finally the good citizens of Lucerne flung it into the lake, fearing to disturb the spirit. In 1307 men were arrested for trying to go to the lake, and even in 1538, when the scholar Vadianus of St. Gall climbed the mountain and viewed the lake, he was led to believe that the story of the presence of Pilate might be true, though he failed to disturb the tyrant.

Gesner had no belief in the story of the lake, nor did he swallow the story that Pilate, dressed in scarlet, was visible one day a year sitting on a rock, and whoever saw him died within a year. Instead of these wonders he found virtues in the mountains, where one can "on a single day observe and pass through the four seasons of the year." He praised the pure air and fragrant smells, the sounds of the birds, the absence of city noise and strife, and declared,

> Give me a man moderately robust in mind and body, liberally educated, and not too much given over to laziness, luxury, or lust; and I should like him also to be a student and admirer of Nature, so that from his contemplation and admiration of the great works of the Architect of the Universe, and of the immense variety of natural phenomena that is to be seen among the mountains, on the slopes of a single eminence, he might enjoy an intellectual pleasure in addition to the symphony of the pleasures of all his senses. What other kind of enjoyment, I ask, will you find within the field of nature which is more honourable, greater or more complete in every respect?[13]

Conrad Gesner, though a medieval professor, had the spirit of a modern mountaineer, and until the last hundred years no author has praised more sweetly than he the delights of the mountain way. Two other continental writers, however, should be noted before we turn our attention to England and to mountain literature there. One of these is Josias Simler, who succeeded Gesner at Zurich, and whose famous volume *De Alpibus Commentarius*, published in Zurich in 1574, describes the difficulties of Alpine travel and deals with methods of crossing snowfields. The other writer, Johann Jacob Scheuchzer, P.R.S. (1672–1733), also a professor at Zurich, but more than a century later, in the first years of the eighteenth century dedicated two bulky and well-illustrated volumes to the Royal Society in London, whose members, including Sir Isaac Newton, had helped defray the expense of publication. The Royal Society since its beginning had had close communication with Swiss scholars about mountain wonders, so that its interest in Scheuchzer's writing is not remarkable. Scheuchzer, however, had strong medieval leanings and his writings, like those of Glanvil on witches, contrast strangely with the inductive logic and scientific methods already employed by so many members of the Royal Society. Scheuchzer describes numerous eyewitness accounts of dragons seen in the Swiss mountains, including views of some who breathe fire and can inhale birds, and others, bright and shining, who throw off sparks as from a red-hot

CONRADVS GESNERVS,
Med. D. et Prof. Phil. Tigur.
nat. 1516.   *denat. 1565.*
Ioh. Iac. Haid excud. Aug. Vind.

Conrad Gesner, although a medieval professor, had the spirit of a
mountaineer. From Gribble, *The Early Mountaineers.*

horseshoe. How the Royal Society must have thrilled over these reports and with what joy Sir Thomas Browne, of the *Pseudodoxia Epidemica*, had he been still alive, would have analyzed them, though how he would have tested the existence of dragons we can only conjecture![14]

England, at the time of Scheuchzer, had no great mountain lovers, such as Conrad Gesner, though Englishmen during previous centuries occasionally had praised mountains in prose and verse. Thomas Churchyard (1520?–1604), for instance, had a true feeling for mountains, even though his experience may have been limited, for he writes,

> *Of mountains now, indeed my muse must runne,*
> *The poets there did dwell as fables fayne:*
> *Because some say, they would be neere the sunne,*
> *And taste sometymes the frost, the cold, the rayne,*
> *To judge of both, which is the chiefe and best.*
> *Who knows no toyle can never skill of rest,*
> *Who alwaies walkes, on carpet soft and gay,*
> *Knows not hard hills, nor likes the mountaine way.*[15]

Churchyard has the right philosophy and expresses it well. And so does Shakespeare, when he kindles the imagination with the lines,

> *Full many a glorious morning have I seen*
> *Flatter the mountaintops with sovereign eye.*[16]

Would that Shakespeare had seen a million mountain mornings and described a few more!

Some medieval English writers, like Sir John Mandeville, mention the mountains, but their observations are not based on personal experience, and when Englishmen first began to travel through mountain regions, they had little good to say of them. Coryat in his *Crudities*, it is true, says some favorable words about mountains, but John Evelyn, who crossed the Simplon Pass in 1646 over "almost inaccessible heights,"[17] is more typical when he describes the Alps as "horrid mountains,"[18] though he did enjoy the sight of snowy summits in the distance. Similarly, half a century later, Addison found in the Alps "an agreeable kind of horror."[19]

During the early eighteenth century few English writers visited the Alps, but among them was young Horace Walpole, who wrote vivid reports of his adventures to his friend Richard West. One of these, written from Turin in 1739 and concerning his crossing of the Mont Cenis Pass in the company of Thomas Gray, was not likely to encourage future travelers:

> Turin
>
> Nov. 11, 1739
>
> So, as the song says, we are in fair Italy! I wonder we are; for on the very highest precipice of Mount Cenis, the devil of discord, in the similitude of sour wine, had got amongst our Alpine savages, and set them a-fighting with Gray and me in the chairs: they rushed him by me on a crag, where there was scarce room for a cloven foot. The least slip had tumbled us into such a fog, and such an eternity, as we should never have found our way out of again. We were eight days crossing the Alps. Such uncouth rocks, and such uncomely inhabitants! My dear West, I hope I shall never see them again! At the foot of Mount Cenis we were obliged to quit our chaise, which was taken all to pieces and loaded on mules; and we were carried in low armchairs on poles, swathed in beaver bonnets, beaver gloves, beaver stockings, muffs and bear-skins. When we came to the top, behold the snows fallen! and such quantities, and conducted by such heavy clouds that hung glouting, that I thought we never could have waded through them. The descent is two leagues, but steep and rough as O's father's face, over which, you know, the devil walked with hobnails in his shoes. But the dexterity and nimbleness of the mountaineers are inconceivable: they run with you down steeps and frozen precipices, where no man as men are now, could possibly walk. We had twelve men and nine mules to carry us, our servants, and baggage, and were above five hours in this agreeable jaunt! The day before, I had a cruel accident, and so extraordinary an one, that it seems to touch upon the traveller. I had brought with me a little black spaniel of King Charles's breed; but the prettiest, fattest, dearest little creature! I had left it out of the chaise for the air, and it was waddling along close to the head of the horses, on the top of the highest Alps, by the side of a wood of firs. There darted out a young wolf, seized poor dear Tory by the throat, and, before we could possibly prevent it, sprung up the side

of the rock and carried him off. The postillion jumped off and struck at him with his whip, but in vain. I saw it and screamed, but in vain; for the road was so narrow that the servants that were behind could not get by the chaise to shoot him. What is the extraordinary part is, that it was but two o'clock, and broad sunshine. It was so shocking to see anything one loved run away to so horrid a death.[20]

Considering these conditions, it is not remarkable that most of Walpole's contemporaries thought of mountainous areas with fear and apprehension. Dr. Johnson was perhaps an exception, for though he had little to say about the Scotch hills, he declared that in his youth he would have climbed them. Richardson actually described a conventional grand tour of the Alps in *Sir Charles Grandison*, but the journey was based on hearsay and no personal feeling was involved. Mrs. Thrale was more enlightened, for she not only traveled but also was pleased with the Mont Cenis and delighted with the Brenner.

Thomas Gray especially was ahead of his time. Even in his somber crossing of the Mont Cenis with Walpole in 1739, he had seen something fine about the mountains, and the idea grew during his lifetime. After a visit to Scotland in 1765 he declared, "The mountains are ecstatic and ought to be visited in pilgrimage once a year. None but these monstrous children of God know how to join so much beauty with so much horror."[21]

Gray's feelings toward mountains probably influenced the great romantic poets, particularly Byron, and also many minor writers of the day. Probably, too, William Windham's account of his visit to Chamonix in 1741 also had an effect on the romantic writers of the latter part of the century. He described the havoc wrought by terrible avalanches and was impressed by the famous Aiguilles, which he pictured as "somewhat resembling old Gothic Buildings or Ruines."[22] He was even courageous enough to walk on the Mer de Glace. In this way, as journeys to the Alps became more common and letters and stories of travelers like William Beckford, Thomas Blaikie, and John Moore became more widely circulated in England, the wonders and terrors of mountains appeared far more frequently as romantic background.

Some of the finest examples of an author's use of mountain scenery in the latter part of the eighteenth century are provided by Mrs. Ann Radcliffe in *The Romance of the Forest* and *The Mysteries of Udolpho*. Generalizations are most skillfully used, while the tenor of her language and her few details harmonize with the accounts of travelers of the period. We hear of "gloomy grandeur" and "mountains of stupendous height shooting into a variety of grotesque forms."[23] She goes on in her description:

> The wild and alpine heights which rose above, were either crowned with perpetual snows, or exhibited tremendous crags and masses of solid rock, whose appearance was continually changing as the rays of light were variously reflected on their surface, and whose summits were often wrapt in impenetrable mists.[24]

The mountain passages in *The Romance of the Forest* are somewhat more effective than those in *The Mysteries of Udolpho*, but together the two novels provide the general attitudes of Mrs. Radcliffe's contemporaries toward the Alps. In *Mysteries* Madam Montoni tells us of the dangers she suffered and hopes she will "soon be beyond the view of these horrid mountains which all the world should not tempt me to cross again."[25] while in *Romance* we learn, "From this point the eye commanded an entire view of those majestic and sublime Alps, whose aspect fills the soul with emotions of indescribable awe, and seems to lift it to a noble nature."[26] Mrs. Radcliffe provides a suitable attitude for everybody, and though we could criticize her lack of uniformity and absence of genuine detail, we must admit that her views of the mountains are far more real than those of many of her contemporaries who had visited the Alps. Perhaps if she had actually been there, she would have found less of the "horrid" and more of the "awe."

Meanwhile, on the Continent, the forerunners of the romantic movement had also been enjoying the mountain scene. Jean-Jacques Rousseau wrote to Julie in 1761 of the marvelous serenity and tranquillity of the hills. His broad outlook showed him the beauties appreciated by Conrad Gesner but realized by so few during the following centuries. Goethe like Rousseau, perceived many of the spiritual and visual beauties of the mountains. In his *Travels in Switzerland* (1779),[27] he sees not only the "savage portals forbidding access" but also the splendor of the surrounding scene. Witness this sunset at Mont Blanc:

> Like a strong body in which death slowly passes from the extremities to the heart, the whole range lost colour nearer and nearer to

Mont Blanc, whose vast bosom raised above the rest retained its crimson flush, and even at the end appeared to keep a rosy tinge— just as life seems to linger when we watch the death of one we love, and it is hard to mark the actual moment when the pulse has ceased to beat.[28]

Rousseau and Goethe, like Wordsworth and Coleridge later, were in their appreciation of natural beauty ahead of their time. Rousseau's contemporaries more generally disregarded objects not shaped and ordered by the hand of man, and it was typical that as Goethe was marveling at the delicate coloring on the upper slopes of Mont Blanc, a literary lady proudly proclaimed her preference for any Paris gutter to the Lake of Geneva.[29] Hers was perhaps the more general spirit of the age. But new interests were stirring. Wordsworth, Byron, Scott, and a host of others were using their eyes and telling the English-speaking world of natural beauty. True, these were not climbers in the modern sense; rather, they were men who viewed the mountains with a romantic eye and who did not scorn what they found there.

Most Englishmen who wrote about mountains in the century preceding the founding of the Alpine Club in London in 1857 were not climbers but travelers. Their eyes had been opened to some of the delights of the mountain way, but they still viewed mountains from afar, and few indeed ever once set foot on a true summit. For instance, Cowper's natural timidity was increased by high places, and he found Sussex alarmingly mountainous. In a letter to Samuel Teedon, dated August 5, 1792, he writes, "I indeed myself was a little daunted by the tremendous height of the Sussex hills, in comparison of which all that I had seen elsewhere are dwarfs."[30] In other letters written at about the same time he tells of the "terrors" of the Sussex "hills or mountains."

Goldsmith used Swiss backgrounds to illustrate his views on freedom, but he shows no true love of the mountains themselves. His literary device of presenting political or philosophical ideas against a background of crude mountain or romantic scenery produced a flood of imitators. Most of this romantic background, however, was vague and insipid for the obvious reason that the poets themselves did not deal with specific and detailed imagery but instead with general material of no emotional appeal. Such treatment reveals why much of the romantic verse of this period fails today to rouse us. In the hands of lesser writers the cataract, the soaring eagle, the deep pine woods, and the gloomy ravine become as stereotyped as the scenery used by a summer theater as background for a dozen widely differing plays. Even so, the cleavage of this verse from the conventions of the preceding period probably made it impressive to its contemporaries, while all critics will admit that in the hands of the greatest poets of the time, romantic imagery was treated with consummate skill. Wordsworth and Shelley wrote magnificent lines about mountains, but their less gifted contemporaries lacked the depth of feeling essential to lyric poetry. Few poems by any but the greatest poets of this period capture the charm of *Grongar Hill* or *The Seasons*, written so much earlier, yet they employ the general terms of the earlier period, such as "horrid" and "grim." In *The Seasons*, for instance, we hear how the dire Andes . . . their hideous deeps unfold," and of the still more "terrible" Alps.[31]

In contrast let us examine briefly the great romantic poets and see to what extent these general remarks apply.

William Wordsworth, who probably spent more time in mountains than any of his romantic contemporaries, wrote about the heights with considerable feeling, though he truly loved only their lower areas, and in his eagerness to convert his reader to his own ideas he normally breaks off his lovely descriptions of the high peaks after one or two lines. Wordsworth was not a climber. He crossed some of the main Alpine passes and on another occasion ascended Snowdon, a climb that, one gathers from *The Excursion*, he did not particularly enjoy. But although Wordsworth probably liked the mountains most when he saw them from afar, he has given us some splendid verses, such as those written on the Simplon Pass, lines that Tennyson considered the finest Wordsworth ever wrote:

> *Brook and road*
> *Were fellow-travelers in this gloomy Pass,*
> *And with them did we journey several hours*
> *At a slow step. The immeasurable height*
> *Of woods, decaying, never to be decayed,*
> *The stationary blasts of waterfalls,*
> *And in the narrow rent, at every turn,*
> *Winds thwarting winds bewildered and forlorn,*
> *The torrents shooting from the clear blue sky,*
> *The rocks that muttered close upon our ears,*

> *Black drizzling crags that spake by the wayside*
> *As if a voice were in them, the sick sight*
> *And giddy prospect of the raving stream,*
> *The unfettered clouds and region of the heavens.*
> *Tumult and peace, the darkness and the light —*
> *Were all like workings of one mind, the features*
> *Of the same face, blossoms upon one tree,*
> *Characters of the great Apocalypse,*
> *The types and symbols of Eternity,*
> *Of first, and last, and midst, and without end.*[32]

This flow of specific images in which Wordsworth saw "types and symbols of Eternity" is inspired. He had been moved by such elements many times before, as he tells us in *The Prelude*, but rarely had they roused him with greater effect. However, almost all of Wordsworth's mountain poetry—and it is considerable—deals characteristically with the valleys or lower slopes. When he does occasionally focus on an area above the line of vegetation, he refers to it with awe but not with love or understanding. In his two poems on Mont Blanc he describes the "white-robed shapes" of the glaciers and contrasts them with "virgin lilies" and "swans descending with the stealthy tide,"[33] beautiful analogies but not figures he would have used had he had experience with glacial ice. In *Descriptive Sketches* he shows admiration for the high snows, but none of the sympathetic and kindred feeling with which he welcomed the wooded slopes below:

> *Bright stars of ice and azure worlds of snow,*
> *Where needle peaks of granite shooting bare*
> *Tremble in ever-varying tints of air,*
> *Great joy by horror tam'd delights his heart . . .*
> *Alps overlooking Alps their state upswell;*
> *Huge Pikes of Darkness named, of Fear and Storms . . .*[34]

The "needle peaks of granite" held no joys for Wordsworth, but elsewhere in most masterly fashion he has depicted the lower Unterwalden, and his charming lines on early morning mists in the Alps reflect the keen observation of a great poet. Each mountain lover prefers some special aspect of the hills, and Wordsworth's preference apparently was for Alpine pastures:

How still! no irreligious sound or sight
Rouses the soul from her severe delight
An idle voice the Sabbath region fills
Of deep that calls to deep across the hills,
And with that voice accords the soothing sound
Of drowsy bells, forever tinkling round;
Faint wail of eagle melting into blue
Beneath the cliffs, and pine-woods! steady sigh;
The solitary heifer's deepened low;
Or rumbling, heard remote, of falling snow.
All motions, sounds, and voices, far and nigh,
Blend in a music of tranquility . . .[35]

In imagery such as this, William may have been aided by his sister, who loved the mountains devotedly and pictured them with great accuracy and charm. Her *Journal of a Tour on the Continent* (1820) gives vivid flashes of description of which any later traveler could be proud.

> The sunshine had long deserted the valley, and was quitting the summits of the mountain behind the village; but red hues, dark as the red of rubies, settled in the clouds, and lingered there after the mountains had lost all but their cold whiteness and the black hue of the crags. The gloomy grandeur of this spectacle harmonized with the melancholy of the vale; yet it was heavenly glory that hung over those cold mountains.[36]

Had Coleridge, like William and Dorothy Wordsworth, traveled in the Alps, he, too, undoubtedly would have produced excellent verse and prose concerning what he saw, but Coleridge, though he had planned a trip from Rome to England through the Alps, was prevented by political unrest from carrying it out and never went beyond Rome, which he had reached by water. What he would have written if he had been subjected to the poetical intoxication of Alpine passes we can only surmise, but it is significant that he could write his fine *Hymn before Sunrise in the Vale of Chamouni* even though his knowledge of Mont Blanc was decidedly secondhand. This fine poetic outburst is all the more remarkable when one realizes that it is a reworking and expansion of a short, colorless poem by Frederica Brun (Munter), a German poet. The outline is the same, but there the connection ceases. Had Coleridge gone to Chamonix and the lordly mountain there, his poem might have been far greater, for he had the temperament of a mountain lover. At this time he had already climbed Etna and done considerable tramping in the Lake country. Of one of these rambles in January 1803, he wrote to Thomas Wedgwood:

> I write with difficulty, with all the fingers but one of my right hand very much swollen. Before I was half way up the Kirkstone mountain, the storm had wetted me through and through . . . I am no novice in mountain mischiefs, but such a storm as this was, I never witnessed, combining the intensity of the cold with the violence of the wind and rain. The rain drops were pelted or slung against my face by the gusts, just like splinters of flint. . . .O, it was a wild business.[37]

Again he declares,

> . . . I think that my soul must have preexisted in the body of a chamois-chaser. . . .The farther I ascend from animated nature, from men and cattle and the common birds of the woods and fields, the greater becomes in me the intensity of the feeling of life. Life seems to me then an universal spirit which neither has nor can have an opposite. . . I do not think that it is possible that any bodily pains could eat out the love of joy, that is so substantially part of me, towards hills and rocks and steep water; and I have had some trial.[38]

Byron, of course, spent considerable time in the Alps and gloried in their beauty, but though he liked mountain scenery, mountains to him were symbolic rather than friends to understand. He frequently used mountain scenery as background for his ideas (as in *He who ascends to Mountain-tops*), and frequently employed it as symbolic of the good things in nature in contrast with the evils of mankind. Byron was a lover of the mountains from afar, but, perhaps because of his physical limitations, not a real mountain poet. He chooses dramatic imagery for considered effect and in *Manfred* great peaks are adjuncts to gloomy melodrama. His kindred feeling for mountain scenery, however, is everywhere evident.

Where rose the mountains, there to him were friends . . .

But in Man's dwellings he became a thing
Restless and worn, and stern and wearisome
Droop'd as a wild-born falcon with clipt wings,
To whom the boundless air alone were home.[39]

This attitude he emphasized strongly and repeatedly in *Childe Harold,* as in the fine lines beginning, "High mountains are a feeling, but the hum of human cities torture."[40] Despite these sentiments, however, he never truly understood mountains. His poem to Mont Blanc is cold, while the lines on *The Apennine,* in which he lists the number of peaks he has seen, merely reveal the extent of his travels. The last lines, however, provide a striking image of Mount Soracte, which,

. . . from out the plain
Heaves like a long-swept wave about to break,
And on the curl hangs pausing . . .[41]

If Byron had not been lame, his natural feeling toward mountains might have ripened into something far stronger.

John Keats, too, had he a more robust physique, might have become a true mountain lover. He was turned back on Helvellyn because of wet rock and attempted Skiddaw instead, only to have the clouds descend when he was nearly at the summit. Later he climbed Ben Nevis in Scotland and sat watching the swirling mists below. His view was hidden but his thoughts remained active as we learn from his sonnet:

Read me a lesson Muse, and speak it loud
Upon the top of Nevis, blind in mist
I look into the chasms, and a shroud
Vaprous doth hide them—just so much I wist
Mankind do know of hell—I look o'erhead,
And there is sullen mist—even so much
Mankind can tell of heaven—mist is spread
Before the earth, beneath me—even such,
Even as vague is man's sight of himself.[42]

Of all the romantic poets, none viewed the mountains so accurately and with such magnificent poetic vision as Shelley. He saw them as they were and his heart was stirred. He needed no vehicle for political ideas to ride on, for he found more in the distant snows themselves than his pen could set down. A lovely picture of Shelley's first rapturous view of the Alps appears in a letter he wrote to Thomas Peacock on July 22, 1816:

> ... Mont Blanc was before us, but it was covered with cloud; its base, furrowed with dreadful gaps, was seen above. Pinnacles of snow intolerably bright, part of the chain connected with Mont Blanc, shone through the clouds at intervals on high. I never knew—I never imagined what mountains were before. The immensity of these aerial summits excited, when they suddenly burst upon the sight, a sentiment of ecstatic wonder, not unallied to madness. And remember this was all one scene, it all pressed home to our regard and our imagination. Though it embraced a vast extent of space, the snowy pyramids which shot into the bright blue sky seemed to overhang our path; the ravine, clothed with gigantic pines, and black with its depth below, so deep that the very roaring of the untamable Arve, which rolled through it, could not be heard above—all was so much our own, as if we had been the creators of such impressions in the minds of others as now occupied our own. Nature was the poet, whose harmony held our spirits more breathless than that of the divinest.[43]

The "wonder," not unallied to madness," the deep emotion engendered by this first ecstatic vision of the silver summits, never entirely left the poet. Repeatedly in letters, in *Prometheus Unbound*, and in later verses he regains the rapturous mood of his first view of Mont Blanc from the valley. Wordsworth, Byron, and Coleridge have all written fine lines on Mont Blanc but none can compare with the rare spiritual beauty of Shelley's stanzas:

> *Far, far above, piercing the infinite sky,*
> *Mont Blanc appears—still, snowy, and serene —*
> *Its subject mountains their unearthly forms*
> *Pile around it, ice and rock; broad vales between*
> *Of frozen floods, unfathomable deeps,*
> *Blue as the overhanging heaven, that spread*
> *And wind among the accumulated steeps. . .*

> *Is this scene*
> *Where the old Earthquake-demon taught her young*
> *Ruin? Were these their toys? or did a sea*
> *Of fire envelop once this silent snow?*
> *None can reply—all seems eternal now.*
> *The wilderness has a mysterious tongue*
> *Which teaches awful doubt, or faith so mild,*
> *So solemn, so serene, that man may be,*
> *But for such faith with nature reconciled;*
> *Thou hast a voice, great Mountain, to repeal*
> *Large codes of fraud and woe; not understood*
> *By all, but which the wise, and great, and good*
> *Interpret, or make felt, or deeply feel.*[44]

Shelley knew none of the emotions of the wanderer among summit snows who bivouacs high on a great mountain and sees on all sides impressive evidence of nature's power: avalanches that toss ice blocks as big as houses, crevasses descending hundreds of feet in glacial ice, winds that can move great boulders or blow a man completely off his feet. In mountains, periods of violence and serene calm alternate in a way not often understood by those who see the great peaks from below, but Shelley had a certain understanding of this perpetual mutability of nature, even though he knew nothing of summit ridges. How much more poetic his treatment of Mont Blanc than Byron's bluntness, Coleridge's beautiful but somewhat stilted apostrophe, or even Wordsworth's quiet and thoughtful comparisons.

Shelley is not always accurate in his description of the upper snows, as, for instance, when he describes the utter stillness of the heights.

> *In the calm darkness of the moonless nights,*
> *In the lone glare of day, the snows descend.*
> *Upon that Mountain; none beholds them there,*
> *Nor when the flakes burn in the sinking sun,*
> *Or the star-beams dart through them:—Winds contend*
> *Silently there, and heap the snow with breath*
> *Rapid and strong, but silently!*[45]

The general impression is magnificent, but had Shelley stood where the winds were heaping the snows or even listened to snow falling or heard the normal and continuous mountain sounds, he would not have written these beautiful lines. From where he saw the upper snows, they naturally appeared serene, but he was looking at them from a distance of several miles. Again, when he says, "I love snow and all the forms of the radiant frost,"[46] he has the proper instincts of a mountaineer, but we would appreciate the idea more if we thought that he knew what some of the "radiant forms of frost" are like when one is actually in the midst of them and not just looking at them from afar. Snow and clouds take on a very different aspect when seen at close quarters.

Again, Shelley writes,

> *The cold earth slept below;*
> *Above, the cold sky shone;*
> *And all around,*
> *With a chilling sound,*
> *From caves of ice and fields of snow*
> *The breath of night like death did flow*
> *Beneath the sinking moon.*[47]

To experienced climbers, night in the mountains does not suggest death, but Shelley, seeing the warm sunset flow die away on the upper slopes to be replaced by pallid white, thinks of extinction much as Goethe had done before, though with a very different image. "The breath of night like death did flow" is a masterly phrase to describe the emotion Shelley felt at the penetrating damp and cold in the valleys when the sunlight had gone. Though he never left the valleys and passes, Shelley was a remarkably keen observer. In *Prometheus Unbound* he captures with magnificent simplicity in a few lines what he saw from his valley belvedere:

> *The point of one white star is quivering still*
> *Deep in the orange light of widening morn*
> *Beyond the purple mountains: through a chasm*
> *Of wind-divided mist the darker lake*
> *Reflects it: now it wanes: it gleams again*
> *As the waves fade, and as the burning threads*
> *Of woven cloud unravel in pale air:*
> *Tis lost! and through yon peaks of cloud-like snow*

The roseate sunlight quivers . . .
And multitudes of dense white fleecy clouds
Were wandering in thick flocks along the mountains
Shepherded by the slow, unwilling wind . . .[48]

Of those who have looked at mountains from afar and written verse about them, none has pictured them more sensitively than Shelley. Had he been able to climb to the high places himself, his verse might have had similar beauty, but it would have had an entirely different quality, based on intimate knowledge of the summit snows. This Shelley was unable to gain, for he was not physically daring and, at the time he wrote *Prometheus Unbound*, fewer than a score of Englishmen had ascended Mont Blanc, an undertaking then considered extremely hazardous, while only one or two of the other first-rank Alpine peaks had even been climbed.

The discovery of these other peaks was to come soon, however, and like Marti and Gesner, thousands of Englishmen were soon to find that there is "great easing of the heart upon high hills."[49] Others, likewise, were to find in improved transportation facilities the opportunity to explore the beauties of still more remote Alpine valleys, so that gradually there grew up a considerable quantity of writing about the mountains. Always there were the two groups: those who looked at the mountains only from afar, and did not climb them; and those who came to grips with the mountains themselves. At first the scene was limited to the Alps or to the British Isles, then to Norway and the Caucasus, and finally expanded to include all the mountainous areas of the globe. From the days of Homer or of the writer of the *Song of Solomon* to Shelley, a long period had elapsed and comparatively little progress been made in the technique of climbing mountains. From this time on, however, great technical advances were to be made, opening untrodden regions and producing a stimulus to the imagination and an impact on English literature worthy of close examination.

The Magic Attraction
of Mont Blanc

I N ORDER TO UNDERSTAND better the changing point of view with regard to mountains—and the vast amount written about them in the middle of the nineteenth century in England, some of it of true literary value—it is well to turn briefly to the mountain ascents that caused this material to be written. Surely no one in London in 1840 could have predicted the swelling interest in the mountains, the natural and direct outgrowth of events a century before, or believed that the inspiration to make Alpine ascents could suddenly develop in churchmen, statesmen, artists, and lawyers delightful and totally unsuspected literary qualities. These were not writers who saw the mountains from afar but men who dared to explore them and face on them unknown dangers.

As we have already noted, Windham's visit to Chamonix in 1741 attracted considerable attention at home and on the Continent, and during the next twenty years several similar visits to Chamonix were made. By far the most important of these was that of young Horace Bénédict De Saussure of Geneva, whose future influence on the sport of mountain climbing and less directly on the literature of the mountains can hardly be overestimated. De Saussure's motive for his visit, we are told, was to collect plants for Albrecht von Haller, the Swiss scholar whose poem on the Alps, written in 1732, gained an international reputation and was later much admired by Byron. When De Saussure reached Chamonix, however, the icy Mont Blanc massif impressed itself so forcibly on him that he nearly forgot his floral specimens, and when he left ordered a "handsome reward" to whomever should reach the summit of Mont Blanc. This reward had no immediate effect on the local fears and superstitions about the higher snows, however, so that although De Saussure returned to

Chamonix again and again, it was not until 1775 that a serious attempt on the peak was made.

From then on, for the next few years, there were repeated attempts and failures. Superstition was gradually giving way as higher mountain areas were reached, but technical skill was still almost completely lacking. For instance, in 1783 a guide seriously advised De Saussure that the only items of equipment that should be taken on Mont Blanc were a parasol and smelling salts. Two years later, with a variety of equipment, the doughty Swiss himself made a determined attempt to ascend the huge snow peak, but was turned back by a fresh snowfall. The following summer, on August 8, 1786, the summit was attained by Dr. Paccard and Jacques Balmat of Chamonix, a crystal seeker, to whose gallant achievement De Saussure pays tribute.

The ascent of Mont Blanc, a peak so long attempted and so often stated to be impregnable, was news in every capital of Europe. De Saussure immediately hastened to Chamonix to talk to the conquerors and to attempt the peak again, but the season was now so far advanced that he was unable to satisfy his burning ambition until the next year. The details of the Paccard-Balmat climb, interesting as they are, need not be discussed here. Suffice it to say that the great peak had finally been ascended, the victors had suffered no serious ill effects, and the way was now found for other climbers.

Next year De Saussure laid siege to Mont Blanc, and on August 3, 1787, after three days of climbing in company with Jacques Balmat and seventeen other guides with a mercurical barometer, reached the summit.[50] There, more interested in his scientific observations than in the view, he felt angered that he was physically unable to complete all his self-appointed tasks. De Saussure did not realize it, but he was making the first of a series of scientific summit observations on Mont Blanc that have continued to the present day. Nor did he realize that his large expedition was setting for future climbers a style to be followed until the "revolt" of the guideless climbers Hudson and Kennedy in 1854. But far more important than De Saussure's personal triumph in reaching the summit of Mont Blanc was the effect of his literary and scientific publications, particularly his *Voyage dans les Alpes* (1779–96). Rousseau had described natural scenery and preached the return to nature, but it was a Swiss scientist who showed another way to appreciate mountains and led people up into them.

Five days after De Saussure's triumph, Mark Beaufoy, a young Englishman,

"Frequent appearance of ice, with bridges of snow." Charles Fellows climbed Mont Blanc in 1825, aided by ten guides. From Fellows, *Narrative of an Ascent to the Summit of Mont Blanc.*

repeated the ascent, to be followed during the next half century by a considerable number of other English climbers. Yet for fifty years the ascent of Mont Blanc was a most perilous undertaking. The climbers were definitely amateurs, often not in the best condition and always lacking the technical skill, acclimatization, and general mountaineering experience of the modern climber. It is no wonder that each ascent was considered extremely hazardous and that most of the conquerors of the summit published dramatic illustrated accounts of their climbs.

Typical of two or three dozen of these accounts between the turn of the century and 1850 are those by Charles Fellows and John Auldjo, which, luridly illustrated, appeared in 1827 and 1828. Fellows's account, typical of the "terror school" of mountain writers, lacks literary merit, but Auldjo is a good observer who writes more clearly and effectively. Each of these young climbers,

"Bridge where the party breakfasted." Auldjo's ascent of Mont Blanc in 1822 created great interest in his book and its exaggerated drawings. From Auldjo, *Narrative of an Ascent of Mont Blanc.*

without restraint, dwells on the discomforts of his position. Fellows, for instance, tells of two of his guides who "fell from faintness" and "copiously vomited blood."[51] After relating "marvelous escapes" in his ascent of Mont Blanc, he feels it his duty to give warning:

> I think, great as certainly is the pleasure of overcoming an acknowledged succession of dangers, that any one who sets the least value upon his own life, or upon theirs who must accompany him on such an expedition, hazards a risk, which, upon calm consideration, he ought not to venture; and if it ever fall to my lot to dissuade a friend from attempting what we have gone through, I shall consider that I have saved his life.[52]

Auldjo, whose ascent won him a gold medal from one king and a diamond ring from another, writes with dignity, sincerity, courage, and determination, but without humor or any true kindred feeling for the mountains. Only rarely do the beauties of the ascent make him forget the dangers:

"Scaling a wall of ice. Drawn on stone from a sketch by Auldjo." From Auldjo.

An extended plain of snow now presented itself, here and there covered with masses of broken ice; sometimes a beautiful tower of that substance raised its blue form, and seemed to mock the lofty, pointed rocks above it; sometimes an immense block, its perpendicular front broken into pinnacles, now bearing a mass of snow, now supporting long and clear icicles, looked like some castle, on whose dilapitated walls the ivy, hanging in clustering beauty, or lying in rich or dark luxuriance, was, by the wand of some fairy, changed into the bright matter which now composed it.[53]

Most of the time, however, he must watch where he is putting his feet:

Taking my steps with the greatest care, I could not prevent myself from slipping . . . I came down on my face, and glided rapidly towards the lower [crevasse]; I cried out, but the guides who held the ropes attached to me did not stop me, though they stood firm. I had got to the extent of the rope, my feet hanging over the lower crevice, one hand grasping firmly the pole and other my hat. The guides called to me to be cool, and not afraid;—a pretty time to be cool, hanging over an abyss, and in momentary expectation of falling into it.[54]

Even before this experience, Auldjo tells us that the blood had curdled in his veins. Despite his graphic descriptions of the ascent, however, he was not by many years the last to make the ascent in the grand manner with much preparation and multiple guides. In 1838, Mlle. Henriette d'Angeville, an aristocratic French lady, forty-four years old, fulfilled her great ambition and reached the summit, though she declared that only five out of 25,000 people sympathized with her wish to climb the mountain. She took six guides and six porters, few indeed in comparison with Empress Josephine, who in 1810 used sixty-eight guides to get her to the Montanvert near the bottom of the mountain. Provisions for Henriette's party were also modest, including only two legs of mutton, two ox tongues, twenty-four fowl, six large loaves of bread, eighteen bottles of St. Jean, one cask of vin ordinaire, plus a few other items, a list worth recalling when reading Mark Twain's ascent to the Riffelberg in *A Tramp Abroad*.

Mille Henriette D'Angeville climbed Mont Blanc in 1838 and continued making ascents for another twenty-five years. From Gribble, *The Early Mountaineers.*

Henriette climbed stoutly but near the top thought she was going to die, and ordered her guides that if she did, they were to drag her body to the top and leave it there—quite the reverse of the normal procedure—stating that her family would reward them for obeying her last wishes. She did not perish, however, and soon after was drinking a health in lemonade at the summit. After the descent, Mlle. Henriette did not rest on the honors she had so pluckily won, and unlike Fellows and Auldjo, who lacked a true feeling for mountains, she for many years afterward continued to climb, ascending twenty-one peaks, including the Oldenhorn (10,250 feet) at the age of sixty-nine. Mlle. d'Angeville writes modestly and with pleasant humor of her expeditions, but as she writes in French she is important to us only for her influence on contemporary mountaineers of both sexes.

Traveling to Chamonix was now becoming somewhat more common, but most of the Alps had as yet neither been climbed nor approached with scientific curiosity. Their isolation was not to last long, however, for James D. Forbes (1809–1868), F.R.S., and others[55] were soon to seek out Alpine mysteries with a scientific or adventurous eye. Forbes, a brilliant scientist—professor of natural philosophy at Edinburgh University at the age of twenty-four—determined to carry on the scientific studies of De Saussure, and like De Saussure made Alpine history in several ways. From 1835 on, this precocious Scot carried out scientific investigations in every major mountain range of western Europe from the Pyrenees to Norway, and was probably the earliest British visitor to the Dolomites, Tyrol, and other later famous mountain areas. Forbes's interests were mainly geologic and topographic and, as one might expect, his writings are more scholarly than literary, though his love for work adds definite charm to the precise accounts of travels and observations:

> Happy the traveller who, content to leave to others the glory of counting the thousands of leagues of earth and ocean they have left behind them, established in some mountain shelter with his books, starts on his first day's walk among the Alps in the tranquil morning of a long July day, brushing the early dew before him, and, armed with his staff, makes for the hill-top—begirt with ice or rock as the case may be—whence he sees the field of his summer's campaign spread out before him, its wonders, its beauties, and its difficulties, to be explained, to be admired, and to be overcome.[56]

Early in his best-known work, *Travels through the Alps of Savoy*, published in 1843, Forbes tells us that his purpose in writing the book is scientific and that he has taken the works of the great De Saussure as his model. Certainly the Geneva scientist would have been proud of his Scotch disciple, for it was Forbes who, after observations, presented his famous and now accepted theory of the viscosity of glacial ice, a subject that for the next few years was to involve the whole scientific world in bitter disputes among Forbes, Agassiz, and Tyndall. The revolutionary character of Forbes's theory is described by his friend and staunch supporter John Ruskin, who writes in *Fors Clavigera*:

> We all knew that glaciers moved . . .that there were cracks all through them and moraines all down them; that some of their ice was clear, and other ice opaque . . . We were all puzzled to account for glacier motion, but never thought of ascertaining what the motion really was . . . None of us ever had the slightest idea of the ice's being anything but an entirely solid substance, which . . . was always rigid and brittle like so much glass or stone. This was the state of affairs in 1841. But in 1842 Forbes solved the problem of glacier motion forever—announcing to everyone's astonishment . . . that glaciers were not solid bodies at all, but semi-liquid ones and ran down in their beds like so much treacle.[57]

This clear analysis by Ruskin indicates the scientific importance of Forbes's work, but the average reader was less interested in his scientific discoveries than in his visits to hitherto unknown mountain regions and his wanderings on the mountains themselves. Although Forbes generally writes objectively and with great restraint (quite the opposite of his contemporaries, who dramatically describe their perils on Mont Blanc), many incidents in his *Travels* thrilled his readers: for instance, the story of the rescue of a solitary American who had fallen on the Trelaporte and become trapped on a narrow ledge, where he spent the night "surrounded by precipices on every side";[58] the measured account of avalanche danger on the first crossing of the Col d'Herens; the decaying corpses he found in crossing the Col de Collon; or the description of the magnificent view from the Stockhorn (11,795 feet), whose first ascent Forbes made in 1842. Later he recognized the popularity of the unscientific parts of his *Travels* and in 1855, under the title *Tour of Mont Blanc and Mont Rosa*, published a new and immediately popular edition, with most of the scientific material delightfully compressed, as the following example shows:

> Poets and philosophers have delighted to compare the course of human life to that of a river; perhaps a still apter simile might be found in the history of a glacier. Heaven-descended in its origin, it

yet takes its mould and conformation from the hidden womb of the mountains which brought it forth. At first soft and ductile, it acquires a character firmness of its own, as an inevitable destiny urges it on its onward career. Jostled and constrained by the crosses and inequalities of its prescribed path, hedged in by impassable barriers which fix limits to its movements, it yields groaning to its fate, and still travels forward seamed with the scars of many a conflict with opposing obstacles. All this while, although wasting, it is renewed by an unseen power—it evaporates, but is not consumed. On its surface it bears the spoils which, during the progress of its existence it has made its own; often weighty burdens devoid of beauty or value—at times precious masses, sparkling with gems or with ore. Having at length attained its greatest width and extension, commanding admiration by its beauty and power, waste predominates over supply, the vital springs begin to fail; it stoops into an attitude of decrepitude; it drops the burdens one by one, which it had borne so proudly aloft; its dissolution is inevitable. But as it is resolved into its elements, it takes all at once a new, and livelier, and disembarrassed form; from the wreck of its members it arises, another, yet the same—a noble, full-bodied, arrowy stream, which leaps, rejoicing over the obstacles which before had stayed its progress, and hastens through fertile valleys towards a freer existence, and a final union in the ocean with the boundless and the infinite.[59]

Forbes's book of travels, perhaps more than any other, stimulated English climbing in the days before the founding of the Alpine Club of London. His lucid, precise yet pleasant style, blending science and mountaineering, looks back to De Saussure and forward to Wills, Hudson, Kennedy, Tyndall, Whymper, Stephen, and the many other young Englishmen who, aroused by Forbes, were already making daring first ascents in the Pennine Alps.

Before we discuss these Alpine pioneers, however, we must consider a final member of the brotherhood who climbed Mont Blanc in the grand manner, for he too, although different in every respect from Professor Forbes, did much to create in young Englishmen a true enthusiasm for the mountains. This was Albert Richard Smith, showman, journalist, and entrepreneur, sometimes

Albert Smith, an original member of the Alpine Club, climbed Mont Blanc in 1851 and
became rich through his illustrated lectures about his climb. From Smith, *Mont Blanc.*

called a vulgarizer of the mountains, but, as has been shown,[60] a man truly
appreciative of mountain beauties. Smith wrote for Punch and was a friend
and contemporary of Dickens and Thackeray, though by no means their literary equal, for he was far more successful as a lecturer and showman than as an
author. After his ascent of Mont Blanc in 1851, accompanied by three other
Englishmen, sixteen guides, and enough food for a regiment,[61] he had painted
dioramas of Mont Blanc, which he used for background during an illustrated
lecture called "The Ascent of Mont Blanc." As the account was based on
Auldjo's ascent and his own, the thrills and horrors lost nothing in the telling,
and Egyptian Hall, London, where the lectures were held, more than once was
besieged by people unable to gain admission.

As one might suspect, Albert Smith's writings have spontaneity and his
anecdotes are delightful, but unfortunately he wrote little of literary worth.
The following quotation from his *Story of Mont Blanc* is typical of his subjective descriptions:

> I have said the Mur de la Cote is some hundred feet high, and is an
> all but perpendicular iceberg. At one point you can reach it from

the snow, but immediately after you begin to ascend it obliquely, there is nothing below but a chasm in the ice more frightful than anything yet passed. Should the foot slip, or the baton give way, there is no chance for life—you would glide like lightning from one frozen crag to another, and finally be dashed to pieces hundreds of feet below in the horrible depths of the glacier. Were it in the valley, simply rising up from a glacier moraine, its ascent would require great nerve and caution; but here, placed fourteen thousand feet above the level of the sea, terminating in an icy abyss so deep that the bottom is lost in obscurity; exposed in a highly rarefied atmosphere, to a wind cold and violent beyond all conception; assailed, with muscular powers already taxed far beyond their strength, and nerves shaken by constantly increasing excitement and want of rest—with bloodshot eyes, and raging thirst, and a pulse leaping rather than beating—with all this—it may be imagined that the frightful Mur de la Cote calls for more than ordinary determination to mount it.[62]

Smith goes on to describe the "guides creeping like flies" and other gruesome details. Like the average journalist of today, he was no blushing violet. Even more colorful according to report were his Egyptian Hall lectures, which inspired hundreds of Englishmen to visit Chamonix. Undoubtedly some of these visitors found the original Chamonix less colorful than Egyptian Hall, and were disappointed not to find large St. Bernard dogs walking over the ice carrying baskets of chocolates, as they did during the intermission in Albert Smith's lectures. Other visitors were more appreciative of the mountains, however, and some even were enticed to explore the upper snows.

Better transportation between London and the Alps, combined with the writings of Forbes, Smith, Ball, and others, was now enabling a record number of Englishmen to visit Mont Blanc. Five years after Albert Smith reached the summit of the highest peak in western Europe, two books describing mountain ascents appeared, and others came hard after them. The first, by Rev. Charles Hudson and E.S. Kennedy, was called *Where There's a Will There's a Way: An Ascent of Mont Blanc*. Despite the Horatio Alger title, this is a modest volume that describes a *guideless* ascent of Mont Blanc in 1855. Kennedy and Hudson, two versatile young Cambridge graduates, provide a striking contrast

210   THE STORY OF MONT BLANC.

"Coming down." Descending Mont Blanc, as seen by Albert Smith. From Smith, *Mont Blanc.*

to Smith and his companions of the 1851 ascent. The sixteen guides, forty-six fowl, and ninety-four bottles of wine and brandy were dispensed with, and the expedition carried out with remarkable simplicity and efficiency. Unfortunately, this attractive volume, the second edition of which gives an account of Hudson's first ascent of Mont Blanc, is not inspired.

In the same year appeared *Wanderings Among the High Alps,* by Alfred Wills, a book of considerable literary value, which vividly describes mountaineering and mountain travel. Wills, who later became Sir Alfred Wills and was for twenty-one years a judge of the High Court, writes with great appreciation of the mountains. *Wanderings Among the High Alps* describes visits to what have long since become the major Alpine centers of the Alps, such as Chamonix, Saas-Fee, Zermatt, Kandersteg, Lauterbrunnen, and Interlaken. In 1853 tourists and mountain climbers were almost entirely unknown in most of these areas and Wills was in every way a pioneer both in the valleys and on the upper snows. He writes with charm and spontaneous enthusiasm of most of what he sees. He is interested in the peasants and their way of living, in the glaciers, the guides, and the magnificence of mountain scenery. Wills has an inquiring mind, and as he is also a good observer, the combination prospers. Despite his enthusiasm, however, he is no Auldjo or Albert Smith. His chapter describing an early ascent of the Wetterhorn has an almost boyish freshness and delight in adventure, yet at the same time dignity and recognition of the dangers. When the party leaves Grindelwald for the Wetterhorn, the landlord of the hotel wrings their hands, begs them "try to return all of you alive,"[63] then breaks down and goes off shaking his head. Despite this inauspicious farewell, a wretched bivouac en route, and the fact that two young chamois hunters with a fir tree join the party, all goes well, and after a long bout of step-cutting they find themselves high on the mountain and under a great overhanging crest of snow:

> The cornice curled over towards us, like the crest of a wave, breaking at regular intervals along the line into pendants and inverted pinnacles of ice, many of which hung down to the full length of a tall man's height. They cast a ragged shadow on the wall of ice beyond, which was hard and glassy, not flecked with a spot of snow, and blue as the "brave o'erhanging" of the cloudless firmament. They seemed the battlement of an enchanted fortress,

framed to defy the curiosity of man, and to laugh to scorn his audacious efforts.

A brief parley ensued. Lauener had chosen his course well, and had worked up to the most inaccessible point along the whole line, where a break in the series of icicles allowed him to approach close to the icy parapet, and where the projecting crest was narrowest and weakest. It was resolved to cut boldly into the ice, and endeavor to hew deep enough to get a sloping passage on to the dome beyond. He stood close, not facing the parapet, but turned half round, and struck out as far away from himself as he could. A few strokes of his powerful arm brought down the projecting crest, which, after rolling a few feet, fell headlong over the brink of the arete, and was out of sight in an instant. We all looked on in breathless anxiety; for it depended upon the success of this assault, whether that impregnable fortress was to be ours, or whether we were to return, slowly and sadly, foiled by its calm and massive strength.

Suddenly a startling cry of surprise and triumph rang through the air. A great block of ice bounded from the top of the parapet, and before it had well lighted on the glacier, Lauener exclaimed: "Ich shaue den blaue Himmel!" (I see the blue sky!) A thrill of astonishment and delight ran through our frames. Our enterprise had succeeded! We were almost on the summit. That wave above us, frozen, as it seemed, in the act of falling over, into a strange and motionless magnificence, was the very peak itself! Lauener's blows flew with redoubled energy. In a few minutes, a practicable breach was made, through which he disappeared; and in a moment more the sound of his axe was heard behind the battlement under whose cover we stood. In his excitement he had forgotten us, and very soon the whole mass would have come crashing upon our heads. A loud shout of warning came from Sampson, who now occupied the gap, was echoed by five other eager voices, and he turned his energies in a safer direction. It was not long before Lauener and Sampson together had widened the opening; and then, at length, we crept slowly on. As I took the last step, Balmat disappeared from my sight, my left shoulder grazed against the angle of the icy embrasure, while, on the right, the glacier fell abruptly away beneath me towards an unknown and awful abyss; a hand from an invisible person grasped mine; I stepped across, and had passed the ridge of the Wetterhorn.[64]

Here is true mountain craft. Like the other climbers we gauge the cornice, debate whether it can be cut through, and stand in great suspense on the small steps chopped in the ice at the top of the tremendous slope while Lauener flogs away at the parapet. He breaks through, and as a great chunk of ice crashes away, blue sky suddenly appears. With considerable skill Wills has recaptured a truly dramatic moment.

Wills, unlike Smith and Auldjo, knows enough about the mountains to realize when there is great peril and when there is not. He understands danger and faces it calmly, as we see later in the description of the storm he, Balmat, and Professor Tyndall face while burying thermometers on the summit of Mont Blanc. This storm is described in his second Alpine book, *'The Eagle's Nest' in the Valley of Sixt*, which appeared three years after the *Wanderings*. Wills's second book is also well written and skillfully records the author's difficulties with suspicious peasants, who, when they learn of his desire to buy land, immediately suspect him of various low designs on the countryside. In general, however, *'The Eagle's Nest'* cannot compare with the charm of its predecessor, though chapter 8, which describes a magnificent sunset with a strange unearthly glow seen from the Grands Mulets, and also Wills's exposure to a storm on the summit of Mont Blanc, is justifiably famous.

Wills, who lived to be eighty-four, was one of the founders of the Alpine Club and later a distinguished contributor to the *Alpine Journal*. Among his other writings must be mentioned his *Passage of the Fenêtre de Saleinaz*, a most delightful article that first appears in the first edition of *Peaks, Passes and Glaciers*, and gives a particularly felicitous description of an unexpected bivouac among Alpine bilberries and rhododendrons.

The year following the publication of Wills's *Wanderings*, another book appeared that also had influence on the now expanding number of British climbers. This was Hinchliff's Summer Months among the Alps, a fresh and charming account of wanderings and occasional climbs among the mountain valleys. Like Wills's book of the year before, it shows the author's keen observation and appreciation of all around him, for he is a man who sees the mountains as they are, not as the imagination of a valley traveler causes him to see them. Hinchliff is continually in good spirits, whether he has just slipped on the Strahleck or had his hat blown off at the top of the Altels, and he laughs at the fearful stories of the effects of altitude on climbers of Mont Blanc: for instance, the gentleman who seriously stated that "the rarefaction of the air causes a relaxation of the ligaments of the knee and hip-joints,"[65]and thereby accounted for his not being able to climb higher on Mont Blanc.

Hinchliff probably did less climbing during his lifetime than did Justice Wills, but he was a real mountaineer and also contributed charming articles for several years to the *Alpine Journal*. With Hinchliff as well as Wills, we identify with the author as he travels into unknown regions, and continually share in his surprise. In Hinchliff's story of the first crossing of the Trift Pass, printed in *Peaks, Passes and Glaciers*, we find him interrupted at luncheon:

> The provision knapsacks were emptied and used as seats; a goodly leg of cold mutton on its sheet of paper formed the center, garnished with hard eggs and bread and cheese, round which we ranged ourselves in a circle. High festival was held under the deep blue heavens, and now and then, as we looked up at the wondrous wall of rocks which we had descended, we congratulated ourselves on the victory with a quiet nod, indicative of satisfaction. M. Seiler's beautiful oranges supplied the rare luxury of a dessert, and we were just in the full enjoyment of the delicacy when a booming sound, like the discharge of a gun far over our heads, made us all at once glance upwards to the top of the Trifthorn. Close to its craggy summit hung a cloud of dust, like dirty smoke, and in a few seconds another and a larger one burst forth several hundred feet lower. A glance through the telescope showed that a fall of rocks had commenced, and the fragments were leaping down from ledge to ledge in a series of cascades. Each block dashed off others at every point of contact, and the uproar became tremendous; thousands of fragments, making every variety of noise according to their size, and producing the effect of a fire of musketry and artillery combined, thundered downwards from so great a height that we waited anxiously for some considerable time to see them reach the snow-field below. As nearly as we could estimate the dis-

tance, we were 500 yards from the base of the rocks, so we thought that, come what might, we were in a tolerably secure position. At last we saw many of the blocks plunge into the snow after taking their last fearful leap; presently much larger fragments followed, taking proportionably larger bounds; the noise grew fiercer and fiercer, and huge blocks began to fall so near to us that we jumped to our feet, preparing to dodge them to the best of our ability. "Look out!" cried some one, and we opened out right and left at the approach of a monster, evidently weighing many hundred-weight, which was coming right at us like a huge shell fired from a mortar. It fell with a heavy thud not more than twenty feet from us, scattering lumps of snow into the circle where we had just been dining; but scarcely had we begun to recover from our astonishment when a still larger rock flew exactly over our heads to a distance of 200 yards beyond us. The malice of the Trifthorn now seemed to have done its worst; a few more blocks dropped around us, and then, after an incessant fire for about ten minutes, the falling masses retired in regular graduation, till nothing remained in transitu but showers of stones and small debris pouring down the side of the mountain; the thundering noise died away into a tinkling clatter; and, though clouds of dust still obscured the precipice, silence was soon restored.[66]

Later writers on the mountains would not have been so surprised at this type of rockfall, nor would they have detailed so accurately the succession of sounds. The point of view is definitely that of a real climber, but one who has been exposed to rockfall so rarely that the experience causes him pained surprise.

Hinchliff and other English climbers, as the books we have just considered show, had now gained firsthand knowledge of the Alps and enough technical proficiency to lead their own guideless climb of Mont Blanc. It is not surprising, then, that in the summer of 1857 William Mathews, E.S. Kennedy, and others were to form in London the Alpine Club, the oldest mountaineering club in existence today. Of course there had been mountain groups before—such as the Tramontane Club of Virginia, whose members in 1712 were agreed to climb Mount George in Virginia annually, and drink to the health of the king—but this was the first climbers' club in the modern sense. It became the source and pattern of later clubs in all parts of the globe.

The first meeting was held December 22, 1857. Shortly afterward, E.S. Kennedy was elected vice president and Hinchliff honorary secretary. The next year John Ball, who had climbed in the Alps since 1845 and was editor of *Peaks, Passes and Glaciers,* the club's first literary production, was selected to be president, with Professor Forbes the first honorary member. In 1862 a new *Peaks, Passes and Glaciers* edition in two volumes appeared under the editorship of Kennedy, and the next year came the first issue of the *Alpine Journal.*

Of the many excellent articles on mountain ascents selected for publication in *Peaks, Passes and Glaciers* in 1859 and 1862, we can mention only a few. The men who wrote them were living in what has been called the "golden age of mountaineering," and each summer they made first ascents that were charmingly described. At this period there was no affectation to prevent the writer from lovingly recounting the simple pleasures or discomforts common to most mountain climbs. Experiences were new and fresh to these authors and their readers, never hackneyed as they often became with later writing. The exaggeration of the earlier "horror school" had gone and the jargon and technical descriptions of route-finding, later so frequent, fortunately had not come in. Perhaps there were too many quotations from earlier writers to express the author's anxieties in critical places, but by and large these papers have literary value. Although only one or two of the contributors to *Peaks, Passes and Glaciers* can be considered a professional writer, the standards were high and the command of the language unusual. Men of other professions, under the stress of recaptured excitement or supreme beauty, rise above their normal levels and write with surprising effect. Indeed, the fact that new editions of Ball's *Peaks* still appear every few years is indicative of the book's sustained value.

Among the writers who should be mentioned, in addition to those already referred to, are William Mathews, F.F. Tuckett, J.F. Hardy, John Tyndall, J. Ormsby, Edward Whymper, and Leslie Stephen, all of whom also wrote in the next few years for the *Alpine Journal.* Most of these men continued their writings on the mountains and will be considered separately later. Practically all of them could describe with delightful touches their night bivouacs, problems of food and drink, boiling water at high places to determine the altitude, and encounters with alpine beasts—not dragons, but bouquetins (steinboch), chamois, sheep, marmots, and even fleas, the last of which Ormsby discusses in detail:

There was but one drop of bitter in our cup, counting the lamp oil as nothing. It was the fleas. Without any inordinate vanity, I may say that I am a judge of fleas. I have given them my attention under various circumstances and in various countries. Not to speak of an intimacy with the ordinary flea of the diligence, founded on having travelled many a league in his company, I have spent nights with hardy mountain fleas in Swiss chalets, with desperate Freischutz Wildjager fleas in the Tyrol, with bold contrabandist fleas in the Spanish Pyrenees, with Arab fleas, restless and lawless, children of the desert, dwellers in tents. But none of these ever impressed me so much as the others in ferocity and physical vigour; they surpass them all in instinct. They even give evidence of a kind of mutual dependence and organization of labour so systematic and well-sustained are their attacks. In the Marmot's Hole we were knee-deep in them. They crept up our trousers and down our necks until we were saturated with them. They lay in wait for us in dark corners and sprang upon us suddenly. They clung to us viciously, and bit us at supper and bit us at breakfast. They bit us sitting and bit us walking. On the mountainside, on the glacier, nay, even on the top of the Grivola, unaffected by the rarefication of the air, unimpressed by the magnificence of the view, there they were, biting away as if they had not broken their fast for twenty-four hours.[67]

As one who has been afflicted with fleas in India, the Alps, and elsewhere, I sympathize with Ormsby and appreciate his outraged feelings. The material is slight enough but the author's description is spirited, as it is with most of the articles in *Peaks*, whether a stoneman is being built, seracs are falling, a fast glissade is being made, or health drunk in red wine at the summit. The same high-spirited good fellowship and stories of lively ascents appear in the early numbers of the *Alpine Journal*, whose publication, as has been stated, began in 1863. Beginning quarterly issues of a magazine solely devoted to mountain travel and mountain ascents undoubtedly seemed rash at this time, for there were many who believed the sport of mountaineering would be short-lived, but the editor (H.B. George) bravely set forth his vindication:

It may, perhaps, be thought rather late to commence the publication of an Alpine Journal when so many of the great peaks of Switzerland have been already climbed, and the successful expeditions described. But we can assure the most skeptical reader that the Alps are not nearly exhausted, even by the many new ascents of last summer, of which we are now recording the first installment. The number of persons who know the mere name of the highest mountain in the great Dauphiné group may be reckoned in tens; and many peaks, that would be considered first-rate but for the proximity of such neighbours as Mont Blanc and the Weisshorn, are as yet untried; while, even if all other objects of interest in Switzerland should be exhausted, the Matterhorn remains (who shall say for how long?) unconquered and apparently invincible. Moreover, the Himalayas, which are daily becoming more accessible to enterprise, offer an unlimited field for adventure and scientific observation, not to mention the numerous ranges in all parts of the world which the Englishman's foot is some day destined to scale. With all these sources from whence to derive a constant supply of narrative and of valuable knowledge, we may defer the prospect of the starvation of the Alpine Journal, for want of matter whereon to feed, to some date beyond the scope of our calculations.[68]

George was correct. There was on hand, and for many years would continue to arrive, interesting material involving mountain ascents. In fact, the *Alpine Journal* has been published without a break from 1863 to the present time, through two world wars, and shows no intention of shutting down its presses. Just as the Alpine Club of London has been the parent of many mountain organizations, so the *Alpine Journal* has inspired publication of the Appalachian Mountain Club's *Appalachia, The American Alpine Journal, The Canadian Alpine Journal, The Sierra Club Bulletin, The Himalayan Journal,* and other mountain publications written in English and other languages the world over. For style, content, literary skill, and high qualities of editing, however, none has been as successful as the original. In this publication, as in the many others, there is great diversity of material: familiar essays, narratives of high adventure, scientific discussions, guidebook material, even verse and humor— all concerning mountains in any of the far reaches of the world.

At the time of the first issue, however, practically all articles were concerned with the Alps, and the writers, typically enough, varied from professionals like Leslie Stephen, to lawyers, doctors, parsons, businessmen, and surveyors like Philip Gossett, who describes a winter accident on the Haut-de-Cry:

> Bennen did not seem to like the look of the snow very much. He asked the local guides whether avalanches ever came down this couloir, to which they answered that our position was perfectly safe ... We were walking in the following order: Bevard, Nance, Bennen, myself, B., and Rebot. Having crossed over about three-quarters of the breadth of the couloir, the two leading men suddenly sank considerably above their waists. Bennen tightened the rope. The snow was too deep to think of getting out of the hole they had made, so they advanced one or two steps, dividing the snow with their bodies. Bennen turned round and told us he was afraid of starting an avalanche; we asked whether it would not be better to return and cross the couloir higher up. To this the three Ardon men opposed themselves; they mistook the proposed precaution for fear, and the two leading men continued their work. After three or four steps gained in the aforesaid manner, the snow became hard again. Bennen had not moved—he was evidently undecided what he should do; as soon, however, as he saw hard snow again, he advanced and crossed parallel to, but above, the furrow the Ardon men had made. Strange to say the snow supported him. While he was passing I observed that the leader, Bevard, had ten or twelve feet of rope coiled round his shoulder. I of course at once told him to uncoil it and get on the arete, from which he was not more than fifteen feet distant. Bennen then told me to follow. I tried his steps, but sank up to my waist in the very first. So I went through the furrows, holding my elbows close to my body, so as not to touch the sides. This furrow was about twelve feet long, and as the snow was good on the other side, we had all come to the false conclusion that the snow was accidentally softer there than elsewhere. Bennen advanced; he had made but a few steps when we heard a deep, cutting sound. The snowfield split in two about fourteen or fifteen feet above us. The cleft was at first quite narrow, nor more than an inch broad. An awful silence ensued; it lasted but a few seconds, and

then it was broken up by Bennen's voice, "Wir sind alle verloren." His words were slow and solemn, and those who knew him felt what they really meant when spoken by such a man as Bennen. They were his last words. I drove my alpenstock into the snow, and brought the weight of my body to bear on it. I then waited. It was an awful moment of suspense. I turned my head towards Bennen to see whether he had done the same thing. To my astonishment I saw him turn round, face the valley, and stretch out both arms. The ground on which we stood began to move slowly, and I felt the utter uselessness of any alpenstock. I soon sank up to my shoulders and began descending backwards. From this moment I saw nothing of what happened to the rest of the party. With a good deal of trouble I succeeded in turning round. The speed of the avalanche increased rapidly, and before long I was covered up with snow. I was suffocating when I suddenly came to the surface again. I was on a wave of the avalanche, and saw it before me as I was carried down. It was the most awful sight I ever saw. The head of the avalanche was already at the spot where we had made our last halt. The head alone was preceded by a thick cloud of snow-dust; the rest of the avalanche was clear. Around me I heard the horrid hissing of the snow; and far before me the thundering of the foremost part of the avalanche. To prevent myself sinking again, I made use of my arms much in the same way as when swimming in a standing position. At last I noticed that I was moving slower; then I saw the pieces of snow in front of me stop at some yards' distance; then the snow straight before me stopped, and I heard on a large scale the same creaking sound that is produced when a heavy cart passes over frozen snow in winter. I felt that I also had stopped, and instantly threw up both arms to protect my head in case I should be crushed to death. This tremendous pressure lasted but a short time; I was covered up by snow coming from behind me. My first impulse was to try and uncover my head—but this I could not do, the avalanche had frozen by pressure the moment it stopped, and I was frozen in. Whilst trying vainly to move my arms, I suddenly became aware that the hands as far as the wrists had the faculty of motion. The conclusion was easy; they must be above the snow. I set to work as

Johann Joseph Bennen, was a famous guide who died in an avalanche on the Haut-de-Cry. From Tyndall, *Hours of Exercise in the
Alps.*

well as I could; it was time, for I could not have held out much
longer. At last I saw a faint glimmer of light. The crust above my
head was getting thinner, but I could not reach it any more with my
hands; the idea struck me that I might pierce it with my breath.
After several efforts I succeeded in doing so, and felt suddenly a
rush of air towards my mouth; I saw the sky again through a little
round hole. A dead silence reigned around me; I was so surprised
to be still alive, and so persuaded at the first moment that none of
my fellow-sufferers had survived, that I did not even think of

shouting for them. I then made vain efforts to extricate my arms, but found it impossible; the most I could do was to join the ends of my fingers, but they could not reach the snow any longer. After a few minutes I heard a man shouting; what a relief it was to know that I was not the sole survivor! to know that perhaps he was not frozen in and could come to my assistance! I answered; the voice approached, but seemed uncertain where to go, and yet it was now quite near. A sudden exclamation of surprise! Rebot had seen my hands. He cleared my head in an instant and was about to try and cut me out completely, when I saw a foot above in the snow, and so near to me that I could touch it with my arms, although they were not quite free yet. I at once tried to move my foot; it was my poor friend's. A pang of agony shot through me as I saw that the foot did not move. Poor B. had lost sensation and was perhaps already dead. Rebot did his best; after some time he wished me to help him, so he freed my arms a little more so that I could make use of them. I could do but little, for Rebot had torn the axe from my shoulder as soon as he had cleared my head (I generally carry an axe separate from my alpenstock—the blade tied to the belt, and the handle attached to the left shoulder). Before coming to me Rebot had helped Nance out of the snow; he was lying nearly horizontally, and was not much covered over. Nance found Bevard, who was upright in the snow, but covered up to the head. After about twenty minutes the two last-named guides came up. I was at length taken out; the snow had to be cut with the axe down to my feet before I could be pulled out. A few minutes after 1 o'clock p.m. we came to my poor friend's face . . . I wished the body to be taken out completely, but nothing could induce the three guides to work any longer, from the moment they saw that it was too late to save him. I acknowledge that they were nearly as incapable of doing anything as I was. When I was taken out of the snow the cord had to be cut. We tried the end going towards Bennen, but could not move it; it went nearly straight down, and showed us that there was the grave of the bravest guide the Valais ever had, and ever will have.[69]

Gossett's description of being cast down in an avalanche illustrates how the tremendous emotion of a dramatic moment in the mountains can so impress itself on a person that even if he lacks literary training, the recaptured tension of the moment may lead him to re-create the event with great effect. Gossett, as has been said, was a surveyor and very definitely not a literary man, yet the passage cited has great suspense: first as we sense Bennen's feeling of anxiety as to the insecurity of the snow, then the great effort made to get off the treacherous slope, the ominous cracking, Bennen's dramatic announcement, and the sensation of falling. As if this is not enough, we are carried down the avalanche with the snow hissing around us and the head of the avalanche preceded by a cloud of powder snow thundering ahead far below us, then the snow creaks to a stop, there is great pressure, and he is buried to the wrists. Finally, there is the almost miraculous escape, ending with the discovery that Bennen has been buried under tons of snow. Hardy or Hemingway, if either had been carried down in an avalanche, may have re-created the event better, but even in the hands of a surveyor the experience produces a fine picture that vividly recaptures the emotion of the moment.

Not every article in the *Alpine Journal*, naturally enough, involves miraculous escapes such as this, nor are the descriptions as vivid. There is in the *Alpine Journal*, however, writing of high caliber, partly because of the educational, professional, or literary background of contributors, but more perhaps because of recaptured dramatic moments that stand out against the drab background of ordinary life and, superimposed on the natural and often latent writing ability of the contributors, produce material of literary value. These moments of emotion need have nothing to do with danger. For instance, examine Wills's description of a mountain bivouac below the glacier de Saleinaz or Thomas Kennedy's climb through broken clouds to the summit of the Dent Blanche. Kennedy states:

> We ascended slowly, kicking steps in the half-consolidated snow. The north wind, charged with icy spiculae, drove fiercely in our faces, and Wigram's hair, unprotected by his hat, became a mass of white icicles. . . . Sometime, when the cornice was higher than our heads, we drove our alpenstocks through its weak part in order to try its condition, and could see white rolling clouds beneath the hole. . . . Thick mists and driving clouds of snow swept over and past us; at one moment we could see the lower rocks and buttresses of the mountain far down in the depths around; another instant,

and all was again hidden, and we seemed to be alone in the midst
of chaos. Vainly we turned our eyes around, wearied by the form-
less glare, in search of some object on which to rest them.
Downwards, to our left, were steep rocks covered with snow—not
even the chamois might venture there; on our right was a seething
abyss, at the bottom of which we knew lay the glaciers of Zinal and
Schönbuhl, but nothing was to be seen except an indescribable
wreathing in the air, like the wind made visible.[70]

This is not literature, but here a writer, clearly not a professional, has given
a very fair description of men with iced eyelashes high on a cloud-swept ridge
of snow gazing below on writhing masses of vapor that were "like the wind
made visible."

A contemporary of Thomas Kennedy, who many times saw curling strands
of mist below him, was A.W. Moore, author of one of the most charming
mountain books of the period, *The Alps in 1864*. This book, published privately for Moore's mountaineering friends, was not written for the general public.
Moore, who later became political secretary at the India Office, introduces
none of the gravity of his profession into his mountain writings. He is on holiday, and though his statements are exact, he is never eloquent and never aims
at effect. Instead there is humor, humanity, and delightful frankness. *The Alps
in 1864* is a private journal, neither scientific nor literary, full of hedonistic
wanderings. In the introduction Moore apologizes that he did not have time to
rewrite it "on a different principle," but we are glad that he did not, for it is the
private-journal, not-for-publication quality that most pleases us today. Had
Moore the statesman written for publication, dignity and restraint might have
caused great changes, charming but intimate incidents probably would have
been removed or treated objectively, and some reason, scientific or otherwise,
would have had to be found for the pleasant excursions. Owing to the generally conservative principles of Moore's time, this thoroughly subjective volume
was not published for public sale until a generation later.

As has been noted, *The Alps in 1864* was not organized for literary effect, but
what it lacks in formality it makes up in variety of incident: Moore chasing
young chamois, watching a giant serac fall across his path on the Biesjoch, strug-
gling up the Mönch with his left arm in a sling, and drinking lemonade with satisfaction after a long day only to find at the bottom of the bottle two dozen blue-
bottle flies "in various stages of decomposition."[71] In his chapter on Mont Blanc

by the Brenva Route we have a particularly amusing description of the whole party "à cheval" on a narrow ledge, Moore wondering whether, if someone slips, the others will jump off the opposite side—and if so what will happen.

Moore did not limit his Alpine writing to his diary, fortunately, and was a frequent contributor to the early *Alpine Journals*. Always an innovator, he was one of the first winter climbers in the Alps and gives a pleasant account of a moonlight ascent of the Finsteraarjoch.[72] Later still he was one of the first mountaineers to visit the Caucasus, climbing Elbrus with Freshfield and Tucker in 1868. On this adventure his sense of humor and innate gallantry impressed his companions.

Moore was not the only unscientific adventurer in these early days of climbing. W.E. Hall, for instance, climbed joyfully during the early 1860s and finds humor in most situations. Typical of other struggles with Alpine provender is his affair with a small black loaf of Alpine bread, which for various reasons had become the major portion of the menu on a climb of the Dent d'Hérens:

> We tried to chop it with an ice axe, and it hopped about the chalet like a marble; we boiled it for four long hours, while we glared greedily at the pot, and at the end a quarter of an inch of the outside was turned into gluey slime, and within it was as hard as ever.[73]

Contrast this with Albert Smith's food supply and one realizes that ascents as well as accounts of them had ceased to be in the grand manner.

Most climbers at this time felt they needed a reason for their mountain wanderings, and selected science, but some, like De Saussure and Professor John Tyndall, who became one of the most distinguished scientific men of the day, did not. Tyndall was one of the first daring explorers of the high snows, and numbered among his mountain achievements first ascents of the Aletschorn, the Weisshorn, and Pic Tyndall on the Matterhorn. He bravely attempted to make the first ascent of the Matterhorn in a period when such an undertaking was considered suicidal, and nearly accomplished it. (In 1868, after the peak had been climbed, he at last reached the actual summit.)

Tyndall loved mountains and loved to climb them, but one scarcely gets this impression from his writing, so careful was he to cloak all his actions under the guise of scientific investigation. Unlike many, who even today use a similar "reason" for mountain travel, Tyndall was a true scientist and an excep-

Tyndall and Bennen saving a porter from a crevasse. From Tyndall, *Hours of Exercise in the Alps.*

tionally keen and observant one, yet beneath his cold scientific reserve he must have been a romantic, too. In fact, he has been likened by a contemporary to an "animated onion," with the "man of science" shell on the outside and under it "the feudal baron who delighted in the pursuit of bears, wolves and foxes in the fastness of the hills."[74]

Tyndall writes lucid prose, reminiscent of that of Forbes, and full of regard for mountain beauties. His courage, ingenuity, and enterprising spirit are as admirable as his scientific discoveries and the literary caliber of his writings. He made his first attempt on the Matterhorn in 1860—a bold man, for even in 1863 in the preface of the *Alpine Journal* doubt is expressed whether the Matterhorn will ever be climbed. From 1856 until 1870 he climbed almost continuously, describing what he saw in articles and in *The Glaciers of the Alps* and *Hours of Exercise in the Alps*. The latter was particularly famous in his own day and has appeared in numerous editions right to the present. *The Glaciers of the Alps* is somewhat disconnected, as it is more or less in journal form, and full of scientific observations and ponderings, but through it all the love of the mountains and of mountain ascents is clear. Professor Tyndall, however, is so imbued with the need for constant scientific justification for his bold adventuring that today he sometimes seems amusing. For instance, after a fine passage describing a daring traverse of a knife-blade of snow on the Weisshorn, thousands of feet above the glaciers, the professor rationalizes his act by quoting Faraday's theory of the compacting of snow under pressure—though he honestly admits that he acted first and thought of the theory afterward. Similarly, in describing a particularly dangerous passage on the Gauli Glacier, he finds himself becoming too subjective and suddenly breaks off the incident. Note the transition:

> Its steepness was greater than that of a cathedral roof, while below us, and within a few yards of us, was a chasm into which it would be certain death to fall. Education enables us to regard a position of this kind almost with indifference; still the work was by no means unexciting.[75]

What restraint! Occasionally, too, but fortunately rarely, he yields to the Victorian impulse to moralize:

> . . . ice crags proclaim from their heights, "Do not trust us; we are

momentary and merciless." They wear the aspect of hostility undisguised; but these chasms of the névé are typified by the treachery of the moral world, hiding themselves under shining coverlets of snow, and compassing their ends by dissimulation.[76]

Tyndall is also a Victorian scientist, who sees in the eroding slopes of the Aeggishhorn an illustration of the changeless laws of nature.[77] Indeed, as early in the morning he looks out over the great Alpine peaks, we don't know whether he will be moved in a scientific or a romantic manner, for he was equally capable of expressing himself in either. For instance, his description of climbing the Jungfrau ends as follows:

> And as I looked over this wondrous scene towards Mont Blanc, the Grand Combin, the Dent Blanche, the Weisshorn, the Dom, and the thousand lesser peaks which seemed to join in celebration of the risen day, I asked myself, as on previous occasions: How was this colossal work performed? Who chiselled these mighty and pic-turesque masses out of a mere protuberance of the earth? And the answer was at hand. Ever young, ever mighty—with the vigour of a thousand worlds still within him—the real sculptor was even then climbing the eastern sky. It was he who raised aloft the waters which cut out these ravines; it was he who planted the glaciers on the mountain slopes, thus giving gravity a plough to open out the valleys; and it is he who, acting through the ages, will finally lay low these mighty mountains, rolling them gradually seaward—
>
> Sowing the seeds of continents to be; so that the people of an older earth may see mould spread and corn wave over the hidden rocks which at this moment bear the weight of the Jungfrau.[78]

None of the mountaineers of scientific inclinations has expressed his views more clearly and effectively than Tyndall, nor perhaps has any been a more daring climber, but the professor, as has been noted, was also a romantic of the first order. Storms, clouds, and other natural phenomena impressed him, as indicated by his description of a lovely sunset he once saw coloring the higher Alpine peaks:

> They seemed pyramids of solid fire, while here and there long stretches of crimson light drawn over the higher snowfields linked

the summits together. An intensely illuminated geranium flower seems to swim in its own colour, which apparently surrounds the petals like a layer, and defeats by its luster any attempt of the eye to seize upon the sharp outline of the leaves. A similar effect was here observed on the mountains; the glory did not seem to come from them alone, but seemed also effluent from the air around them.[79]

Many passages of this sort could be quoted, but enough have probably been given to show Professor Tyndall's descriptive capacity. One minute he is gleefully describing a companion wearing a red nightcap and squatting over a meager fire like a demon; later he is elucidating with professional geologic diction the complex ice honeycombs of a nearby icefall. Soon after the narrative of a narrow escape from an avalanche of the type that had killed his former guide Bennen, he can turn with great equanimity to a scientific problem, such as why the sky is blue. Only on top of the Weisshorn does he put away his notebook, feeling that notes in such a place are too profane. But whether this brilliant and romantic scientist is rescuing a porter from a crevasse, toasting his cheese in a mountain bivouac, or bolstering his determination by recalling the stubborn and unyielding qualities of the English in battle, he knows he can excuse himself by the statement that it is all grand discipline for mind and body.

Professor Tyndall's great rival for the first ascent of the Matterhorn was less cultured and sensitive to convention, had less scientific and literary ability, and was probably only slightly more skilled as a climber, yet Edward Whymper not only first climbed the Matterhorn, but also became the world's most famous mountaineer and the author of the best-known mountain book.

To do justice to the conqueror of the Matterhorn, one must go back a few years. Edward Whymper was the son of a book illustrator. Like his father, he became an artist, and in 1860, at the age of twenty, was commissioned to go to the Alps to make illustrations for an edition of *Peaks, Passes and Glaciers*. Taking naturally to life in the mountains, and being hardy and possessed of considerable initiative and ingenuity, Whymper returned to the Alps year after year to climb and sketch, and soon became one of the most experienced mountaineers of his day. As he was not wealthy, he was forced to climb frequently without guides, a fact that doubtless increased his self-reliance and craftsmanship, but at the same time nearly caused his death in a fall down an ice slope during an early attempt on the Matterhorn:

... I slipped and fell.... The knapsack brought my head down first, and I pitched into some rocks about a dozen feet below; they caught something and tumbled me off the edge, head over heels, into the gully; the baton was dashed from my hands, and I whirled downwards in a series of bounds, each longer than the last; now over ice, now into rocks; striking my head four or five times, each time with increased force. The last bound sent me spinning through the air, in a leap of fifty or sixty feet, from one side of the gully to the other, and I struck the rocks, luckily, with the whole of my left side. They caught my clothes for a moment, and I fell back on to the snow with motion arrested. My head fortunately came the right side up, and a few frantic catches brought me to a halt, in the neck of the gully, and on the verge of the precipice. Baton, hat and veil skimmed by and disappeared, and the crash of the rocks— which I had started—as they fell on to the glacier, told how narrow had been the escape from utter destruction. As it was, I fell nearly 200 feet in seven or eight bounds. Ten feet more would have taken me in one gigantic leap of 800 feet on to the glacier below.[80]

He goes on to describe his injuries and how "the blood jerked out in blinding jets at each pulsation," but he managed to stop the flow and get down off the mountain. This is moving description, comparable with Gossett's account of his tremendous fall in an avalanche, but why is Whymper still the most read of all mountain writers? There is a reason, though one must know a little about his life or read the whole of his *Scrambles*, not merely a passage from it, to understand.

Whymper, a very ambitious youth from a middle-class family of eleven children, found in the unclimbed Alps a challenge, and for five years he climbed with great skill and determination. His first goal had been to climb the Weisshorn or the Matterhorn, but when he learned that Professor Tyndall had reached the summit of the Weisshorn, his ambitions concentrated furiously on the Matterhorn, in many ways the most dramatic and awe-inspiring peak in the Alps. Seven times he unsuccessfully attempted it from the Italian side, both with and without guides, and on one of these forays, as we have seen, he nearly lost his life. Meanwhile, however, he had been developing techniques and improving the then existing equipment, so that by 1865 he was probably as

"We saw a toe - it seemed to belong to Moore - we saw Reynaud a flying body." From Whymper, *Scrambles Amongst the Alps*.

experienced as any English mountaineer, including Hudson, Tyndall, and
Tuckett. To justify this claim one must point out that though Whymper had
climbed fewer peaks than one or two other Englishmen, he had personally
done more than any of them in route-finding and reconnoitering difficult rock
and snow, while his bivouac equipment, developed through methodical preparation and trial and error, excelled that of any of his contemporaries.

For five years, then, Whymper's burning ambition was to climb the
Matterhorn, a desire not dampened by the bold efforts of his many rivals, especially the Italian guide Jean-Antoine Carrel and Professor Tyndall. Throughout
this period Whymper showed amazing courage in continually believing that
the Matterhorn could be climbed, for in his day the stupendous precipices had
psychologically persuaded nearly all guides and mountaineers that the ascent
was impossible.

Writing about the Matterhorn, he tells us of the "terror inspired by its
invincible appearance," and goes on to say, "There seemed to be a cordon
drawn around it, up to which one might go, but no farther. Within that invisible line gins and affreets were supposed to exist—the Wandering Jew and the
spirits of the damned. The superstitious natives in the surrounding valleys
(many of whom firmly believed it to be not only the highest mountain in the
Alps, but in the world) spoke of a ruined city on its summit wherein the spirits dwelt; and if you laughed, they gravely shook their heads; told you to look
yourself to see the castles and the walls, and warned one against a rash
approach, lest the infuriate demons from their impregnable heights might hurl
down vengeance for one's derision."[81]

Despite this attitude Whymper was always optimistic, and his systematic and
determined planning was in marked contrast to the pessimism of those about
him. Carrel, as has been said, also believed in the peak's accessibility, and but for
his loyalty to Italy he, with Whymper, probably would have made the first ascent,
and one of the most famous Alpine tragedies would have been prevented.

This is what happened: Undeterred by his previous failures and those of
Professor Tyndall, Whymper planned to attack the Matterhorn again in the
summer of 1865, but this time from Zermatt, as he had noted that the slant of
the strata favored assaults from this side. At nearly the last moment Carrel and
his brother, who Whymper thought had agreed to accompany him, suddenly
refused to go, for their plan was to lead an Italian party to the summit from the
Italian side, making the first ascent for the honor of Italy. Left without guides in

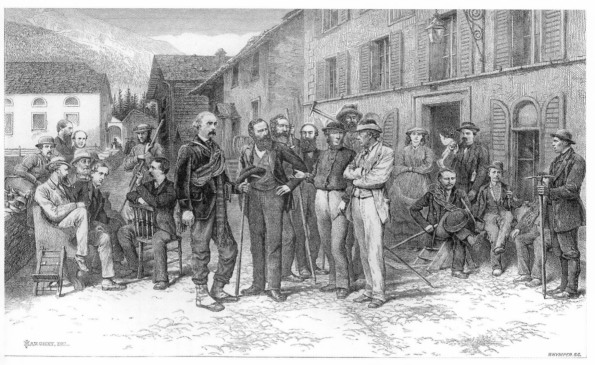

"The Club Room of Zermatt in 1894." outside the Monte Rosa Hotel. Among the guides shown are Peter Perrn (far right), Peter Taugwalder (upon the bench), J. J. Maguignaz (leaning against the door post), Franz Andermattten (on the steps) and Ulrich Lauener "towers in the background." From Whymper, *Scrambles Amongst the Alps.*

this manner, most men would have conceded defeat, but not Whymper. On his way to Zermatt, he fell in with young Lord Francis Douglas and later with Charles Hudson, one of the best English climbers, who was also about to attempt the Matterhorn and had with him Jean Croz, Whymper's former guide.

The parties joined forces, determined to prevent the rival Italians from gaining the first ascent, and accordingly on the morning of July 13, 1865, eight men left Zermatt to try to ascend the great Valais pyramid by the Hörnli ridge. In addition to those mentioned was Douglas Hadow, a young and inexperienced climber companion of Charles Hudson, together with the old guide Taugwalder and his two sons. This large party would today be considered unwieldy, but in 1865 the technique of climbing was still in the formative period. At about 11,000 feet a bivouac was established from which one of the Taugwalder boys returned to Zermatt. The next day the route was found to be easier than anticipated, and though Hadow needed frequent assistance, the whole party was soon at the base of the final snow slope and wondering whether the Italians had preceded them. Whymper tells us:

> You must now carry your thoughts back to the seven Italians who started from Breuil on the 11th of July. Four days had passed since their departure, and we were tormented with anxiety lest they should arrive on the top before us. All the way up we had talked of them, and many false alarms of "men on the summit" had been raised. The higher we rose, the more intense became the excitement. The slope eased off, at length we could be detached, and Croz and I, dashing away, ran a neck-and-neck race, which ended in a dead heat. At 1:40 p.m. the world was at our feet, and the Matterhorn was conquered. Hurrah! Not a footstep could be seen.
>
> It was not yet certain that we had not been beaten. The summit of the Matterhorn was formed of a rudely level ridge, about 360 feet long, and the Italians might have been at its farther extremity. I hastened to the farther end, scanning the snow right and left eagerly. Hurrah! again; it was untrodden. "Where are the men?" I peered over the cliff, half doubting, half expectant, and saw them immediately—mere dots on the ridge, at an immense distance below. Up went my arms and my hat. "Croz! Croz!! Come here!!" "Where are they, Monsieur?" "There, don't you see them, down there?" "Ah! the Coquins, they are low down." "Croz, we must make those fellows hear us." We yelled until we were hoarse. The Italians seemed to regard us—we could not be certain. "Croz, we must make them hear us; they shall hear us!" I seized a block of rock and hurled it down, and called upon my companion, in the name of friendship, to do the same. We drove our sticks in, and prised away the crags, and soon a torrent of stone poured down the cliffs. There was no mistake about it this time. The Italians turned and fled.
>
> Still, I would that the leader of that party [Carrel] could have stood with us at that moment, for our victorious shouts conveyed to him the disappointment of the ambition of a lifetime. He was the man of all those who attempted the ascent of the Matterhorn,

who most deserved to be the first upon its summit. He was the first to doubt its inaccessibility, and he was the only man who persisted in believing that its ascent would be accomplished. It was the aim of his life to make the ascent from the side of Italy, for the honor of his native valley. For a time he had the game in his hands; he played it as he thought best; but he made a false move, and he lost it.[82]

Whymper had won. The great moment of his life had arrived. For five years he had thought and planned to achieve this conquest and now he had succeeded. Note his actions as the party arrives at the summit. Does he congratulate the others, gaze rapturously at the view, or dig into the rucksacks to get food to refresh the more weary members of the party? No. Plenty of time for that later. Instead he races for the top, to be the first to plant his foot on the actual summit. Then he must be sure that the Italians have not preceded him, for this he considers his mountain and he must have complete victory.

To Whymper, the Matterhorn is his opponent in a gigantic duel. Nothing else really matters. His own ascents of the Aiguille Verte, the Ponte des Écrins, and other peaks are a sideshow; the attempts of Professor Tyndall and J.A. Carrel on the Matterhorn are highly significant moves to defeat him. He is determined to overcome all obstacles, human and geologic, to win his way to the top. *Scrambles Amongst the Alps* rarely deviates from this tremendous struggle. As G.W. Young graphically describes it, we have "the flash-light representation of a flinty mountain and of a steely Whymper in continuous concussion; all illuminated by the sparks of perilous incident they struck out of one another."[83]

The struggle for the Matterhorn did not last as long as that for Mount Everest, but there is nothing in later mountain literature as epic and dramatic as Whymper's personal fight against great odds to conquer the Matterhorn. In it is symbolized man's struggle against mountains, or if you like, man's combat against nature, for it is both. Whymper's courageous spirit and determination keep him going when any "sensible" man would have given up. The determination of the guides that the peak cannot be climbed; Professor Tyndall's bold attempt followed by his agreement that it cannot be climbed; the injuries inflicted on Whymper by the mountain when, as we have seen, he fell from it on the return from an unsuccessful attempt—none of these reasons for giving up seriously dashed his spirits. It seemed as if he and the mountain were ordained to fight it out until one or the other succumbed.

In *Scrambles Amongst the Alps* Whymper is in the center of the picture at all times. He accurately observes the peasants and the various peaks he climbs, but always there is the underlying struggle between him and the Matterhorn, and it is this epic struggle that has made the book so popular. As can be noticed from the quotations already given, Whymper is more subjective than the other Victorian writers we have considered, but there is none of the hedonistic good humor that distinguishes Moore nor the strange mixture of professional scientific analysis mixed with descriptive outbursts of Professor Tyndall. Instead we have a serious and determined account, larded with lively and interesting incidents, which focuses attention on the author himself. Wills, Hinchliff, Hudson, E.S. Kennedy, John Ball—not one of these contemporaries could so separate himself from convention and write about himself as Whymper does. Had any done so, probably the writing would have been circulated privately among a small group only, as was the case with Moore's *The Alps in 1864*.

But we have left Edward Whymper and his companions on the summit of the Matterhorn, no place to linger long. After a colorless description of the summit panorama and "one crowded hour of glorious life,"[84] the descent is begun. Unfortunately, Whymper goes back to leave the climbers' names in a bottle, and when he returns all eight are roped together, contrary to modern practice, and through mistake a link of weak rope is substituted for the strong Manila one used on the ascent.

Whymper's account of the descent in *Scrambles* continues:

> A few minutes later, a sharp-eyed lad ran into the Monte Rosa hotel, to Seiler, saying that he had seen an avalanche fall from the summit of the Matterhorn on to the Matterhorn Gletscher. The boy was reproved for telling idle stories; he was right nevertheless, and this was what he saw.
>
> Michel Croz had laid aside his axe, and in order to give Mr. Hadow greater security, was absolutely taking hold of his legs, and putting his feet, one by one, into their proper positions. So far as I know no one was actually descending. I cannot speak with certainty, because the two leading men were partially hidden from my sight by an intervening mass of rock, but it is my belief, from the movements of their shoulders, that Croz, having done as I have said, was in the act of turning round, to go down a step or two

Guide Michel-August Croz, 1865. From Whymper, *Scrambles Amongst the Alps.*

himself; at this moment Mr. Hadow slipped, fell against him, and knocked him over. I heard one startled exclamation from Croz, then saw him and Mr. Hadow flying downwards; in another moment Hudson was dragged from his steps, and Lord F. Douglas immediately after him. All this was the work of a moment. Immediately we heard Croz's exclamation, old Peter and I planted ourselves as firmly as the rocks would permit; the rope was taut between us, and the jerk came on us both as on one man. We held; but the rope broke midway between Taugwalder and Lord Francis Douglas. For a few seconds we saw our unfortunate companions sliding downwards on their backs, and spreading out their hands, endeavoring to save themselves. They passed from our sight uninjured, disappearing one by one, and fell from precipice to precipice on to the Matterhorn gletscher below, a distance of nearly 4,000 feet in height. From the moment the rope broke it was impossible to help them.

So perished our comrades! For the space of half an hour we remained on the spot without moving a single step. The two men, paralyzed by terror, cried like infants, and trembled in such a manner as to threaten us with the fate of the others. Old Peter rent the air with exclamations of "Chamounix! Oh, what will Chamounix say?" He meant, who would believe that Croz could fall? The young man did nothing but scream or sob, "We are lost!" "We are lost!" Fixed between the two, I could neither move up nor down. . . . At last old Peter summoned up the courage, and changed his position to a rock to which he could fix the rope; the young man then descended, and we all stood together. Immediately we did so, I asked for the rope which had given way and found, to my surprise—indeed, to my horror—that it was the weakest of the three ropes. It was not brought, and should not have been employed, for the purpose for which it was used. It was old rope, and compared with the others, was feeble. It was intended as a reserve, in case we had to leave much rope behind, attached to rocks. I saw at once that a serious question was involved, and made him give me the end. It had broken in mid-air, and it did not appear to have sustained previous injury.

For more than two hours afterwards I thought almost every moment that the next would be my last; for the Taugwalders, utterly unnerved, were not only incapable of giving assistance, but were in such a state that a slip might have been expected from them at any moment. After a time, we were able to do that which should have been done at first, and fixed rope to firm rocks, in addition to being tied together. These ropes were cut from time to time, and were left behind. Even with their assurance the men were afraid to proceed, and several times old Peter turned with ashy face and faltering limbs, and said, with terrible emphasis, "I cannot!"[85]

The passage quoted is one of the best known in Alpine writing. Whymper's *Scrambles* has received its fame largely for two reasons: the intense five-year struggle between Whymper and the Matterhorn, and his beautifully drawn and exciting illustrations. It would be unfair to Whymper, however, to deny that though his famous work has little organization, his observation is excellent and the book deservedly famous. Above all, *Scrambles* holds the interest amazingly well, partly because of the carefully recorded dialogue and colorful incidents. He gives us the personality of the people he meets: good-hearted landlords like Seiler, cheerful peasants like the hunchback Luc Meynet, and guides like Almer the steady man and Croz the strong man. Little incidents remain in the memory, such as troubles in clearing Alpine equipment through the French customs and M. Reynaud's delayed leap of a Bergschrund on the Col de Pilatte. Against these vivid moments may be weighed the digressions to discuss glacial theories or equipment, somewhat similar to those that interrupted Professor Tyndall's more smooth-flowing narratives. But despite these organic faults and the excessively journalistic style, with its exclamation points and dashes, we can delight in the bold, confident record of a man rising above himself and recording the great period of his life.

Whymper's success on the Matterhorn and the ensuing tragedy quickly made him the outstanding mountain figure of the day. From then on he was famous, and great things were expected of him. His later career, however, was not particularly successful, although be visited Greenland and the Canadian Rockies, and made the first ascents of Mount Chimborazo (21, 425 feet) in Ecuador, and other South American peaks. His later writings, like his book on South America, *Travels Amongst the Great Andes of the Equator,* are sometimes dull and clearly lack the inspiration of his "great period," so successfully recaptured in the *Scrambles*. This Alpine book will be remembered long after his other writings have been forgotten, the personal record of a climber who fought stoutly and alone against a great foe, and, undisturbed by psychological fears or scientific problems, carried on to victory. Even as mountaineering fashions of the day meant nothing to him, so literary conventions requiring reticence, suppression, and objectivity were likewise discarded, and he gives us

"The whirling snow mocked our efforts." Whymper and his companions attempt to erect a tent on Mount Cotocachi. From Whymper, *Travels Among the Great Andes of the Equator.*

a personal account of his duel with the Matterhorn that grips the imagination as it is held by none of his more skillful but more inhibited literary contemporaries.

Others who climbed during this great period should be mentioned briefly, although most are less sensational and far more objective than Whymper. Too often geographical matters bulk large in the author's mind and interfere with literary worth. Like Sir Alfred Wills, most climbers are reticent about describing personal danger. For instance, all that William Mathews has to say about his brother falling into a crevasse and catching on the edge is that "he had a most providential escape and described the sensation of his legs dangling in the cleft in something the reverse of agreeable."[86] The same author, however, is more personal in describing his intense enjoyment at getting away from the "ceaseless millwork of England in the nineteenth century,"[87] as can be seen in a paper read before the Alpine Club in 1880:

> No occupation in the world could have been more fascinating than our threading our upward way among the seracs of the Eiger Glacier. . . . Now we are cutting hand and foot holds up a huge pyramid of ice; now seated astride of a long wedge and creeping along it hand over hand; but the most delightful moment of all is when, every other method proving unavailing, we descend into the labyrinthic caverns of the glacier, and pause a moment to admire the strange beauty of our position. We are standing in a grotto, or rather, a corridor, whose walls tinted with delicate shades of blue and green rise high over our heads, and curl over into cornices fringed with pendent icicles; overhead is a long rift of sky, of the profoundest Alpine blue, while down the glacier the crevasse opens out into several branches, disclosing glimpses of distant pine woods and green pastures, scattered chalets and silver streaks of falling water, thus forming a series of exquisite pictures each set in its crystal frame. In the opposite direction the crevasse closes overhead; but we see that it is open beyond, and creeping through the icy tunnel we climb up again on to the glacier surface farther on.[88]

Here is true delight in Alpine wanderings, and the same joy, though with another source, that Hinchliff has when high on the Trift Pass he carols, "Never was cold mutton sweeter; never did the good Beaujolais flow more mellifluously from the leathern cup."[89]

C.E. Mathews, later the author of the conventional and somewhat unin-spired *Annals of Mont Blanc*, in 1870 could give a graphic description of climb-ing the Matterhorn in a storm that clogged his eyelashes and made Melchior Anderegg look like "Father Christmas."[90] He could enjoy the fight against the storm as much as his brother William could delight in the beauties of a cre-vasse or Hinchliff in his luncheon on the Trift, for life in the mountains holds different pleasures for different people. The fact that Mathews could glory in his struggle against a furious storm marks a fine breaking away from the con-ventions of ten years before when the Reverend J.L. Davies apologizes in *Peaks, Passes and Glaciers* for not contributing to geology or botany during his climb-ing but merely having fun.

Another who climbed during this period should be mentioned, A.C. Ramsay, who begins an account of some interesting glacial studies as follows:

> In the good old days of pigtails and bagwigs the tourist world cared nothing for glaciers, and only a few philosophers, like De Saussure, ever dared voluntarily to face the privations and dangers of the High Alps; their effigies in many an engraving is something very like full court costume, with a crowd of attendant guides, still bear-ing witness to the interest they took in Alpine glaciers. . . . Rash writers still held that the far-borne boulder drift, so widely spread over the cold and temperate regions of Europe, Asia and America, had been scattered abroad by mighty sea-waves, set in motion by the sudden upheaval of hypothetical northern continents; and the polish and striation of the rocks in the mountain valleys—the ver-itable signs of vanished glaciers—were attributed by flippant writ-ers and talkers to cartwheels, hob-nailed boots, and the nether integuments of Welshmen sliding down the hills; as if the country had been inhabited in the famous armor of stone worn by Loupgarou and his giants, when they fight with the heroic Pantagruel—their sole occupation for illimitable ages having con-sisted in the performance of titanic glissades upon the rocks.[91]

Far more important than Ramsay, however, was T.M. Bonney, whose *Alpine Regions of Switzerland and the Neighboring Countries* came out in 1868 and was helpful later in his pleasant but stately and somewhat ponderous *Building of the Alps*. Bonney's style lacks the freshness and humor that make the words of so many of his contemporaries a delight to read. He was one of many prolific Alpine writers, such as John Ball, author of the first Alpine guidebook, and H.B. George, first editor of the *Alpine Journal,* while Adams-Reilly, the Pendlebury brothers, and F.F. Tuckett wrote many colorful accounts of early climbs. It was George, typically enough, who discovered that his Islamic bearers in the Caucasus, though they could not drink liquor, would consume champagne with great satisfaction if he called it sherbet.[92]

Tuckett was probably the most active climber of his day in the Alps and was known so widely that Leslie Stephen declared Tuckett's name would become a legend:

> At some distant period, when the Alpine Club is half forgotten, and its early records are obscured amongst the mist of legends and popular traditions, then is one great puzzle in store for the critical inquirer. As he tries to disentangle truth from fiction, and to ascertain what is the small nucleus of fact round which so many incredible stories have gathered, he will be specially perplexed by the constant recurrence of one name. In the heroic cycle of Alpine adventures, the irrepressible Tuckett will occupy a place similar to that of the wandering Ulysses in Greek fable, or the invulnerable Siegfried in the lay of the Niebelungs. In every part of the Alps, from Monte Viso and Dauphiné to the wilds of Carinthia and Styria, the exploits of this mighty traveler will linger in the popular imagination. In one valley, the peasant will point to some vast breach in the everlasting rocks, hewn, as his fancy will declare, by the sweep of the mighty ice-axe of the hero. In another, the sharp, conical summit, known as the Tuckett-spitze, will be regarded as a monument raised by the Eponymous giant, or possibly as the tombstone piled above his athletic remains. In a third the broken masses of a descending glacier will fairly represent the staircase which he built in order to scale a previously inaccessible height.
>
> That a person so ubiquitous, and distinguished everywhere by such romantic exploits, should have been a mere creature of flesh and blood will, of course, be rejected as an absurd hypothesis. Critics will rather be disposed to trace in him one more example of that universal myth whose recurrence in diverse forms

proves, amongst other things, the unity of the great Aryan race. Tuckett, it will be announced, is no other than the sun, which appears at earliest dawn above the tops of the loftiest mountains, gilds the summits of the most inaccessible peaks, penetrates the remotest valleys, and passes in an incredibly short space of time from one extremity of the Alpine chain to the other.[93]

Here is Victorian humor with skillfully modulated phrases and a perfect subject, for the good-natured and lightning-gaited Tuckett was fair game. As for Tuckett himself, most of his writings were left in journal form until his death, with the exception of encyclopedias of Alpine material, publications in German, and articles in the *Alpine Journal*. Several of the latter are especially interesting, though Tuckett's literary ability was not so great as that of his friend Leslie Stephen. One of his well-known articles describes a narrow escape from a vast avalanche on the Eiger; another relates a close call from lightning in a storm on the Roche Melon.

While on the summit of the latter peak, he writes:

> Without a moment's warning, a perfect mitraille of hail smote the roof above us, tore through the mist like grape-shot through battle-smoke, and whitened the ground like snow. . . .
> As the clouds swept by, every rock, every loose stone, the uprights of the rude railing outside the chapel, the ruined signal, our axes. . . and even my fingers and elbows, set up "a dismal universal hiss." It was as though we were in a vast nest of excited snakes, or a battery of frying pans, or listening at a short distance to the sustained note of a band of cigali in a chestnut wood.[94]

Down from the summit the party races and, abandoning their axes outside, they push into a small chapel part of the way down the mountain:

> The wind roared and the hail hissed in fiendish rivalry, and yet both seemed silenced when the awful crashes of thunder burst above and about us. We were in the very central track and focus of the storm, and, as we sat crouched upon the floor, the ground and the building seemed to reel beneath the roar of the detonations, and our heads almost to swim with the fierce glare of the lightning. I had carefully closed the door, not only to keep the wind and the

hail out, but also because lightning is apt to follow a current of air, and, to the right on entering, at about the height of a man, was a small unglazed window some two feet square. Opposite the door was the altar, on the step of which I seated myself. Imseng took a place at my side, between me and the window, whilst Christian perched himself on the coil of rope with his back to the wall, not far from the door and between it and the window. A quarter of an hour may have gone by, when a flash of intense vividness seemed almost to dart through the window, and so affected Imseng's nerves that he hastily quitted his seat by me and coiled himself near Christian remarking that "that was rather too close to be pleasant." Then came four more really awful flashes, followed all but instantaneously by sharp, crackling thunder, which sounded like a volley of bullets against a metal target, and then a fifth with a slightly increased interval between it and the report. I was just remarking to Christian that I thought the worst was past, and that we should soon be liberated, adding "how fortunate we are for the second time today, to get such shelter just in the nick of time," when— crash! went everything, it seemed, all at once . . If someone had struck me from behind on the bump of firmness with a sledge-hammer, or if we had been in the interior of a gigantic percussion shell which an external blow had suddenly exploded, I fancy the sensation might have resembled that which I for the first instance experienced. We were blinded, deafened, smothered, and struck, all in a breath. The place seemed filled with fire, our ears rang with the report, fragments of what looked like incandescent matter rained down on us as though a meteorite had burst, and a suffocating, sulphurous odour—probably due to the sudden production of ozone in large quantities—almost choked us. What my companions' ideas were I cannot tell: mine were few and simple—I had been struck, or was being struck, or both; the roof would be down upon us in another moment; inside was death, outside our only safety. The door opened inwards, and our simultaneous rush delayed our escape; but it was speedily thrown back, and, dashing out into the blinding hail, we plunged, dazed, and almost stupefied, into the nearest shed . . .

> The lightning had first struck the iron cross outside, and smashed in the roof, dashing fragments of stone and plaster upon us which, brilliantly illuminated, looked to our dazed and confused vision like flakes of fiery matter. It had then encountered the altar, overturning the iron cross and wooden candlesticks only three feet from the back of my head as I sat on the step, tearing the wreath of artificial flowers or worsted rosettes strung on copper-wire which surrounded the figure of the Virgin and scattering the fragments in all directions.[95]

Fortunately no one was seriously injured, but the interior of the chapel was wrecked.

Tuckett, who in the characteristic manner of mountain climbers lived to be nearly eighty, was less writer than climber, but under the stress of emotion he writes more graphically here. The storm and crash of the lightning are very vivid, and we can overlook some of the past expressions.

Tuckett's friend Leslie Stephen (1832–1904), though he did not experience as many thrills in the mountains as the human meteor, had his share, and, as we have already seen in his comparison of Tuckett to the sun myth, was well able to express himself. In fact, of all the climbers who have described their emotions in English, perhaps none has made a greater contribution to mountain literature or done more to establish the dignity of mountain wanderings than Leslie Stephen.

Stephen returned to Cambridge to take orders shortly after his undergraduate studies were ended, but he was far more interested in literature than in the church and soon began to write for the *Saturday Review* and *Pall Mall Gazette*. For some years thereafter he edited *The Cornhill Magazine* and in 1882 became editor of the *Dictionary of National Biography*. Long before this he had married Thackeray's younger daughter and had also written most of the scholarly works that firmly established his reputation on both sides of the Atlantic. Here, we are concerned only with his mountain literature, *The Playground of Europe*.

Before discussing this charming group of essays, it may be well to examine Stephen as a representative of the mid-Victorian era. Like so many other climbers of the age, he could not ignore the disapproval that his contemporaries held for climbing, and himself felt called upon to defend mountaineering against calumny. This he did with such great tact and diplomacy that more than anyone else he was able to justify climbing in the eyes of a frowning world. His justification, it should be pointed out, was far more intelligible to the average Victorian than the defense made by others that they were climbing purely to aid science. At a time when Queen Victoria was considering attempting to forbid mountain climbing as dangerous, it was well that such a tactful writer of such established position should so simply and sincerely state the case for the mountain way.

Stephen's justification means little to us today, but the charming style and pawky humor with which he accompanies us to the hills makes us long for more of his Alpine wanderings. Stephen writes clearly and simply, restraining the lyric feelings that the mountains evoke in him. Only occasionally will he emotionally let himself go, and then he is quick to cover his embarrassment by changing the subject with a joke or blunt remark. He is also extremely modest and takes great pains to claim no credit, except for "following better men than myself with decent ability"[96] —a small claim for one of the pioneers who explored the Alps, made first ascents and crossed new passes, and was called by Whymper "the fleetest of foot of all the Alpine brotherhood."[97] His modesty is also shown in his failure to play up in any way the dangers of a mountain ascent. He knows the penalties the mountains can exact, but he sees them squarely, often with a grim sort of humor, and never lingers over them as so many of his contemporaries liked to do. On the Eigerjoch he simply states,

> The ice was very hard, and it was necessary, as Lauener observed, to cut steps in it as big as soup-tureens, for the result of a slip would in all probability have been that the rest of our lives would have been spent in sliding down a snow-slope, and that that employment would not have lasted long enough to become at all monotonous.[98]

This is a marked change from Albert Smith or Auldjo, as is his sincerity in describing his arrival at the top of the Jungfraujoch:

> The top of the Jungfraujoch comes rather like a bathos in poetry. It rises so gently above the steep ice-wall, and it is so difficult to determine the precise culminating point, that our enthusiasm oozed out gradually instead of producing a sudden explosion; and that instead of giving three cheers, singing "God Save the Queen,"

or observing any of the traditional ceremonial celebrations of a simpler generation of travellers, we calmly walked forwards as though we had been crossing Westminster Bridge, and on catching sight of a small patch of rocks near the foot of the Mönch rushed precipitately down to it and partook of our third breakfast.[99]

Except when he suppresses his feelings, Stephen tells exactly how the mountains impress him. In their presence he often feels humble or is left with deep and serious thoughts:

> The mountains represent the indomitable force of nature to which we are forced to adapt ourselves; they speak to man of his littleness and his ephemeral existence; they rouse us from the placid content in which we may be lapped when contemplating the fat fields which we have conquered and the rivers which we have forced to run according to our notions of convenience. And, therefore, they should suggest not sheer misanthropy, as they did to Byron, or an outburst of revolutionary passion, as they did to his teacher Rousseau, but that sense of awe-struck humility which befits such petty creatures as ourselves.[100]

How many of us who have stood on the tops of great mountains and gazed on thousands of square miles of wild or untrodden peaks and glaciers have felt this same sense of humility and awe at the vastness of our surroundings, the apparent endlessness of time, and our temerity in thinking that anything we do can ever be important. Also, sometimes, even on top of a remote peak, one feels too obvious, as if watched by some mysterious being, a feeling that John Buchan describes effectively in an article in the *Scottish Mountaineering Club Journal*.[101] Stephen also mentions this feeling on the Schreckhorn, but his immortal being is a calm spirit and not the threatening one that chased Buchan down a mountain:

> One felt as if some immortal being, with no particular duties upon his hands, might be calmly sitting upon those desolate rocks and watching the little shadowy wrinkles of the plain, that were really mountain ranges, rise and fall through slow geological epochs.[102]

More than once the mountains impress Stephen with their timelessness. For instance, an Alpine boulder on a knoll recalls to him an Eastern legend:

There is a stone column in Ceylon, if I remember rightly, which is now about six feet in length. Formerly, it is said, it was twice its present size; but once in every century, or, for it matters little, in every thousand years, an angel passes and just touches the corner of the pillar with the extreme hem of his aerial garment. The degradation produced by this contact has been the one cause of decay, and when the column is quite worn out something will happen—which does not much matter to the existing generation. The boulder wears away a little faster, but it, too, takes the mind back into a giddy abyss of years sufficient to crush the human imagination. It is pleasant to look at some minute channel on its surface and guess that when the rain first began to trace it, the Roman empire may still have been flourishing, and that a knob on its surface has been in process of carving ever since the pyramids were erected. The boulder marks a definite epoch, in that vast abyss of time, as distinctly as the seaweed washed ashore by the last tide. The great ice-wave reached just this point some inconceivable number of centuries back, and then began its slow retreat towards the central peaks. Meanwhile the old boulder is sleeping peacefully in the sun, whether at some remote future again to be lifted on the shoulders of a new glacier in another icy period, or to melt away like a lump of snow, and descend piecemeal into the lake.[103]

The boulder that gives rise to the weighty thoughts in Stephen would have caused scientific reveries in Professor Tyndall, but Stephen had no use for science. He once, contrary to his normal nature, at the request of a friend carried a thermometer to the top of a mountain, but when he accidentally dropped it he was highly pleased that he was relieved of the responsibility of doing anything scientific. That Stephen felt this way was important to his fellow mountaineers, because he justified mountaineering for itself alone. Stephen thought Tyndall somewhat pompous, just as he considered Ruskin too elaborate—criticism by a man who exemplified truth and simplicity in all things. He loved the mountains for their scenery and the exercise and excitement they afforded, for, as Douglas Freshfield has said, they were both cathedral and playground to him.

When Stephen was in the playground, his mood could change as quickly as the weather. Just as Tyndall blends scientific and romantic feelings, so Stephen blends a lyric appreciation of mountain scenery with a conventional fear that he is becoming too subjective and emotional. Unlike Tyndall, however, Stephen always has recourse to dry humor, as in his discussion of sleep in the mountains in "A Bye-Day in the Alps" or his comparison of the English climber and the Italian in "The Baths of Santa Catarina." For instance, he somewhat autocratically analyzes the average British tourist in the Alps:

> I studied with a philosophic eye the nature of that offensive variety of the genus of *primates*, the common tourist. . . . He likes a panoramic view in proportion to the number of peaks which he can count, which, I take it, is a method of telling his beads; he is doomed to see a certain number of objects, and the more he can take in at one dose, the better. Further, he comforts himself for his sufferings under sublime scenery by enjoying those conundrums in stone—if they may be so called—which are to be found even in the mountains. A rock that imitates the shape of the Duke of Wellington's nose gives him unspeakable delight; and he is very fond of a place near Grindelwald where St. Martin is supposed to have thrust his staff through one hill and marked the opposite slope by sitting down with extreme vigour.[104]

This is the Stephen of the playground, reproving mankind in the Victorian manner but consciously enjoying himself and criticizing with a twinkle in his eye. When in his cathedral mood, however, there is utter simplicity and none of this conscious artistry:

> If I were to invent a new idolatry (rather a needless task) I should prostrate myself, not before beast or ocean, or sun, but before one of these gigantic masses to which, in spite of all reason, it is impossible not to attribute some shadowy personality. Their voice is mystic and has found discordant interpreters; but to me at least it speaks in tones at once more tender and more awe-inspiring than that of any mortal teacher. The loftiest and sweetest strains of Milton or Wordsworth may be more articulate, but do not lay so forcible a grasp upon my imagination.[105]

Again, in a description of the Wengern Alp, he shows how deeply he feels the beauty of the mountains and how inadequate are words to express his feelings:

To me the Wengern Alp is a sacred place—the holy of holies in the mountain sanctuary, and the emotions produced when no desecrating influence is present and old memories rise up, softened by the sweet sadness of the scenery, belong to that innermost region of feeling which I would not, if I could, lay bare. Byron's exploitation of the scenery becomes a mere impertinence; Scott's simplicity would not have been exalted enough; Wordsworth would have seen this much of his own image; and Shelley, though he could have caught some of the finer sentiments, would have half spoilt it by some metaphysical rant. The best modern describers cannot shake off their moralising or their scientific speculation or their desire to be humorous sufficiently to do justice to such beauties. A follower in their steps will do well to pass by with a simple confession of wonder and awe.[106]

Stephen himself, however, cannot always merely pass by the places of beauty he sees, such as the Alpine pastures heavy with the scent of anemones and rhododendrons where one can lie on the grass and gaze upward at the delicately curving snow ridges across the valley, or the view at sunset from the summit of Mont Blanc:

Peak by peak the high snowfield caught the rosy glow and shone like signal-fires across the dim breadths of delicate twilight. Like Xerxes, we looked over the countless host sinking into rest, but with the rather different reflection, that a hundred years hence they would probably be doing much the same thing, whilst we should long have ceased to take any interest in the performance. . . . And suddenly began a more startling phenomenon.

A vast cone, with its apex pointing away from us, seemed to be suddenly cut out from the world beneath; night was within its borders and the twilight still all around; the blue mists were quenched where it fell, and for the instant we could scarcely tell what was the origin of this strange appearance. Some unexpected change seemed to have taken place in the programme; as though a great fold in the curtain had suddenly given way, and dropped on to part of the scenery. Of course a moment's reflection explained the meaning of this uncanny intruder; it was a giant shadow of

Mont Blanc, testifying to his supremacy over all meaner eminences. It is difficult to say how sharply marked was the outline, and how startling was the contrast between this pyramid of darkness and the faintly-lighted spaces beyond its influence; a huge inky blot seemed to have suddenly fallen upon the landscape. As we gazed we could see it move. It swallowed up ridge by ridge, and its sharp point crept steadily from one landmark to another down the broad valley of Aosta. We were standing, in fact, on the point of the gnomon of a gigantic sundial, the face of which was formed by thousands of square miles of mountain and valley. So clear was the outline that, if figures had been scrawled on glaciers and ridges, we could have told the time to a second; indeed, we were half inclined to look for our own shadows at a distance so great that whole villages would be represented by a scarcely distinguishable speck of colouring. The huge shadow, looking ever more strange and magical, struck the distant Becca di Nona, and then climbed into the dark region where the broader shadow of the world was rising into the eastern sky. By some singular effect of perspective, rays of darkness seemed to be converging from above the apex of the shadowy cone. For a time it seemed that there was a kind of anti-sun in the east, pouring out not light, but deep shadow as it rose. The apex soon reached the horizon, and then to our surprise began climbing the distant sky. Would it never stop, and was Mont Blanc capable of overshadowing not only the earth but the sky? For a minute or two I fancied, in a bewildered way, that this unearthly object would fairly rise from the ground and climb upwards to the zenith. But rapidly the lights went out upon the great army of mountains, the snow all round took the livid hue which immediately succeeds an alpine sunset, and almost at a blow the shadow on Mont Blanc was swallowed up in the general shade of night.[107]

This magnificent natural phenomenon is most simply and effectively described as I myself can vouch, having seen a similar dramatic event from the top of a snow peak in Alaska long before I had ever heard of Leslie Stephen. In the latter instance the great shadow of Mount Crillon swept the Pacific until it reached the horizon, then climbed above the horizon onto the rose-tinted clouds above, higher and higher, until it vanished. The rays of *black* light, if they can be so described, were most unearthly and portentous, and the whole panorama had no rival that I have ever seen for supernatural mystery and awe.

Leslie Stephen's shadow, similarly impressive, is so effectively linked to the figure of a vast sundial that the great bulk of Mont Blanc is most forcibly etched on the reader's imagination. Stephen's analogies are extremely effective, and more than anything else stamp an individuality on his very personal descriptions of mountain places, setting them apart and above hundreds of less imaginative attempts to give a similar effect. This ability reaches its peak, perhaps, in his essay "A Bye-Day in the Alps" or in "The Alps in Winter," a masterly description of how wintry magic casts a spell on the Alps and keeps them in a state of trance until they can be freed by the summer sun. It must be admitted, however, that although this essay is particularly fine, Stephen's point of view would have been broader had he visited more of the higher slopes in winter, but in this as in some other respects, he was hindered by the techniques and conventions of his time.

Leslie Stephen's essays still are among the finest examples of mountain literature. They impart the flavor of the high hills, whether he is among the peasants in a Carinthian village, idling through flowery Dolomite pastures below the snow line, or battling joyfully against the steep defenses of an unclimbed peak in the Alps.

He rolls the flavor of any particular mountain moment on his tongue and savors what it is that sets it apart from any other. In him we have come a long way from the more or less frightened one-peak climbers like Fellows and Auldjo, and from Forbes, Tyndall, and others who climbed primarily for science. Also evident, despite moments of self-consciousness and inhibition, is a style far more deft and imaginative than anything Bonney or Whymper ever achieved. In fact, in Leslie Stephen we have the most skilled writer of the "golden age of mountaineering": the delightful combination of true mountaineer and imaginative man of letters.

"The guide Couttet ascending the ice cliff to gain the Grand Mulet Rock, below him a Chasm of unknown depth." The drawing shows head guide Joseph Couttet with "axe" and baton leading, and Michal Balmat on the other end of their rope. From Barry, *Ascent to the Summit of Mont Blanc in 1834.*

Watchers From Afar

What power is this? what witchery wins my feet
To peaks so sheer they scorn the cloaking snow,
All silent as the emerald gulfs below,
Down whose ice-walls and wings of twilight beat?
What thrill of earth and heaven-most wild, most sweet -[108]
                                        —Theodore Watts-Dunton

S WE HAVE SEEN, mountains and mountain scenery more and more captured the imagination of English poets and prose writers throughout the eighteenth century, culminating in the respectful admiration of the romantics. Byron, Coleridge, Wordsworth, and Shelley were among the foremost English literary men to travel the mountain valleys, watching the living snows above them and letting their thoughts be lifted far and beyond the white-capped summits. Wordsworth and Shelley, in particular, felt the impact on the spirit and imagination made by mountain scenery, and it is a great pity that neither ventured during the period when men learned to climb among the far-off peaks. Perhaps with Shelley it is just as well that he never climbed onto the upper snows, for the physical discomforts surely would have diverted his attention, but he would have loved the Alpine pastures, where he could lie among the saxifrage and watch the clouds "shepherded by the slow, unwilling wind."[109]

Shelley, like Wordsworth, was many years ahead of his time in his appreciation of natural objects, for in the early nineteenth century, as has been noted, the average Englishman still viewed the Alps with mixed feelings of admiration, respect, and dismay. For instance, Thomas Jefferson Hogg, Shelley's old friend and fellow conspirator at Oxford, wrote from the Alps to Thomas Love Peacock in 1825:

> With respect to Switzerland I was rather foreign than English in my feelings: the English admire that scenery extravagantly; foreigners and T.J.H., look upon it as a frightful wilderness. . . . I experienced a dread and dismay, of which I could have had no notion, when I was in those horrible regions, where vegetation has ceased, and where there is nothing but bare, unchanging rock, perpetual snow and everlasting ice; I cannot describe the satisfaction I used to feel, when I descended to flowers and vines and fruit trees and felt a genial air, and saw the clouds in their proper places, above my head, and not beneath my feet. The fatigue of ascending to these abodes of the damned is beyond all conception, and the recollection adds to my dislike of the Alpine passes; the Simplon is bad enough, but St. Bernard, and especially St. Gotthard, will always be remembered with pain and terror.[110]

Thomas Hogg, unlike his brother the naturalist, who admired mountains, was generally unathletic and unimpressed by natural beauty. What a contrast between his peevish, unhappy letter to Peacock and Shelley's spirited outburst to the same correspondent a decade earlier. Men greater than Hogg, and equally as intellectual and urbane, were now entering the mountains for the first time, however, and glowing with delight at the experience. Charles Lamb, for instance, was thrilled at climbing Skiddaw:

> We have clambered up to the top of Skiddaw, and I have waded up to the bed of Lodore. In fact, I have satisfied myself that there is such a fine thing as that which tourists call *romantic*, which I very much suspected before; they make such a sputtering about it, and toss their splendid epithets around them, till they give as dim a light as at four o'clock next morning the lamps do after an illumination. . . . Oh, its fine black head, and the bleak air atop of it, with a prospect of mountains all about and about, making you giddy; and then Scotland afar off, and the border countries so famous in song and ballad! It was a day that will stand out, like a mountain, I am sure, in my life. But I have returned (I have now been come home near three weeks; I was a month out), and you cannot conceive the degradation I felt at first, from being accustomed to wander free as air among mountains, and bathe in rivers without being

controlled by any one, to come home and *work*. I felt very *little*. I had been dreaming I was a very great man. . . . I feel that I shall remember your mountains to the last day I live. They haunt me perpetually. I am like a man who has been falling in love unknown to himself, which he finds out when he leaves the lady.[111]

It is always pleasant to watch the reaction of the city dweller when he is first exposed to the beauty of the mountains, and also to observe the ruminative, educated man when he is removed from the petty disturbances of city life and set down amid scenes of great natural grandeur. Thomas Carlyle was not as confirmed a haunter of city streets as Charles Lamb, and one does not generally consider him a wanderer in the mountains, yet in many ways the following passage is typical of the man and of the reactions of many other thoughtful men who, viewing the strength and timelessness of the mountains, have sensed their own triviality and frailty:

> From such meditations is the Wanderer's attention called outwards for now the valley closes in abruptly, intersected by a huge mountain mass, the strong water-worn ascent of which is not to be accomplished on horseback. Arrived aloft, he finds himself again lifted into the evening sunset light, and cannot but pause, and gaze round him.. . . No trace of man now visible; unless indeed it were he who fashioned that little invisible link of high-way, here, as would seem, scaling the inaccessible, to unite province with province. But sunwards, lo you! how its towers sheer up, a world of mountains, the diadem and centre of the mountain region! A hundred and a hundred savage peaks, in the last light of day; all glowing, of gold and amethyst, like giant spirits of the wilderness; there in their silence, in their solitude, even on the night Noah's Deluge first dried! Beautiful, nay solemn was the sudden aspect, to our Wanderer. He gazed over those stupendous masses with wonder, almost with longing desire; never till this hour had he known Nature, that she was One, that she was his Mother and divine. And as the ruddy glow was fading into clearness in the sky, and the Sun had now departed, a murmur of Eternity, and Immensity, of Death and of Life, stole through his soul; and he felt as if Death and Life were one, as if the Earth were not dead, as if the Spirit of the Earth

had its throne in that splendour, and his spirit were therewith holding communion.[112]

What a lyric outburst from the author of *Sartor Resartus*, the old curmudgeon of Craigenputtock! Had Carlyle spent more time high in the hills, he would have found much to ponder in the depths of his spirits, even as Leslie Stephen did later high on the slopes of the Schreckhorn; for any man's reaction to the aesthetic inspiration of mountain scenery is likely to reveal a good deal about the man himself. As we have seen, Hogg and Shelley reacted very differently when similarly exposed for the first time to the beauties of the Alps, and each revealed something typical of the man himself. This idea should not be carried to extremes, but it is true that under the stress of sincere emotion, a writer is most likely to express his honest and unaffected feelings.

We shall find other writers like Carlyle and Lamb, who, though their experience with the mountains is small, are greatly moved by what they see, but for the present let us consider some of the valley travelers who wrote of mountain scenes but were less inspired by them. Sir Walter Scott, for instance, cannot be claimed as a mountaineer, or even as a mountain writer, though he climbed Helvellyn and wrote a somewhat dull poem about his ascent. The Scottish Highlands, which he knew and loved, and Westmoreland appear repeatedly as background in his novels from the time of *Waverly* on, and also in his poems. Scott's somewhat Ossian-like descriptions of the heather-clad hills are very real, but the atmosphere he creates is strangely sad and ominous. For some reason the reader usually has a foreboding that tragedy is inevitable. Glens are always dark and wild, and joy in the beauties of the bens is severely curtailed. "The Lay of the Last Minstrel," "The Lady of the Lake," "Lord of the Isles," and shorter poems like "The Trossachs" and "Coriskin," among many others, employ Scottish Highland scenery with accuracy and effectiveness but without particular emphasis on the mountains themselves.

Similarly, Samuel Rogers was writing numerous poems about Switzerland, most of which merely employ Swiss background. These are generally dull, even "Lauterbrunnen," where the Swiss hunter shoots an eagle who "chances" to be passing with the hunter's child in his talons. Of course the child falls unhurt to the ground. "In the Alps" has good feeling in its first lines but cannot in any way be termed inspired.

Thomas Moore has more vigor than Rogers in his verses on Switzerland, but he also makes use of the mountains mainly as background. Though he tries often, he fails to capture the beauty of the peaks themselves. In the following lines from "Rhymes on the Road," somewhat jingly and vaguely reminiscent of Byron when not at his best, Moore describes his first sight of Mont Blanc:

> *Mighty Mont Blanc! thou wert to me*
> *That minute, with thy brow in heaven,*
> *As sure a sign of deity*
> *As e'er to mortal gaze was given.*
> *Nor ever, were I destined yet*
> *To live my life twice o'er again,*
> *Can I the deep-felt awe forget,*
> *The dreams, the trance that rapt me then!*[113]

Ebenezer Elliot, at about the same time, wrote a few good verses about the British uplands, of which *Win-Hill*, despite conventional diction, has a certain freshness.

> *King of the Peak! Win-Hill! thou, throned and crowned,*
> *That reign'st o'er many a stream and many a vale!*
> *Star-loved, and meteor-sought, and tempest-found!*
> *Proud centre of a mountain-circle, hail!…..*
> *Blow, blow, thou breeze of mountain freshness, blow!*
> *Stronger and fresher still, as we ascend*
> *Stronger and fresher still, as we ascend*
> *Strengthen'd and freshen'd, till the land below*
> *Lies like a map!…..*
> *Now expectation listens, mute and pale,*
> *While, ridged with sudden foam, the Derwent brawls;*
> *Arrow-like comes the rain…..*[114]

John Stuart's Blackie, who knew the Highlands intimately, also shows good feeling in his verses, especially in "Ben Greig":

> *Why climb the mountains? I will tell thee why…..*
> *I love to leave my littleness behind*
> *In the low vale where little cares are great,*
> *And in the mighty map of things to find*

A sober measure of my scanty state,
Taught by the vastness of God's pictured plan
In the big world how small a thing is man![115]

Like Thomas Moore and Samuel Rogers, Aubrey de Vere, who had considerable popularity in his day, wrote of Alpine scenery. Many of his lines are bad and little that is favorable can be said for his verses on Mont Blanc, but he occasionally shows poetic ability, as in "The Mountain Language."

John Campbell Shairp is more convincing than is de Vere in his verses on the mountains. "Schihallion" is a somewhat melodramatic but effective description of a sunset in the Highlands, and "The Moore of Rannoch," despite its meter, has a few good lines. Even better is Christopher North's "Midnight on Helm Crag."

In many ways, of course, the finest verses written about the heights in this period are by Alfred Tennyson, for the poet laureate spent considerable time in the mountains. He particularly liked the Pyrenees and the Vale of Cauteretz, and enjoyed visits to Grenoble, Pontresina, the Val Anzasca, and the Dolomites. He climbed the Pic du Midi in the Pyrenees and later at Grenoble the Dent du Chat, but he was temperamentally better suited to the valleys than the heights, and like Shelley describes the summits beautifully, as seen from below. One morning in Milan he climbed the great cathedral and watched the dawn color the crests of Monte Rosa:

I climb'd the roofs at break of day;
Sun-smitten Alps before me lay.
I stood among the silent statues,
And statued pinnacles mute as they.
How faintly flushed, how phantom-fair,
Was Monte Rosa, hanging there
A thousand shadowy-pencill'd valleys
And snowy dells in a golden air.[116]

The last quatrain is particularly fine, but he does well with other mountain scenes. Cauteretz he describes beautifully in "The Lotos-Eaters":

A land of streams! some, like a downward smoke,
Slow-dropping veils of thinnest lawn, did go;
And some thro' wavering lights and shadows broke,

Rolling a slumbrous sheet of foam below.
They saw the gleaming river seaward flow
From the inner land; far off, three mountain-tops,
Three silent pinnacles of aged snow,
Stood sunset-flush'd . . .[117]

This description of mountain waterfalls, comparable to others by Ruskin and Clough, is particularly effective, as in the familiar opening of Oenone,

There lies a vale in Ida, lovelier
Than all the valleys of Ionian hills.
The swimming vapor slopes athwart the glen,
Puts forth an arm, and creeps from pine to pine,
And loiters, slowly drawn. On either hand
The lawns and meadow-ledges midway down
Hang rich in flowers, and far below them roars
The long brook falling thro' the clov'n ravine
In cataract after cataract to the sea.
Behind the valley topmost Gargarus
Stands up and takes the morning . . .[118]

These lines also are better then Ruskin's prose about lush mountain slopes below the snow line.

While at Val Anzasca in the Alps, in another beautiful mountain region, Tennyson, who was kept awake by the nearby glacier stream, wrote "The Voice and the Peak," but its verses lack the musical and sensitive imagery of "The Lotos-Eaters," "Oenone," and "The Princess." In this late "medley of poems," Tennyson describes snow-tipped Alps and hanging glaciers, but without the sympathetic feelings with which he treats the Alpine meadows and wooded ravines of the lower slopes. The following passage, written before the form-stion of the Alpine Club, shows the conventional Victorian disapproval of mountain climbing:

Come down, O maid, from yonder mountain height:
What pleasure lives in height (the shepherd sang),
In height and cold, the splendour of the hill?
But cease to move so near the Heavens, and cease
To glide a sunbeam by the blasted Pine,

To sit a star upon the sparkling spire;
And come, for Love is of the valley, come,
For Love is of the valley, come thou down
And find him; by the happy threshold, he,
Or hand in hand with Plenty in the maize
Or red with spirted purple of the vats,
Or foxlike in the vine; nor cares to walk
With Death and Morning on the silver horns,
Nor wilt thou snare him in the white ravine,
Nor find him dropt upon the firths of ice,
That huddling slant in furrow-cloven falls
To roll the torrent out of dusky doors.[119]

The normal reaction of Victorian society to the actions of the Alpine Club, which was formed later, was an indignant "Come down before you hurt yourself," so Tennyson's lines on walking "with Death and Morning" are not surprising. The description of the glacier is fairly effective but cannot compete with the beautiful lines on Monte Rosa quoted earlier. As with other watchers from the valleys, Tennyson is best when describing areas he knows from personal and intimate experience.

And so is Robert Browning, who writes,

Here, here's his place, where meteors shoot, clouds form
Lightnings are loosened
Stars come and go![120]

One notes, however, the lack of specific detail, for Browning never knew the high peaks from personal experience, although he did write "Two on a Mountain," climbed Calvano on a mule, and in "The Englishman in Italy" jerkily but effectively describes the changing vegetation as the mule climbs upward:

Over all trod my mule with the caution
Of gleaners o'er sheaves,
Still, foot after foot like a lady,
Till, round after round,
He climbed to the top of Calvano,
And God's own profound

Was above me, and round me the mountains,
And under, the sea
And within me my heart to bear witness
What was and shall be.
Oh, heaven and the terrible crystal!
No rampart excludes
Your eye from the life to be lived
In the blue solitudes.
Oh, those mountains, their infinite movement!
Still moving with you;
Ever some new head and
Breast of them thrusts into view
To deceive the intruder.[121]

This is not great poetry, but it is a sincere personal reaction and to me more effective than the better-known lines in "Saul" on the coming of spring to the mountains, or those of "In the Heart of Things." Browning doesn't pose or pretend to be doing great things, but in "The Englishman in Italy" we get the succinct picture of the upward progress of the poet and his mule and the surge of pleasure the writer felt at the summit.

Elizabeth Barrett Browning in "Mountaineer and Poet" is noteworthy mainly for her reference to the Brocken, that spectral phenomenon of the mist occasionally seen high in the mountains, and also referred to by De Quincey. Of minor importance also is Arthur Hugh Clough, whose letters are full of praise for the Alps, and who deals pleasantly with mountain streams below the snow line in "Bather's Pool."

Matthew Arnold, however, knew the Alps far better than the Brownings or Clough, and for a short period was actually a member of the Alpine Club. He climbed the Titlis, crossed some of the more common Alpine passes, and visited Zermatt, Chamonix, and other climbing centers, yet his most effective descriptions of the mountains are made from the valleys. "Rugby Chapel," of course, has a mountaineering background, but it so completely lacks reality that it could be quoted only as an example of what not to do. Arnold was more interested in presenting an idea than in describing a storm or avalanche, but his motive fails to excuse his lack of verisimilitude.

In most of Arnold's poems about the Alps there is sadness, caused partly perhaps by the memory of an affair he had in 1848 at Thun with a French girl named Marguerite. He pays pleasant tribute to her in "The Terrace at Berne." Far more celebrated, however, are his two poems mourning Obermann, with their fine descriptions of the Lake Geneva country.

In both "Obermann" and "Obermann Once More" exist lines with good imagery picturing verdant slopes dominated by their guardian Mount Jaman. "Switzerland" is somewhat jingly, but the rush of the wind sweeps it along well:

> *Hark! fast by the window*
> *The rushing winds go,*
> *To the ice-cumber'd gorges,*
> *The vast seas of snow!*
> *There the torrents drive upward*
> *Their rock-strangled hum;*
> *There the avalanche thunders*
> *The hoarse torrent dumb.*
> *I come, O ye mountains!*
> *Ye torrents, I come.*[122]

The Pre-Raphaelites were interested in the mountains, and describe them occasionally, though none of the poets could be considered a true mountain climber. Rossetti's "The Hill Summit" is among the best:

> *This feast-day of the sun, his altar there*
> *In the broad west has blazed for vesper-song;*
> *And I have loitered in the vale too long*
> *And gaze now a belated worshipper.*
> *Yet may I not forget that I was 'ware,*
> *So journeying, of his face at intervals*
> *Transfigured where the fringed horizon falls,*
> *A fiery bush with coruscating hair.*
> *And now that I have climbed and won this height,*
> *I must tread downward through the sloping shade*
> *And travel the bewildered tracks till night.*
> *Yet for this hour I still may here be stayed*
> *And see the gold air and the silver fade*
> *And the last bird fly into the last light.*[123]

Rossetti's "fiery bush with coruscating hair" is vivid, as is the general atmosphere of sunlight in the mountains long after it has disappeared in the valleys, an effect that William Morris describes somewhat less effectively in "Sigurd the Volsung":

> *Cloudless the mountain riseth against the sunset sky,*
> *The sea of the sun grown golden, as it ebbs from the day's desire;*
> *And the light that afar was a torch is grown a river of fire,*
> *And the mountain is black above it, and below it is dark and dun;*
> *And there is the head of Hindfell as an island in the sun.*[124]

This sunset is real enough, but Sigurd wishes to climb the mountain to "behold the earth at its best," and the easy way he makes the night ascent will not satisfy any mountaineer. What the hero sees from the summit also appears somewhat jumbled in the poet's mind, but he clearly describes the lovely lower clouds.

Swinburne occasionally mentions the mountains too, as in "Atlanta in Calydon," but never in detail, for they were foreign to his nature. About the same period Robert Buchanan was writing verse about the Highlands, but he deals more with the lakes and valleys than the heights and is not inspired. George Eliot does better with "Sanct Margen," as does Sydney Dobell with "Balder":

> *I am the sun, I am above the mountains,*
> *My joy is on me, I will give you the day!*
> *I will spend day among you like a king!*
> *Your water shall be wine because I reign!*
> *I stave my golden vintage on the mountains,*
> *And all your rushing rivers run with day!*[125]

This joyful outburst with its lovely line about the wine is in a far lighter vein than Theodore Watts-Dunton's "New Year's Eve in the Alps," where the beauties of the mountains gradually dispel the hero's gloom and sorrow. This poem has some fine lines regarding the healing power of nature. Watts-Dunton's "Natura Maligna" and "Natura Benigna" also have spirit and a feeling for the mountains:

> *The lady of the Hills with crimes untold*
> *Followed my feet with azure eyes of prey;*

By glacier-brink she stood – by cataract-spray –
When mists were dire, or avalanche-echoes rolled.
At night she glimmered in the death-wind cold,
As if a footprint shone at break of day,
My flesh would quail, but straight my soul would say:
"Tis hers whose hand God's mightier hand doth hold."
I trod her snow-bridge, for the moon was bright,
Her icicle-arch across the sheer crevasse,
When lo, she stood!….. God made her let me pass,
Then felled the bridge!….. O, there in sallow light,
There down the chasm, I saw her cruel, white,
And all my wondrous days as in a glass.[126]

This somewhat grim picture is in complete contrast with his "Natura Benigna," in which his pulse leaps for joy at the "ruddy eastern glow Where, far away, the skies and mountains meet."[127]

These verses have more spirit and poetic imagery than Charles Kingsley's earnest lines of confession in "Palinodia":

Ye mountains, on whose torrent-furrowed slopes,
And bare and silent brows uplift to heaven,
I envied oft the soul which fills your wastes
Of pure and stern sublime, and still expanse
Unbroken by the petty incidents
Of noisy life . . .
Mountains, and winds, and waves, take back your child.[128]

Kingsley did not write extensively about the hills, but he knew them well— much better than did Alfred Austin, who does some absurd things with his Zermatt Shepherdess in his play *Prince Lucifer*. Austin blends Adam, Eve, and Lucifer with a Swiss love story and personifies the Matterhorn, Weisshorn, and other local phenomena as chorus. Needless to say, the whole closet drama shows almost complete lack of knowledge of the mountains.

Most poets of the period were equally uninitiated concerning the mountains. The prose writers do better. Before returning to the latter, however, let us consider one more sample of Victorian verse.

Following the famous accident on the Matterhorn in 1865, a storm of protest rose against any form of mountain climbing. As few non-climbers then could see anything remotely justifying mountaineering, Alpine Club members found it all the more gratifying when, shortly after the Matterhorn accident, the poem by A.G. Butler quoted below appeared in the *London Times*:

They warred with Nature, as of old with gods
The Titans; like the Titans too they fell,
Hurled from the summit of their hopes, and dashed
Sheer down precipitous, tremendous crags,
A thousand deaths in one . . .
Yet, too, methinks, we were not what we are
Without that other fiery element—
The love, the thirst for venture, and the scorn
That aught should be too great for mortal powers;
That yet one peak in all the skyey throng
Should rise unchallenged with unvanquished snows.
Virgin from the beginning of the world.
Such fire was theirs; O not for fame alone—
That coarser thread in all the finer skein
That draws adventure, oft by vulgar minds
Deemed man's sole aim—but for the high delight
To tread untrodden solitudes, and feel
A sense of power, of fullest freedom, lost
In the loud vale where Man is all in all.
For this they dared too much . . .
One clear, cold morn: they climbed the virgin height.....
Then they turned homeward, yet not to return.
It was a fearful place, and as they crept
Fearfully down the giddy steep, there came
A slip—no more—one little slip, and down
Linked in a living avalanche they fell,
Brothers in hope, in triumph, and in death,
Nor dying were divided . . .[129]

True understanding of the climbers' spirit is expressed here, for the poet visualizes the keen delight and sense of power in their struggle against a magnificent opponent.

It is unfortunate that the outstanding novelists of the period lacked A.G. Butler's understanding spirit. Charles Dickens, for instance, though his letters show that he was considerably affected by Alpine scenes of natural beauty, almost entirely disregards the mountains in his novels. During his lifetime, however, Dickens spent considerable time in the Alps, wrote *Dombey and Son* while at Lausanne, and much enjoyed a visit to Chamonix in August 1846, as shown by the following letter to John Forster, later his biographer:

> Mont Blanc, and the Valley of Chamounix, and the Mer de Glace, and all the wonders of that most wonderful place, are above and beyond one's wildest expectations. I cannot imagine anything in nature more stupendous or sublime. If I were to write about it now, I should quite rave—such prodigious impressions are rampant within me. . . . Going by that Col de Balme pass, you climb up and up and up for five hours and more, and look—from a mere unguarded ledge of path on the side of the precipice—into such awful valleys, that at last you are firm in the belief that you have got above everything in the world, and that there can be nothing earthly overhead. Just as you arrive at this conclusion, a different (and oh Heaven! what a free and wonderful) air comes blowing on your face; you cross a ridge of snow; and lying before you (wholly unseen till then), towering up into the distant sky, is the vast range of Mont Blanc, with attendant mountains diminished by its majestic side into mere dwarfs tapering up into innumerable rude Gothic pinnacles; deserts of ice and snow; forests of fir on mountain sides, of no account at all in the enormous scene; villages down in the hollow, that you can shut out with a finger; waterfalls, avalanches, pyramids and towers of ice, torrents, bridges, mountain upon mountain until the very sky is blocked away, and you must look up, overhead, to see it. Good God, what a country Switzerland is, and what a concentration of it is to be beheld from that one spot! . . . I went into all sorts of places; armed with a great pole with a spike on the end of it, like a leaping-pole, and with pointed irons buckled onto my shoes; and am all but knocked up. I was very anxious to make the expedition to what is called "The Garden": a green spot covered with wild flow-

ers, lying across the Mer de Glace, and among the most awful
mountains; but I could find no Englishman at the hotels who was
similarly disposed, and the Brave wouldn't go.[130]

It is pleasant to speculate whether Dickens, if he had made the crossing of the
Mer de Glace, as he wished, would have continued to make use of his leaping pole
and his pointed irons, and become genuinely interested in mountain travel.
Probably, unless he had met Forbes or some other of the early pioneer climbers,
he would not, for in 1846 mountain travel was practically unknown as a sport. As
far as we know, Dickens's desire for glacier travel never seriously returned.

In *Pictures from Italy*, written in the same year, there is a nice description of
his crossing of the Simplon Pass, material that he also uses two years later in
No Thoroughfare, a potboiler on which Wilkie Collins collaborated. Here
Dickens is at his worst, and it seems hardly fair to quote him. The blizzard on
the Simplon, the St. Bernard dogs, and the mountaineering heroine who res-
cues the hero after his murder has been attempted and he has been thrown off
the mountain—all are pure melodrama without a trace of reality. Generality
follows generality and Dickens's normally vivid and specific descriptions
become vague:

> Far and high above them glaciers and suspended avalanches over-
> hung the spots where they must pass by-and-by; deep and dark
> below them on their right, were awful precipice and roaring tor-
> rent; tremendous mountains rose in every vista. The gigantic land-
> scape, uncheered by a touch of changing light or a solitary ray of
> sun, was yet terribly distinct in its ferocity.[131]

Moments later an avalanche barely misses them, but this terrible, nerve-wrack-
ing experience is passed off lightly:

> They were yet in the midst of their dangerous way, when there
> came a mighty rush, followed by a sound as of thunder.
> Obenreizier clapped his hand on Vendale's mouth and pointed to
> the track behind them. Its aspect had been wholly changed in a
> moment. An avalanche had swept over it, and plunged into the tor-
> rent at the bottom of the gulf below.

Dickens did not feel at home in the mountains and, as Mr. H.E. Cooke has
recently shown,[132] like many other Victorians disapproved of the practice of

mountain climbing. In 1865 in *All the Year Round*, a magazine that Dickens edited, two articles, probably by Dickens, appeared criticizing the accident that occurred on the first ascent of the Matterhorn and strongly condemning climbing in general. These essays indicate clearly the popular reaction toward mountaineering at the time of the founding of the Alpine Club and show why Stephen, Tyndall, Whymper, and other climbers were constantly defending or apologizing for their sport.

Other writers of the period may have been less sensitive to public opinion than was Dickens, for in any event most of them who were exposed to the mountains reacted in an individual and personal manner. George Borrow was not greatly affected by popular fashions and his reaction to the mountains is what one might expect. He liked the wild, constantly changing vistas and the mountain people who so frequently resist change, preserve the old customs and dialects, and present a wanderer like Borrow with delightful opportunities for philological and etymological musings. According to his statement in *Lavengro*, he became "a daring cragsman,"[133] and indeed in *Wild Wales*, as in *Lavengro* and *The Romany Rye*, we have good but brief descriptions of mountain scenery. Borrow's ascent of Snowdon does not demonstrate his ability as a mountaineer but is typical of the man. Arm in arm with a young girl, he starts upward, lustily singing a Welsh song about the mountain. Instead of describing the details of the ascent, in Borrow fashion he muses why the peak across the valley is called by a Welsh name, which signifies the hill of counselors. When he reaches the top he mentions the frightful precipices below him, but his description generalizes, for he is more interested in having climbed this famous peak than in the view from it:

> "Here," said I to Henrietta, "you are on the top crag of Snowdon," which the Welsh consider, and perhaps with justice, to be the most remarkable crag in the world; which is mentioned in many of their old wild romantic tales, and some of the noblest of their poems, amongst others in the Day of Judgment, by the illustrious Goronwy Owen, where it is brought forward in the following manner:
>
> " 'Ail I'r ar ael Eryri
> Cyfartal hoewal a hi' "
>
> The brow of Snowdon shall be levelled with the ground, and the eddying waters shall murmur round it.[134]

Somehow Borrow's description of his climb of Snowdon does not make us feel that he was greatly impressed by what he saw, for as usual he is more interested in the association with other events than in the event itself. Certainly his description of ascending Snowdon cannot compare with Wordsworth's picture of his climb in *The Excursion*. Perhaps had Borrow known the lovely Alpine meadows with their rhododendrons and anemones and crocuses, he would have chosen such a place for Mr. Petulengro's pleasant dictum, "Life is very sweet, brother"[135]—and what is more, would have given us fine descriptions of the jagged skylines around him.

To Borrow and Dickens mountains were unimportant, but to arrogant John Ruskin they became almost a religion and certainly a source of inspiration throughout his career. In *Praeterita* he tells us that his first memory is of being taken to the edge of Friar's Crag on Derwentwater.[136] Thereafter, mountain excursions molded and colored his whole life.

All his writings show that he detested flat places and intensely admired mountains. For instance, he wrote,

> To myself, mountains are the beginning and the end of all natural scenery; in them, and in the forms of inferior landscape that lead to them, my affections are wholly bound up; and though I can look with happy admiration at the lowland flowers, and woods, and open skies, the happiness is tranquil and cold, like that of examining detached flowers in a conservatory, or reading a pleasant book; and if the scenery be resolutely level, insisting upon the declaration of its own flatness in all the detail of it, as in Holland or Lincolnshire, or Central Lombardy, it appears to me like a prison, and I cannot long endure it . . .
>
> I know that this is in great part idiosyncrasy; and that I must not trust to my own feelings in this respect, as representatives of the modern landscape instinct; yet I know it is not idiosyncrasy, in so far as there may be proved to be indeed an increase of the absolute beauty of all scenery in exact proportion to its mountainous character . . .[137]

Again and again in his works, Ruskin states that the mountains are the sources of endless good. This theory he carries to extremes, as we shall soon see, but first let us consider a few facts that led Ruskin to become one of the greatest literary worshippers of the mountains and yet the condemner of mountain climbers. In *Praeterita* he gives a splendid description of his first view of the Alps, when, aged fourteen, he spent the summer in Switzerland with his parents and visited Chamonix. Immediately the Alpine splendors stimulated and impressed him so strongly that for the rest of his life mountains were never far from his thoughts. During the next four years he continued to travel frequently to the mountains, crossing the Col de la Faucille to Geneva in 1835 and climbing both Scafell and Helvellyn two years later. He was not an athletic boy, however, and his docile obedience to his parents' wishes frequently prevented his climbing.

In 1842 he visited Chamonix again and two years later at Simplon he met James Forbes, who greatly impressed him with his personal knowledge of the mountains and his geological theories as to their origins. Although Ruskin never saw Forbes again, he supported his views vehemently during the disputes between Tyndall, Agassiz and Forbes which later disrupted the scientific world. In 1844 Ruskin crossed to the base of the Aiguille d'Argentière, no small expedition in those days, and also climbed the Bel Alp, probably the first traveler to do so. Later he traversed the Buet, but the weather changed during the climb and he made a wretched and fatiguing descent in a heavy rain. It was following this journey that he wrote that "the Alps were, on the whole, best seen from below,"[138] but as he tells us later, he had planned more difficult climbs and would have gone on and done them if the weather had not remained bad.

This account of Ruskin's ascents is given because he is normally considered a writer who saw the mountains only from below and at a distance. Such was not the case. Ruskin in 1844 may have been as capable a climber as some of the pioneers who later founded the Alpine Club. If his family's influence on him had not been so strong, Ruskin might have continued to climb and might have given us more of the excellent analyses and descriptions of mountain scenery which appear in *Modern Painters*. As Ruskin knew the Alpine valleys well, was an excellent observer, and had exceptional command of the language, it is no wonder that his prose descriptions of the mountains are unusually strong. In "The Mountain Glory" he states:

> Of the greater grandeur or expressions of the hills I have not spoken; how far they are great, or strong, or terrible, I do not for the moment consider, because vastness, and strength, and terror, are

not to all minds subjects of desired contemplation. It may make no difference to some men whether a natural object be large or small, whether it be strong or feeble. But loveliness of colour, perfectness of form, endlessness of change, wonderfulness of structure, are precious to all undiseased human minds; and the superiority of the mountains in all these things to the lowland is, I repeat, as measurable as the richness of a painted window matched with a white one, or the wealth of a museum compared with that of a simply furnished chamber. They seem to have been built for the human race, as at once their schools and cathedrals; full of treasures or illuminated manuscript for the worker, quiet in pale cloisters for the thinker, glorious in holiness for the worshiper. And of these great cathedrals of the earth, with their gates of rock, pavements of cloud, choirs of stream and stone, altars of snow, and vaults of purple traversed by the continual stars—of these, as we have seen, it was written, not long ago, by one of the best of the poor human race *for whom they were built* (Ed. Italics), wondering in himself for whom their Creator could have made them, and thinking to have entirely discerned the Divine intent in them—"They are inhabited by the Beasts."*139*

What an exaggerated, romantic defense of mountains against the cold, literal-minded evaluation of the eighteenth century! To Ruskin mountain grass is sweeter, mountain trees grown in more visible and beautiful patterns, and mountain water has an infinite variety unknown to the lowlander.

Ruskin's colorful descriptions of mountain beauties are those of a valley walker, not one who has ever climbed high. In fact in 1865, though a minor climber himself, shortly after the Matterhorn tragedy he criticized the Alpine Club severely in *Sesame and Lilies*,

> You have despised nature; that is to say, all the deep and sacred sensations of natural scenery. The French revolutionists made stables of the cathedrals of France; you have made race-courses of the cathedrals of the earth. The Alps themselves, which your own poets used to love so reverently, you look upon as soaped poles in a bear-garden, which you set yourselves to climb, and slide down again, with 'shrieks of delight.' When you are past shrieking, having no

articulate human voice to say you are glad with, you fill the qui-
etude of their valleys with gunpowder blasts, and rush home, red
with cutaneous eruption of conceit, and voluble with convulsive
hiccough of self-satisfaction.[140]

Ruskin resented the influx of tourists into the mountain valleys he had
known when they were almost completely untraveled. Perhaps it was the natural resentment that one feels in such circumstances, or possibly the intense
disgust recalled from a visit to Chamonix at the time when Albert Smith and
his companions had just returned from the summit of Mont Blanc and were
extravagantly celebrating their achievement far into the night. Whatever the
cause, Ruskin, who always felt a high moral purpose, became convinced that
the Alpine Club was full of vain men who could not appreciate the beauties of
the mountains.

What an avalanche of Victorian scorn, morality, and self-righteousness!
But "articulate human voices" did exist in the youthful Alpine Club as Ruskin
was soon to find, for Leslie Stephen, Professor Tyndall, and a host of others
analyzed his complaints coldly and logically, until Ruskin, who was prone to
both exaggerations and inconsistencies in his generalizations, was overwhelmed.

Never again was he able to forget his remarks about the "soaped poles" or
his statement in the preface to the first edition of *Sesame and Lilies* that "the
real beauty of the Alps is to be seen, and seen only, where all may see it, the
child, the cripple, and the man of gray hairs."[141] This was too much for the
Alpine Club, whose members rightfully resented the critic's evaluation of what
he had never seen, and for several years the most vigorous literary battle in
mountaineering history was waged. Some animosities remained, but in 1869
Ruskin joined the Alpine Club and remained a member for most of the rest of
his life. Whatever the cause, Ruskin's criticisms were undoubtedly valid concerning some Englishmen in the Alps and some climbers, and so the end result
was undoubtedly salutary.

Ruskin's attacks were made because he loved the mountains sincerely and
was carried away by his own feelings. In "Modern Painters," for instance, he so
greatly stresses the influence of the mountains on art, sculpture, literature, and
religion, that though much of what he says is true, he harms his case by his
overstatement. His essay on "The Mountain Gloom," try as he will, cannot

compare with his impassioned essay on "The Mountain Glory," for the prophet of mountain love feels too intensely the good qualities of the hills to write effectively about the bad ones.

> The Alps were alike beautiful in their snow and their humanity, and I wanted, neither for them nor myself, sight of any throne in heaven but their rocks, or of any spirit in heaven but their clouds.
> *142*

Again he says,

> The only days I can look back to as rightly and wisely in entireness spent, have been in sight of Mont-Blanc, Mont-Rosa, or the Jungfrau.*143*

Although most of Ruskin's works lack humor and do not describe the upper heights as do Leslie Stephen or Geoffrey Winthrop Young, he has described the beauty of mountain lowlands as no one has done before or since. Nor can we forget his descriptions of aiguilles, such as the Blaitière, or of precipices like the north face of the Matterhorn, carved by a "daring sword-sweep and standing like an Egyptian temple."144

Unlike Ruskin, Leigh Hunt scarcely concerned himself with the mountains in his literary work, and yet his *Autobiography* indicates the tremendous first impression that they made on him, too.

> The Alps! It was the first time I had seen mountains. They had a fine sulky look, up aloft in the sky—cold, lofty, and distant. I used to think that mountains would impress me but little; that by the same process of imagination reversed, by which a brook can be fancied a mighty torrent, with forests instead of verdure on its banks, a mountain could be made a mole-hill, over which we step. I found I could elevate better than I could pull down and was glad of it. It was not that the sight of the Alps was necessary to convince me of "the being of God," as it is said to have done somebody, or to put me upon any reflections respecting infinity and first causes, of which I have had enough in my time; but I seemed to meet for the first time a grand poetical thought in a material shape—to see a piece of one's book-wonders realized, something very earthy, yet

standing between earth and heaven, like a piece of the antidiluvian world looking out of the coldness of ages . . . The first sight of the Alps startles us like the disproof of a doubt, or the verification of an early dream—a ghost, as it were, made visible by daylight, and giving us an enormous sense of its presence and materiality.[145]

Hunt here gives vent to the sincere emotions of a sensitive person who is suddenly confronted by great natural objects. It is interesting to contrast his feelings with those of Shelley, Lamb, Ruskin, Hilaire Belloc, and other writers whose first sight of the mountains greatly moved them. George Meredith for instance, like Hunt, was deeply moved and abstractly thought of what the Alps signified rather than of their visible beauty, thus revealing the strong philosophic aspect of his nature.

My first sight of the Alps has raised odd feelings. Here at last seems something more than earth, and visible, if not tangible. They have the whiteness, the silence, the beauty and mystery of thoughts, seldom unveiled within us, but which conquer Earth when once they are. In fact they have made my creed tremble. – Only for a time. They have merely dazzled me with a group of symbols. Our great error has been (the error of all religion, I fancy) to raise a spiritual system in antagonism to Nature. What though yonder Alp does touch the Heavens? Is it a rebuke to us below? In you and me there may be lofty virgin points, pure from what we call fleshiness.[146]

Meredith was to gain more than an intellectual interest in abstractions raised by the Alps for he later crossed many of the cols of Dauphiné and became familiar with mountain scenery in several other regions. He never became a true mountain climber like his friend Leslie Stephen, whom he describes as Vernon Whitford in the *Egoist* ("Phoebus Apollo turned fasting friar"),[147] but from him he probably drew encouragement to love the mountains. In 1871 in *The Adventures of Harry Richmond* he boldly sings of one aspect of the joys of the mountaineer – a most surprising passage, too, for one primarily a walker and not a climber:

Carry your fever to the Alps, you of minds diseased; not to sit down in sight of them ruminating; for bodily ease and comfort will trick the soul and set you measuring our lean humanity against

yonder sublime and infinite; but mount, rack the limbs, wrestle it
out among the peaks; taste danger, sweat, earn rest; learn to dis-
cover ungrudgingly that haggard fatigue in the fair vision you have
run to earth, and that rest is your uttermost reward. Would you
know what it is to hope again, and have all your hopes at hand?
hang upon the crags at a gradient that makes your next step a
debate between the thing you are and the thing you may become.
There the merry little hopes grow for the climber like flowers and
food, immediate, prompt to prove their uses, sufficient if just within the grasp, as mortal hopes should be. How the old lax life closes
in about you there! You are the man of your faculties, nothing
more. Why should a man pretend to be more? We ask it wonder-
ingly when we are healthy. Poetic rhapsodists in the vale below may
tell you of the joy and grandeur of the upper regions; they cannot
pluck you the medical herb. He gets that for himself who wanders
the marshy ledge at nightfall to behold the distant Sennhüttchen
twinkle, who leaps the green-eyed crevasses, and in the solitude of
an emerald Alp stretches a salt hand to the mountain kine.[148]

This unusually vivid brief for the mountaineer would make one imagine
that Meredith did considerable climbing. He did not, however, but during his
lifetime he saw many fine mountain scenes, some of which he describes in
Vittoria and *Beauchamp's Career*. In the latter we view from a ship on the
Mediterranean a magnificent sunset:

The Adriatic was dark, the Alpshad heaven to themselves.
Crescents and hollows, rosy mounds, white shelves, shining ledges,
domes and peaks, all the towering heights were in illumination
from Friuli into farthest Tyrol; beyond earth to the stricken senses
of the gazers. Colour was steadfast on the massive front ranks; it
wavered in the remoteness, and was quick and dim as though it fell
on beating wings; but there too divine colour seized and shaped
forth solid forms, and thence away to others in uttermost distances
where the incredible flickering gleam of new heights arose, that
soared, or stretched their white uncertain curves in sky like wings
traversing infinity.[149]

The last phrase gives with poetic beauty the impression, so often felt, so difficult to describe, that the sunset, touching the tops of distant peaks, has unchained them from the dark earth and by its touch sent them flying off to join the colored clouds on the horizon beyond. The above quotation clearly indicates Meredith's ability to picture the mountains as seen from below. Now for another brief but highly colored piece of prose, this time from *Vittoria*, showing a similar view from high ground:

> Long arms of vapour stretch across the urn-like valleys, and gradually thickening and swelling upward, enwrap the scored bodies of the ashen-faced peaks and the pastures of the green mountain, till the heights become islands over a forgotten earth. Bells of herds down the hidden run of the sweet grasses, and a continuous leaping of its rivulets, give the Motterone a voice of youth and homeliness amid that stern company of Titan-heads, for whom the hawk and the vulture cry. The storm has beaten at them until they have got the aspect of the storm. They have colour from sunlight and are joyless in colour as in shade. When the lower world is under pushing steam, they wear the look of the revolted sons of Time, fast chained before scornful heaven in an iron peace. Day at last brings vigorous fire; arrows of light pierce the mist-wreaths, and the mountain of piled pasturages is seen with its foot on the shore of Lago Maggiore. Down an extreme gulf the full sunlight, as if darting on a jewel in the deeps, seizes the blue-green lake with its isles. . . . Farther away, over middle ranges that are soft and clear, it melts, confusing the waters with hot rays, and the forests with darkness, to where, wavering in and out of view like flying wings, and shadowed like wings of archangels with rose and with orange and with violet, silverwhite Alps are seen. You might take them for mystical streaming torches on the border-ground between vision and fancy.[150]

Writing at about the same period, but about Scotland instead of the Alps, Alexander Smith also vividly describes the mist in the hills. Like Sir Walter Scott he gives the impression of gloom and sadness in the Cuchullins, and also of their wildness, ". . . the Cuchullins—the outline wild, splintered, jagged, as if drawn by a hand shaken by terror or crazy,"[151] Again he catches their changing moods,

In the morning they wear a white caftan of mist; but that lifts away before noon, and they stand with all their scars and passionate torrent-lines bare to the blue heavens, with perhaps a solitary shoulder for a moment gleaming wet to the sunlight.[152]

Alexander Smith was not a climber, but at least he knew Skye and the Highland valleys well, and in this way knew more about mountains than William Hazlitt, who translated *Israel of the Alps* from French to English. Samuel Butler, however, knew more than either, though one would hardly gather this from reading his *Alps and Sanctuaries*, the story of his delightful wanderings through picturesque mountain villages of France and Italy. Yet in *Erewhon*, we quickly realize that the author has lived in the mountains and knows country like the fabulous ranges he pictures. Actually, as John Pascoe clearly shows in his *Unclimbed New Zealand*, Samuel Butler in 1861 made the first crossing of the Rakaia Mountains in New Zealand into the completely unknown Westland country on the opposite side of the range. This material he used most effectively in the early chapters of *Erewhon*, picturing vividly and accurately his crossing of Whitcombe Pass and the Rakaia River in company with his surveyor friend John Taker, the Chowbok of his famous satire:

How often have I sat on the mountain side and watched the waving downs, with the two white specks of huts in the distance, and the little square of garden behind them; the paddock with a patch of bright green oats above the huts, and the yards and wool-sheds down on the flat below; all seen as through the wrong end of a telescope, so clear and brilliant was the air, or as upon a colossal model or map spread out beneath me. Beyond the downs was a plain, going down to a river of great size, on the farther side of which there were other high mountains, with the winter's snow still not quite melted; up the river, which ran winding in many streams over a bed some two miles broad, I looked upon the second great chain, and could see a narrow gorge where the river retired and was lost. I knew that there was a range still farther back; but except from one place near the very top of my own mountain, no part of it was visible; from this point, however, I saw, whenever there were no clouds, a single snow-clad peak, many miles away, and I should think about as high as any mountain in the world.

Never shall I forget the utter loneliness of the prospect—only the little far-away homestead giving sign of human handiwork—the vastness of mountain and plain, of river and sky; the marvelous atmosphere effects—and then again, after cold weather, white mountains against a black sky—sometimes seen through breaks and swirls of cloud—and sometimes, which was best of all, I went up my mountain in a fog, and then got above the mist; going higher and higher, I would look down upon a sea of whiteness, through which would be thrust innumerable mountain tops that looked like islands.[153]

This passage seems unusually simple and uninspired after the vivid phrases of Meredith, but, like Jonathan Swift, Butler uses simplicity and accuracy in small details to secure acceptance of his fabulous story. And as numerous New Zealanders will attest, in doing so he gives a most precise and sensitive account of the Rakaia country.

Just as some may be surprised that the first literary account of New Zealand mountains comes from Samuel Butler, so others may not realize that the best description of Armenian mountains was written by the famous historian James Bryce. Bryce, though he cannot be called a great mountain climber, loved the high hills and spent considerable time in them. For instance, in his *South America* he gives good descriptions of the great Andes, and in *Memories of Travel* we hear of mountain wanderings in Iceland and many other parts of the globe, including a wonderful summer spent with Leslie Stephen in the Tatra of Austria-Hungary. Bryce, who was a member of the Alpine Club, contributed occasionally to the *Alpine Journal*, and gives an excellent account of his ascent of Mount Ararat in his book *Transcaucasia and Ararat*. This book beautifully describes the mountain, lists legends regarding its inaccessibility, and gives a detailed account of his successful expedition. At the summit, his beard one huge icicle, he finds "a snow-filled hollow, just large enough to have held the Ark comfortably, raised 15,000 feet above the surrounding country."[154]

Few people today probably realize that James Bryce climbed any mountains, but probably not many more know that John Addington Symonds, critic and essayist, was also extremely fond of the mountains and frequently climbed them. Symonds moved to Switzerland for his health when he was only thirty-seven, and from that time on spent many years there. During his lengthy

sojourn he became thoroughly familiar with the Swiss people and with the valleys and easier peaks in every season. The mountain air gradually restored his
good health, and his life in the mountains gave him a love for the Alps that he
pours forth eloquently in his poems, in *Our Life in the Swiss Highland*, and in
Sketches and Studies in Italy and Greece. Among his first mountain poems, of
which there are a considerable number, should be mentioned "A Night upon
the Schwartzhorn," "Bodensee," "The Crocus and the Soldanella," "Davos
Revisited," "The Alpine Wreath," and "I Stood at Sunrise on an Alpine Height."
The latter describes a Brocken that Symonds saw from the summit of Monte
Generoso. This scene he pictures better in prose in *Sketches and Studies*, but
"The Alpine Wreath" has the true feeling of spring in the Alps:

> *A garland I will weave of mountain flowers;*
> *Pure golden-hearted dryas, silvery*
> *Touched o' the nether leaf; androsace,*
> *That deepens from cream-white through summer hours*
> *To crimson; with the dark soul-nourishing powers*
> *Of azure gentian, bright-eyed auphrasy,*
> *Pink alpine clover, pale anemone,*
> *And saxifrages fed by flying showers.*
> *These I love best; for these when snows withdraw,*
> *When down the vexed paths of the avalanche*
> *Sky deities of spring renew their dance,*
> *Cheer those gaunt crumbling cliffs that tempests blanch,*
> *Where black streams thunder through the glacier's jaw*
> *And sun-gleams o'er the world-old cembra glance.*[155]

Strange as it seems to visitors, the spring flowers in the Alps are often nour-
ished by avalanches and frequently bloom with great beauty where the ruin of
the previous winter has been greatest. In the same volume Symonds vividly
describes the different types of avalanches, such as the terrible Schlag-Lawine
and the Staub-Lawine, and lists various accidents and miraculous escapes. The
last chapters of *Our Life in the Swiss Highlands* give magnificent descriptions of
the winter landscape hushed by the voice of winter. The soft outlines of the
hills are sensitively treated together with the violent color contrasts that are so
much more striking in the winter than at any other season. We see the snow in
one direction sparkling as if strewn with brilliants, while in another region, not

yet touched by the sun, the whole spectrum of blues, violets, and purples is boldly revealed:

> Spires and pinnacles of burnished silver smite the flawless blue of heaven. The vapour clinging to their flanks and forests melts imperceptibly into amber haze; and here and there broad stripes of dazzling sunlight turn the undulating snowfields round our path to sheets of argent mail, thickly studded with diamonds—crystals of the night. Every leafless larch or alder by the streambed is encrusted with sparkling frost-jewels, and the torrents, hurrying to the Rhine, chafe and foam against gigantic masses of gray-green ice, lipped with fantastically curving snow-wreaths.[156]

In *Sketches and Studies in Italy and Greece,* Symonds blends poetic descriptions of natural objects with philosophic musings. The Brocken that he sees from Monte Generoso, and beautifully depicts, makes him think of the "old formula for an anthropomorphic Deity—the Brocken-spectre of the human spirit projected on the mists of the Non-ego,"[157] a saying that he then goes on to examine. Another brilliant philosophic discussion begins, "What, after all, is the love of the Alps, and when and where did it begin?"[158] This question he examines closely, and finds that in medieval times mountains were not loved, because life was harsh and mountains meant fatigue and cold and robbers, material hardships that prevented appreciation of the immaterial. But he asks, "Why do the slopes gleam with flowers, and the hillsides deck themselves with grass, and the inaccessible ledges of black rock bear their tufts of crimson primroses and flaunting tiger-lilies? Why, morning after morning does the red dawn flush the pinnacles of Monte Rosa above cloud and mist unheeded? Why does the torrent shout, the avalanche reply in thunder to the music of the sun, the trees and rocks and meadows cry their 'Holy, Holy, Holy'? Surely not for us."[159]

He cannot answer his questions, but he does show how the sight of the great beauty in the mountains is not forgotten: "When our life is most commonplace, when we are ill or weary in city streets,"[160] we can be strengthened by recalling the magnificent mountain scenes of the past and feel that life is really good.

Symonds's *Sketches* are as full of loveliness as of philosophy. From a Lombard peak he sees the sunset lighting the crest of Monte Rosa and the Mischabelhorner:

The pyramid of distant Monte Viso burns like solid amethyst far, far away. Mont Cervin beckons to his brother, the gigantic Finsteraarhorn, across tracts of liquid ether. Bells are rising from the villages, now wrapped in gloom, between me and the glimmering lake. A hush of evening silence falls upon the ridges, cliffs, and forests of this billowy hill, ascending into wavelike crests, and toppling with awful chasms over the dark waters of Lugano. It is good to be alone here at this hour. Yet I must rise and go—passing through meadows, where white lilies sleep in silvery drifts, and asphodel is pale with spires of faintest rose, and Narcissus dreams of his own Beauty, loading the air with fragrance sweet as some love-music of Mozart. . . . Downward we hurry, on pathways where the beeches meet, by silent farms, by meadows honey-scented, deep in dew. The columbine stands tall and still on those green slopes of shadowy grass. The nightingale sings now, and now is hushed again. Streams murmur through the darkness, where the growth of trees, heavy with honey-suckle and wild rose, is thickest. Fireflies begin to flit above the growing corn. At last the plain is reached, and all the skies are tremulous with starlight.[161]

Robert Louis Stevenson, like his friend Symonds, visited the Alps to regain his health, and together they spent the winter of 1881–82 at Davos. Though he knew the mountains there only as an invalid at a sanitarium, Stevenson beautifully described the crisp Alpine winter weather in some of his letters and in *Essays of Travel.* From Davos he wrote,

One thing is undeniable – that in the rare air, clear cold, and blinding light of Alpine winters, a man takes a certain troubled delight in his existence which can nowhere else be paralleled. He is perhaps no happier, yet he feels he is stingingly alive. It does not perhaps come out of him in work or exercise, yet he feels an enthusiasm of the blood unknown in more temperate climates. . . . There is nothing more difficult to communicate on paper than this baseless ardor, this stimulation of the brain, this sterile joyousness of spirits. You wake every morning, see the gold upon the snow peaks, become filled with courage, and bless God for your prolonged existence. The valleys are but a stride to you! you cast your shoe over the hilltops; your ears and your heart sing . . .*162*

"Sterile joyousness of spirits" we might dispute, but he goes on to describe "the odd stirring silence—more stirring than a tumult" where "a man walks in a strong sunshine of the mind, and follows smiling insubstantial meditations." Here, he declares, "the fountain of Juventus plays . . . and possibly nowhere else."[163]

These spontaneous observations show the effect of the bracing mountain air of Switzerland on a sensitive nature, for Stevenson has beautifully captured the God-like lift of the spirits that the cold air brings. Similarly, as shown by the following passage, he felt the shock of the astounding color values always present in the sun-swept winter mountain landscape:

> . . . a world of black and white-black pinewoods, clinging to the sides of the valley, and white snow flouring it, and papering it between the pinewoods, and covering all the mountains with a dazzling curd. . . . Day after day breaks with the rarest gold upon the mountain spires, and creeps, growing and flowing, down into the valley. From end to end the snow reverberates the sunshine; from end to end the air tingles with the light, clear and dry like crystal. . . .
>
> An English painter, coming to France late in life, declared with natural anger that "the values were all wrong." Had he got among the Alps on a bright day he might have lost his reason. And even to any one who has looked at landscape with any care, and in any way through the spectacles of representative art, the scene has a character of insanity. The distant shining mountain peak is here beside your eye; the neighbouring dull-colored house in comparison is miles away; the summit, which is all of splendid snow, is close at hand; the nigh slopes, which are black with pine-trees, bear it no relation, and might be in another sphere.
>
> Here there are none of those delicate gradations, those intimate, misty joinings-on and spreadings-out into the distance, nothing of that art of air and light by which the face of nature explains and veils itself in climes which we may be allowed to think more lovely. A glaring piece of crudity, where everything that is not

white is a solecism and defies the judgment of the eyesight; a scene
of blinding definition; a parade of daylight, almost scenically vulgar, more than scenically trying, and yet hearty and healthy, making the nerves to tighten and the mouth to smile; such is the winter daytime in the Alps.[164]

The harsh glare of brilliant mountain sunshine and the inevitable distor-
tion it causes are beautifully observed here. Had Stevenson been physically able
to climb the high peaks, what superb material he would have found on which
to employ his sense of perspective!

Lafcadio Hearn, who was also a great traveler and a skillful describer of
what he saw, was able once in his life to do what Stevenson never was able to
accomplish: He climbed a high mountain. Hearn clearly was no born climber,
yet through sheer will power and the aid of his guides he took himself to the
crater of Fujiyama, an ascent that he describes most vividly in *Exotics and
Retrospectives.* Before the climb, he pictures the mountain:

The most beautiful sight in Japan, and certainly one of the most
beautiful in the world, is the distant apparition of Fuji on cloudless
days—more especially days of spring and autumn, when the
greater part of the peak is covered with late or with early snows.
You can seldom distinguish the snowless base, which remains the
same color as the sky; you perceive only the white cone seeming to
hang in heaven; and the Japanese comparison of its shape to an
inverted half-open fan is made wonderfully exact by the fine
streaks that spread downward from the notched top, like shadows
of fan-ribs. Even lighter than a fan the vision appears—rather the
ghost or dream of a fan—yet the material reality a hundred miles
away is grandiose among the mountains of the globe.[165]

He tells us the legends of the holy peak, whose shape is like "the white bud
of the sacred Flower": of the "shower of pierced-jewels once flung down from
it . . . of the Luminous Maiden that lured to the crater an Emperor who was
never seen afterward . . . of the sand that daily rolled down by pilgrim feet
nightly reascends to its former position."[166] Then he begins the ascent.

At first the peak rises above him in graceful sleeping lines like the shoulders
of a beautiful woman, but soon he is on the scoriaceous lava of the mountain
itself:

Fuji has ceased to be blue of any shade. It is black—charcoal black—a frightful extinct heap of visible ashes and cinders and slaggy lava. . . . Most of the green has disappeared. Likewise all of the illusion. The tremendous naked black reality—always becoming more sharply, more grimly, more atrociously defined—is a stupefaction, a nightmare. . . . Above—miles above—the snow patches glare and gleam against that blackness—hideously. I think of a gleam of white teeth I once saw in a skull—a woman's skull—otherwise burnt to a sooty crisp.

. . . I am perspiring and panting. The guide bids me keep my honorable mouth closed and breathe only through my honorable nose.[167]

Zigzagging upward and slipping frequently, Hearn moves above the clouds, so that the vast slope of the mountain disappears in the mists below. That night he watches the sunset from a small hut two miles above the earth:

Brighter and brighter glows the gold. Shadows come from the west—shadows flung by cloud-pile over cloud-pile; and these, like evening shadows upon snow, are violaceous blue. . . . Then orange-tones appear in the horizon; then smouldering crimson. And now the greater part of the Fleece of Gold has changed to cotton again—white cotton mixed with pink . . . Stars thrill out. The cloud-waste uniformly whitens; thickening and packing to the horizon. . . . It is no longer the Sea of Cotton. It is a Sea of Milk, the Cosmic Sea of ancient Indian legend—and always self-luminous, as with ghostly quickenings.[168]

The night slowly passes,

Dawn: a zone of pearl grows round the world. . . . Rivers appear but as sun-gleams on spider-threads; fishing-sails are white dust clinging to the grey-blue glass of the sea.[169]

Again he starts upward and in two hours reaches the Shinto shrine with the carved tiger at the summit:

Some hideous over-hanging cusps of black lava—like the broken edges of a monstrous cicatrix—project on two sides several hundred feet above the opening; but I certainly shall not take the trouble to climb them. Yet these—seen through the haze of a hundred miles—through the soft illusion of a blue spring-weather—appear as the opening snowy petals of the bud of the Sacred Lotus! No spot in this world can be more horrible, more atrociously dismal, than the cindered top of the Lotus as you stand upon it.

But the view—the view for a hundred leagues—and the light of the far faint dreamy world—and the fairy vapors of morning—and the marvelous wreathing of cloud: all this, and only this, consoles me for the labor and the pain. . . . Other pilgrims, earlier climbers—poised upon the highest crag, with faces turned to the tremendous East—are clapping their hands in Shinto prayer, saluting the mighty Day. . . . The immense poetry of the moment enters into me with a thrill. I know that the colossal vision before me has already become a memory ineffaceable—a memory of which no luminous details can fade till the hour when thought itself must fade, and the dust of these eyes be mingled with the dust of the myriad million eyes that also have looked, in ages forgotten before my birth, from the summit supreme of Fuji to the Rising of the Sun.[170]

Hearn's story of his climb of Fujiyama gives one of our finest pictures of a mountain ascent and suggests what Stevenson, Kipling, and other great contemporary writers might have penned had they, too, been climbers. Significant also is Hearn's disappointment at finding the cusp of the lotus, which looked so beautiful at a distance, only hideous black lava. So it is that the man in the valley and the mountaineer see a peak with different eyes. The valley watcher imagines that he knows what is on the high slopes but he rarely does, whereas the veteran can read the peaks and understand it as a scholar of the ancient Babylonians will read a cuneiform tablet.

An additional illustration of the non-climber's false ideas about mountains and a fine parallel to Hearn's account is furnished in *Tidemarks,* by H.M. Tomlinson, who ascended 5,200-foot Mount Tidore at Ternate in the Dutch East Indies. Leaving the nutmeg groves in the early dawn, Tomlinson soon found himself lost in a canebrake of ten-foot-high elephant grass, through which his guide slashed a spiky tunnel. Grass bayonets cut his clothes and tore his skin, but Tomlinson, as inexperienced as Hearn, enjoyed the experience of finding himself "in a light which was as fixed and greenish as a rare fluid that no wind could stir." In this green world he found "giant leaves even more fantastic than the succuba of roots; banners of wild plantain, pendent epiphytes, and the crowns of tree ferns which suggested in that light that we were lost in time and not in space, and had worked backwards to the Mesozoic epoch."[171]

It seems strange to find a mountaineer lost in a world of green, but Tomlinson passed through the jungle and soon reached the "fuliginois" summit with its "footstool of blackened ruin."[172] There, like Hearn on Fujiyama, he was impressed by the desolation of the scene and also by the power of the giant slumbering beneath his feet. Gazing out over the islands of the Pacific, he, too, could scarcely tell the real world from the imaginary:

> But where was the sea? As soon as we turned from the crater and looked outwards we forgot the nether fires. There was no sea, however. There was no sky. There was only a gulf of light which was blue to infinity. We were central in space. We looked southwards for the cluster of the Moluccas, but in that blue vacancy the islands and the clouds were all immaterial; the isles of Motir, Makian, and distant Batchian were mere conjectures, though in that clear and tranquil light I imagined I could see as far as Paradise and the solution of sorrow.[173]

As we have previously shown, Tomlinson is not the only climber whose thoughts on a mountain top have drifted far from the world of the present. Most of Hearn's literary contemporaries, however, were denied this experience, even if some of them did not scorn the mountains. Rudyard Kipling, for instance, though not a climber, in *Kim* gives us the feeling of the valleys leading up into the great peaks of Garhwal. "Surely the Gods live here,"[174] Kim once tells us, and mountain lovers of any land will agree. Kipling goes on to give a thrilling picture of the terraced heights of the Himalayas:

> Above them, still enormously above them, earth towered away toward the snow-line, where from east to west across hundreds of miles, ruled as with a ruler, the last of the bold birches stopped. Above that, in scarps and blocks unheaved, the rocks strove to fight their heads above the white smother. Above these again, changeless since the world's beginning, but changing to every mood of sun

and cloud, lay out the eternal snow. They could see blots and blurs on its face where storm and wandering wulli-wa got up to dance. Below them, as they stood, the forest slid away in a sheet of blue green for mile upon mile; below the forest was a village in its sprinkle of terraced fields and steep grazing grounds; below the village they knew, though a thunderstorm worried and growled there for a moment, a pitch of twelve to fifteen hundred feet gave to the moist valley where the streams gather that are the mothers of young Sutlej.[175]

Kipling can describe anything well, of course, and an example of what he might have done with mountain scenery appears in *From Sea to Sea*, where he describes the vastness and variegated coloring of Yellowstone Canyon:

All I can say is that without warning or preparation I looked into a gulf seventeen hundred feet deep with eagles and fish-hawks circling far below. And the sides of that gulf were one wild welter of colour—crimson, emerald, cobalt, ochre, amber, honey splashed and silver-grey, in wide lashes. The sides did not fall sheer, but were graven by time and water and air into monstrous heads of kings, dead chiefs, men and women of the old time. So far below that no sound of its strife could reach us the Yellowstone River ran—a finger-wide strip of jade-green. The sunlight took those wide walls and gave fresh hues to those that nature had already laid there. Once I saw the dawn break over a lake in Rajputana and the sun set over the Oodey Saga amid a circle of Holman Hunt hills. This time I was watching both performances going on below me—upside down you understand—and the colours were real! The canyon was burning like Troy town; but it would burn forever . . .[176]

Kipling had interests other than mountains, as did Sir Arthur Conan Doyle, who finishes one of his famous Sherlock Holmes stories in the Alps near Meiringen. At the Reichenbach Falls, which Conan Doyle describes in considerable detail, Sherlock Holmes and the infamous Professor Moriarty have their death struggle, and when Dr. Watson returns to join his friend, he finds only Holmes's alpenstock with a last note to him. The glacial torrent where Holmes has apparently disappeared is vividly pictured:

It is indeed a fearful place. The torrent, swollen by the melting snow, plunges into a tremendous abyss from which the spray rolls up like the smoke from a burning house. The shaft into which the river hurls itself is an immense chasm, lined by glistening, coal-black rock, and narrowing into a creaming, boiling pit of incalculable depth, which brims over and shoots the stream onward over its jagged lip. The long sweep of green water roaring for ever down, and the thick, flickering curtain of spray hissing for ever upwards turn a man giddy with their constant whirl and clamour.[177]

What a place to dispose of a body! In all fairness to Conan Doyle it must be admitted that in 1902 he had skied from Davos to Arosa and was quite at home among mountain scenes.

Joseph Conrad, as far as I know, wrote no great descriptive passages about the Alps, but, as he tells us in *A Personal Record*, at the top of the Furca Pass in 1873 he made one of the great decisions of his life. His tutor had been doing his best to argue him out of his ambition to go to sea and was succeeding when Conrad suddenly saw a strong and capable English mountain climber coming toward him. The romantic appearance of the "ardent and fearless traveler"[178] so inspired Conrad that he pulled himself together and made the basic decision that come what would, he was going to sea. He gives much credit for this decision to the fortuitous appearance of the English adventurer, whom he describes with vigor and exactness.

Although Kipling and Conrad turned their attentions elsewhere, a few of their contemporaries did otherwise. A.E.W. Mason, for instance, author of *The Four Feathers*, wrote of the mountains in many of his stories, particularly in *A Romance of Wastdale* and *Running Water*. Mason, who lived long after Tennyson, was a member of the Alpine Club and an experienced climber, as is shown by his fine novel *Running Water*, in many ways the best extended piece of mountaineering fiction. Fully half of the book deals with mountain climbing: the hero and heroine meet at Chamonix, climb the Aiguille d'Argentiere together, fall in love there, marry, and finally at Courmayeur succeed in preventing a murder high on the slopes of Mont Blanc. The mountain scenes lack the masterly descriptive touches of George Meredith or Lafcadio Hearn, but they are real and help the story move with sureness. The final scenes of the drama on the Brenva Ridge are absorbing. *Running Water* is good fiction with tingling suspense and an ideal mountain heroine, but it is not great literature. The heroine, Sylvia Thesiger, who does the Aiguille d'Argentière as her first climb, puts to shame most fictional woman climbers and Dickens's unreal Alpine girl. Sylvia's reactions at the summit are not those normal to a heroine of fiction but are those of a mountaineer:

> Sylvia lay upon the eastern slope of the Argentière looking over the brow, not wanting to speak, and certainly not listening to any word that was uttered. Her soul was at peace. The long-continued tension of mind and muscle, the excitement of that last ice-slope, both were over and had brought their reward. She looked out upon a still and peaceful world, wonderfully bright, wonderfully beautiful, and wonderfully colored. Here a spire would pierce the sunlight with slabs of red rock interspersed amongst its gray; there ice-cliffs sparkled as though strewn with jewels, bulged out in great green knobs, showed now a grim gray, now a transparent blue. At times a distant rumble like thunder far away told that the ice-fields were hurling their avalanches down. Once or twice she heard a great roar near at hand, and Chayne pointing across the valleys would show her what seemed to be a handful of small stones whizzing down the rocks and icefalls of the Aiguille Verte. But on the whole this new world was silent, communing with the heavens.[179]

Mason's work, which reads better than it quotes, is fiction of a fairly high order. Even better fiction, however, though it does not dwell so continuously on the mountains, was written by John Buchan, governor-general of Canada and a member of the Alpine Club. In several of his novels there is well-worded reference to the mountains and often to mountaineering. Buchan, who climbed brilliantly as a young man, gave up the sport to spare his family anxiety, but his love of the mountains never left him. In several of his books, such as *Mountain Meadow, The Three Hostages,* and *Mr. Standfast,* there are good descriptive passages. In *Mountain Meadow,* with its fine pictures of northern Canada and the chain of the Rockies, we have views of "cliffs and towers as fantastic as the Dolomites, black and sinister against a background of great snowfields."[180]

Even better are the passages in *Mr. Standfast* where Cornelius Brandt does some expert rock climbing in the Coolins while on the trail of a German spy.

Buchan clearly brings out the dark, gloomy sense of foreboding in the Coolins that so impressed Sir Walter Scott and later writers:

> Mountains have always been a craze of mine, and the blackness and mystery of those grim peaks went to my head. I forgot all about Fosse Manor and the Cotswolds. . . . But that dark mountain mass changed my outlook. I began to have a queer instinct that that was the place, that something might be concealed there, something pretty damnable. I remember I sat on a top for half an hour raking the hills with my glasses. I made out ugly precipices, and glens which lost themselves in primeval blackness. When the sun caught them—for it was a gleamy day—it brought out no colours, only degrees of shade. No mountains I had ever seen—not the Drakensberg or the red Kopjes of Damaraland or the cold, white peaks around Erzerum—ever looked so unearthly and uncanny.[181]

Quite different from Buchan's descriptions, though picturesque, are Maurice Hewlett's glimpses of the Greek mountains in his letters, though he nowhere reaches the emotional heights attained by Hilaire Belloc when he first saw the Alps from the Weissenstein. Belloc was not a climber, but he could perceive great beauty and describe the emotional tumult it created inside him:

> I saw between the branches of the trees in front of me a sight in the sky that made me stop breathing, just as great danger at sea, or great surprise in love, or a great deliverance will make a man stop breathing. I saw something I had known in the West as a boy, something I had never seen so grandly discovered as was this. In between the branches of the trees was a great promise of unexpected lights beyond. . . .
>
> There was brume in it and thickness. One saw the sky beyond the edge of the world, getting purer as the vault rose. But right up—a belt in that empyrean—ran peak and field and needle of intense ice, remote, remote from the world. Sky beneath them and sky above them, a steadfast legion, they glittered as though with the armour of the immovable armies of Heaven. Two days' march, three days' march away, they stood up like the walls of Eden. I saw it again, they stopped my breath. I had seen them. . . .

To what emotion shall I compare this astonishment? So, in first love once finds that *this* can belong to *me*. . . .

These, the great Alps, seen thus, link one in some way to one's immortality. Nor is it possible to convey, or even to suggest, those few fifty miles, and those few thousand feet; there is something more. Let me put it thus: that from the height of Weissenstein I saw, as it were, my religion. I mean humility, the fear of death, the terror of height and of distance, the glory of God, the infinite potentiality of reception whence springs that divine thirst of the soul; my aspirations also towards completion, and my confidence in the dual destiny.[182]

Elsewhere in *The Path to Rome, Hills and the Sea, The Pyrenees,* and other books of Belloc, there are fine passages descriptive of the mountains, but nowhere is there such a rhapsodic, mystic utterance as this. It is as if the sight from the Weissenstein had suddenly revealed to Belloc his own soul and the will of God. Nowhere in mountain literature do I know a more emotional outburst at the first sight of great mountains, though we must remember Shelley's letter to Peacock, and Ruskin's gasp when he first saw the Alps, "Suddenly—behold—beyond!"[183]

In recent years British poets, essayists, and novelists who are not true mountaineers have in general failed to treat the mountains vividly and subjectively. I repeat non-mountaineers, for there are many mountaineering writers who will be discussed elsewhere. Of the non-climbers, however, we should mention C.M. Doughty and Norman Douglas, while James Hilton in *Lost Horizon* and *Good-bye, Mr. Chips* also pictures mountain scenery, though without special power or insight. These examples could be multiplied. Many stories of fictional adventure among the peaks have also appeared in recent years, of which Newton Gayle's *Sinister Crag* and Dorothy Sayers's *The Five Red Herrings* are excellent illustrations.[184] In many ways the best, however, is Ralph Bates's *43rd Division,* a thrilling story of patrol actions in the Pyrenees during the Spanish Civil War. The hero, a good mountaineer and skilled rock climber, makes a magnificent ascent up a rock face rising from a valley where enemy patrols are active, shooting some of his foes as they climb precariously up the sheer rock after him. In this story, with its excellent suspense, Bates reveals himself as both a climber and writer of no mean ability.

As might be expected, much good mountain verse has been written, rang-
ing from a line or two in T.S. Eliot to whole poems of considerable length.
W.H. Auden, who has traveled extensively in mountainous country, has written some vivid and beautiful verses, though his satire *The Ascent of F-6*, written with Christopher Isherwood, is less impressive. Several little-known poets
have written excellent single poems on the mountains and even John Masefield
in *The Dauber* has some fine lines, beginning,

> *Silent the finger of the summit stood*
> *Icy in pure, thin air, glittering with snows,*
> *Then the sun's coming turned the peak to blood,*
> *And in the rest-house the muleteers arose.*
> *And all day long where only the eagle goes*
> *Stones, loosened by the sun, fall; the stones falling*
> *Fill empty gorge on gorge with echoes calling.*[185]

Masefield, though no mountaineer, has beautifully captured the loud
silence of the hills broken so harshly and suddenly by falling stones.

Like the poet laureate, Walter de la Mare has also captured the calm and
composure so frequently found in snowy uplands in winter:

> *Still, and unblanched, and cold, and lone,*
> *The icy hills far off from me*
> *With frosty ulys overgrown*
> *Stand in their sculptured secrecy.*
> *Yea, in my mind those mountains rise,*
> *Their perils dyed with evening's rose*
> *And still mine ghost sits at mine eyes,*
> *And thirsts for their untroubled snows.*[186]

Most of the writers considered during this chapter on valley travelers had
only slight personal contact with the heights, though this is not true of
Symonds, Mason, and Buchan. As can be seen, the distinction between the
writer and the climber is often difficult to draw, and some may feel that those
mentioned above should be considered primarily as mountaineers. Be that as
it may, in considering American writers whom we have hitherto avoided, the
borderline cases do not occur, for Whittier, Thoreau, Mark Twain, and other
Americans to be mentioned can scarcely be considered mountaineers.

Retracing our steps a little, we find mountain scenes by Washington Irving in *The Conquest of Granada*, *The Rocky Mountains or the Adventures of Captain Bonneville,* and in many fine stories about the Catskills. Irving was, of course, no mountaineer, but he writes pleasantly of rugged Spanish valleys and of the trials of the fur traders in the Rockies. For obvious reasons, however, in neither does he give the specific detailed descriptions that appear in his stories of the Catskills, which he knew so well. *The Rocky Mountains*, written at the suggestion of John Jacob Astor and based on his fur trader's journals, is lengthy but decidedly not one of Irving's best works.

At a somewhat later period, when Mrs. Hemans was writing her verses to Snowdon and the Alps, Celia Thaxter was expressing, perhaps more sensitively, her emotions at the sight of the White Mountains in poems like "Enthralled." Meanwhile, Lucy Larcom was writing numerous uninspired though sometimes sweet, realistic verses on the granite New Hampshire hills.

Ralph Waldo Emerson, though not a mountain climber, liked the White Mountains as well as Mount Monadnock, and wrote two poems about the latter. The earlier one is uneven and with the exception of one or two lines not notable, while the latter, "Monadnock from Afar," is merely a double quatrain that starts well but ends insipidly. The same mountain was also the subject of a poem by Emerson's friend William Ellery Channing, but faulty lines mar his efforts also.

More polished than any of these is "Nearing the Snow-Line" by Oliver Wendell Holmes, an American who did some climbing. Holmes's poetic talents, however, scarcely were equal to those of Henry Wadsworth Longfellow, who wrote widely, both in prose and verse, of various summits in New Hampshire, Switzerland, France, and Italy. "Enceladus" has pleasant verses on Mount Etna, but it is typical of Longfellow that he does not discuss specific peaks in intimate detail as a mountaineer would do, for though mountains stirred subjective impulses in him, he failed to see the personality of individual peaks. In "Excelsior" he is more interested in the idea than in any imagery of the mountain, and if the poem succeeds it is despite of the lack of realistic, concrete details upon which the mountaineer would insist. Similar in object are some fine lines in the *Masque of Pandora,* which speak nobly of the mountains in very general terms, telling of "the mysterious voice of the mountains":

Centuries old are the mountains;
Their foreheads wrinkled and rifted....
From their bosoms untossed
The snows are driven and drifted,
Like Tithonus' beard
Streaming disheveled and white.[187]

In *Hyperion*, the first American novel in an Alpine setting, we have Alpine background. Longfellow knew the Alps well as a valley watcher and gives nice descriptions of the Furka Pass, the St. Gothard Pass, and Mont Blanc. Of the latter he tells us,

> Before me lay the whole panorama of the Alps; pine forests standing dark and solemn at the base of the mountains, and half way up a veil of mist, above which rose the snowy summits and sharp needles of rock which seemed to float in the air like a fairy world. . . . Then the mists began to pass away; and it seemed as if the whole firmament were rolling together. It recalled to my mind that sublime passage in the Apocalypse, "I saw a great white throne, and Him that sat thereon; before whose face the heavens and the earth fled away, and found no place!" I cannot believe that upon this earth there is a more magnificent scene.[188]

Longfellow liked the mountains but he never rejoiced in them so continually and delightedly as did John Greenleaf Whittier. The latter, not in any way a climber, loved the mountains and was inspired by them with many a lofty and serene thought. His verses on the White Mountains are numerous and include descriptions of many well-known New Hampshire landmarks. Among his longer poems there are fine lines in "Among the Hills" and "The Bridal of Pennacook," while among the shorter ones "Mount Agiochook," "Summer by the Lakeside," "Sunset on the Bearcamp," "Monadnock from Wachusett," and "Franconia from Pemigewasset" are noteworthy. All show careful observation, high moral purpose, and a genuine delight in mountainous country. These poems represent a variety of themes and meters, but the following quotation is fairly representative:

Once more, O Mountains of the North, unveil
Your brows, and lay your cloudy mantles by!

And once more, ere the eyes that seek ye fail,
Uplight against the blue walls of the sky
Your mighty shapes, and let the sunshine weave
Its golden net-work in your belting woods,
Smile down in rainbows from your falling floods,
And on your kingly brows at morn and eve
Set crowns of fire! So shall my soul receive
Haply the secret of your calm and strength,
Your unforgotten beauty interfuse
My common life, your glorious shapes and hues
And sun-dropped splendours at my bidding come.....[189]

Whittier knew the hills better than Longfellow, describes them with more personal feeling than William Cullen Bryant in his "William Tell" and "To the River Arve," and has more beauty in his verses than James Russell Lowell has in his poems of the mountains, such as "Above and Below" and "To a Pine-Tree (on Mt. Katahdin)." It does not follow, however, that for this reason Whittier was a greater poet than those just mentioned, though most of us would place him far ahead of Helen Hunt Jackson and Bayard Taylor, who wrote many poems about the mountains during a slightly later period. Not one of these, however, is distinguished by great depth of perception or particularly sensitive treatment. "The Pass of Ampezzo," describing a short climb made by Miss Jackson, lacks both reality and poetic feeling, but "Cheyenne Mountain" has surer lines. Of Bayard Taylor's mountain verses, "The Two Homes" and "The Mountains" must be mentioned, the latter being the more effective and ending stronger than it begins. Yet none of these is as simple and unaffected as Thomas Bailey Aldrich's inconsequential but delightful poem "An Alpine Picture." More recently Mary Brent Whiteside and Kenneth Rexroth have written verses with fine understanding of the climber's feelings and of mountains.

Have there been no American prose writers who wrote about the mountains? Yes, Starr King wrote well about the White Mountains of New Hampshire and Clarence King brought the Sierras to national notice. Most writers, however, describe mountains as background for other material. Nathaniel Hawthorne, for example, uses a New Hampshire background in "The Great Stone Face" and "The Ambitious Guest," but unfortunately he does not include passages about the hills themselves. Henry Thoreau in *The Maine Woods*, though he gives us a long essay called "Ktaadn," says very little about the mountain. Thoreau's companions did not like to climb and when he trudged up the peak, a cloud cap covered the summit and he had no view. He tells us,

> The mountain seemed a vast aggregation of loose rocks, as if some time it had rained rocks, and they lay as they fell on the mountain sides, nowhere fairly at rest, but leaning on each other, all rocking stones, with cavities between, but scarcely any soil or smoother shelf. They were the raw materials of a planet dropped from an unseen quarry, which the vast chemistry of nature would anon work up, or work down, into the smiling verdant plains and valleys of earth. This was an undone extremity of the globe; as in lignite, we see coal in the process of formation . . .
>
> Now the wind would blow me out a yard of clear sunlight, wherein I stood; then a grey, dawning light was all it could accomplish, the cloud-line ever rising and falling with the wind's intensity. . . . It was like sitting in a chimney and waiting for the smoke to blow away. . . .
>
> The tops of mountains are among the unfinished parts of the globe, whither it is a slight insult to the gods to climb and pry into their secrets, and try their effect on our humanity. Only daring and insolent men, perchance, go there.[190]

Thoreau, under more fortunate circumstances, could have done better with Katahdin.

Farther west, in earlier years, Lewis and Clark, Fremont, and other travelers had forced their way across the Rockies, but the explorers' comments on the peaks are brief, for they were not searching out descriptive material. Somewhat later, however, a hardy soul on the extreme westward slope of the continent began to realize the beauty of his surrounding mountains. This was John Muir, who for many years wrote with loveliness and enthusiasm, extolling the virtues of the mountains in *My First Summer in the Sierra*, *The Yosemite*, *The Mountains of California*, and *Travels in Alaska*. Muir, of course, loved everything about the Sierras: the deep forests of Douglas spruces, sugar pines, and silver firs; the mountain uplands with their beds of flowers; the water ouzels and woodpeckers; and the glacial lakes reflecting the glittering summits thrust heavenward. At times his spontaneous overflow of emotions pour forth:

> Then it seemed to me the Sierra should be called not the Nevada, or Snowy Range, but the Range of Light. And after ten years spent in the heart of it, rejoicing and wondering, bathing in its glorious floods of light, seeing the sunbursts of morning among the icy peaks, the noonday radiance on the trees and rocks and snow, the flush of the alpenglow, and a thousand dashing waterfalls with their marvelous abundance of irised spray, it still seems to me above all others the Range of Light, the most divinely beautiful of all the mountainchains I have ever seen.[191]

Muir's letters glow with a delightful surprise at the bountiful wonders of life. His was an optimistic, kindly, and benevolent spirit. Note the joy in his picture of Yosemite:

> Awful in stern, immovable majesty, how softly these rocks are adorned, and how fine and reassuring the company they keep; their feet among the beautiful groves and meadows, their brows in the sky, a thousand flowers leaning confidingly against their feet, bathed in floods of water, floods of light, while the snow and waterfalls, the winds and avalanches and clouds shine and sing and wreathe about them as the years go by, and myriads of small winged creatures—birds, bees, butterflies—give glad animation and help to make all the air into music.[192]

Too many ecstatic outbursts become cloying and make us prefer to view the mountains as did our great humorist Mark Twain, whose accounts of Zermatt, Chamonix, and other climbing centers are the high spots in more ways than one in *A Tramp Abroad*. This book was not the first nor the most humorous book on the Alps, however; Daudet's *Tartarin sur les Alpes* is the pronounced masterpiece.

Mark Twain, having heard that glaciers move, decided "to take passage for Zermatt on the great Gorner Glacier,"[193] but was disappointed in its slowness and blamed the government. After reading Hinchliff to learn about the mountains, he organized an expedition to ascend the Riffelberg. He was prepared for siege tactics and his "Bandobast" consisted of "198 persons including the mules; or 205, including the cows."[194] He also had seventeen guides, fifteen bar keepers, and four surgeons, together with two thousand cigars, twenty-two barrels of whiskey, and 143 pairs of crutches. During a pause in the ascent he boiled his thermometer and found to his surprise that it indicated he had reached the height of 200,000 feet above sea level. As there was no snow, this scientific measurement immediately proved to him that "the eternal snowline ceases somewhere above the 10,000-foot level and does not begin any more."[195] He next decided to boil a guide to see if it would help him determine his position, but the guides didn't love science and refused. Still later, at the top of the Gorner Grat, he boiled his thermometer again, and found that he was 9,000 feet lower than his hotel, thus demonstrating clearly "that, *above a certain point, the higher a point seems to be, the lower it actually is.*"[196] All Twain's ascents were immediately recorded on stone monuments, and he judiciously tells us,

> There is probably no pleasure equal to the pleasure of climbing a dangerous Alp; but it is a pleasure which is confined strictly to people who can find pleasure in it.[197]

Climbing and Writing

On the high snows it seemed as if magical fires were lit in your blood; the flame of life burned amazingly; something was added unto a man as divine as whatever it is that makes its way into the vapid juice of a fruit and turns it to wine. Nowhere else in the world was the taste of success so wholly and indefeasibly sweet as it was on the tip of some spire of granite and ice that had all but turned you back in despair by the Daphnean rigour of its resistance.[198]

— C.E. Montague

SINCE THE DAYS when Leslie Stephen stoutly defended mountain climbers to a suspicious and indignant Victorian audience, the attitude toward climbing adopted by the public in Europe and much of America has changed. Although most people do not know why men climb, they recognize that some reward in beauty, health, or adventure must be the inspiration for so much strenuous labor and accepted risk. Large numbers of mountaineers have tried to explain their reasons for going to the mountains, of course, but as their feelings vary, even among climbers of a single party, it is not remarkable that the general public fails to understand.

In the material that follows, great differences in point of view will be shown, even as there were tremendous differences among the stimuli that actuated the climbing of Whymper, Stephen, and Tyndall. With these individuals some of the same fundamentals were there, but the proportion varied and the emphasis was never the same. Freshfield, Conway, Mummery, and Geoffrey Winthrop Young also all had differing interests within the same field, and although the mountains were the greatest influence in the life of each man, the attitude of

125

each changed and matured through a lifetime of climbing experience.

In recent years, as mountains have become better known, men in most areas have lost the invigorating sensation of exploring that so delighted the first climbers in any district. Indeed, fostered by guideless climbers, there has appeared a growing interest in new routes and more technically arduous achievements. This development was perfectly natural and did no harm so long as men could gauge their own abilities, the strength of the mountain, and the type of weather, but climbers were not always capable of judging such matters competently and as a result many accidents in the Alps and elsewhere began to occur. In addition, many climbers became more interested in their own techniques or in equipment problems than in the beauties of the places to which their technique enabled them to go. Climbers' interests in this way had a definite influence on their writings, for many began to write only of routes and techniques. The joys of life in the mountains became scarcely mentioned lest the writer seem to be an amateur or a technically unskillful climber. In the same way, philosophical thoughts and lyric feelings were often sternly compressed, to the detriment of much of the writing about mountains from 1880 to the present. This criticism, however, though it applies to the great bulk of writing done for climbers' clubs, does not apply to those writers who were not self-conscious or so conservative that they blindly followed a conventional pattern without expressing what they actually felt and thought. It is the latter— writers who resisted the conventions of repression—with whom the rest of this book is mainly concerned.

At the time when Leslie Stephen was editing the *Alpine Journal,* a young geologist, not many years out of Yale, was beginning to write about his experiences with the California Geological Survey. He was Clarence King, whose essays on the Sierras in the *Atlantic Monthly* brought an enthusiastic response not only from William Dean Howells and American readers in general, but also from the Alpine Club, which welcomed his writings as giving new reasons why Englishmen should visit the United States. King's *Mountaineering in the Sierra Nevada* (1872) is today a classic. Well written, humorous, and full of colorful descriptions of many kinds, it was immediately popular, and the way was prepared for similar successes if the author wished to continue his literary efforts. Unfortunately, however, King's plans for more mountain stories never matured.

Henry Adams, who greatly admired King, once wrote, "He had in him something of the Greek—a touch of Alcibiades or Alexander. One Clarence King only existed in the world."[199] This rugged geologist, born with ability in many lines, had great zest for life, whether furiously attacking Mount Tyndall or Mount Shasta, risking his neck to carry heavy transits up mountain ridges, eating rabbit pie when the meat supply was short, or sliding down a steep slope roped to a companion by a lasso. Of Mount Whitney he writes,

> Silence reigns on their icy heights, save when scream of Sierra eagle or loud crescendo of avalanche interrupts the frozen stillness or when in symphonic fullness a storm rolls through vacant canyons with its stern minor. It is hard not to invest these great dominating peaks with consciousness, difficult to realize that, sitting thus for ages in presence of all nature can work of light-magic and color beauty, no inner spirit has kindled, nor throb of granite heart once responded, no Buddhistic nirvana-life even has brooded in eternal calm within these sphinx-like breasts of stone.[200]

King knew and loved the Sierras: the deep forests, the tumultuous watercourses and the dry upper solitudes. Though he viewed mankind with a twinkle, he saw nature with the unblinking eye of the scientist:

> Spread out below us lay the desert, stark and glaring, its rigid hill-chains lying in disordered grouping, in attitudes of the dead. The bare hills are cut out with sharp gorges, and over their stone skeletons scanty earth clings in folds, like shrunken flesh; they are emaciated corpses of once noble ranges now lifeless, outstretched as in a long sleep. Ghastly colors define them from the ashen plain in which their feet are buried. Far in the south were a procession of whirlwind columns slowly moving across the desert in spectral dimness. A white light beat down, dispelling the last trace of shadow, and above hung the burnished shield of hard, pitiless sky.[201]

Clarence King's literary successes were not at once copied by other Americans, as his climbs were, but his works are well known today. In the United States at the time of King's ascents, few books about mountains had been written, but in England a steady stream of climbing books poured forth in the 1870s and '80s. For instance, *The High Alps without Guides*, by the Rev. Arthur Girdlestone, had great popularity in its day, but more for its delightful spirit of adventure than for its literary quality. Crauford Grove's *Frosty Caucasus* also was popular in the 70s. This deals with Grove's expedition to Elbruz in 1874 with Moore, Walker, and Gardiner, and is more of a travel guide than a climbing book. It does, however, vividly picture the rugged Caucasus and its wild inhabitants, as well as the desolate crater of Elbruz, which loftily surveys the boundary between Asia and Europe. Grove was not seriously affected by the rarity of the air on Elbruz, but he tells us, "It may be taken for granted that no human being could walk to the top of Mount Everest."[202] Then, no one had proved him wrong, though many Englishmen were soon to try.

Meanwhile, W.A.B. Coolidge gradually, by accretion, was compiling his weighty encyclopedias of the Alps; Slingsby was pioneering in Norway; Douglas Freshfield, in addition to editing the *Alpine Journal*, was climbing in many countries and writing beautifully of what he saw; and Clinton Dent was making his vigorous assaults on some of the more difficult Pennine routes.

Of all climbers who have written of the mountains in English, however, none worked more steadfastly than W.A.B. Coolidge (1850–1926), an American who attended Oxford and spent most of his life in Europe and the Alps. Coolidge climbed the Niesen, Benoit Marti's beloved peak, at the age of fifteen, and not only went on to make further ascents the same season, but also returned to the Alps again and again until he had climbed almost every pass and peak possessing the least historic reference. Coolidge apparently was never particularly gregarious. During his early climbs he was known as "the young American who climbs with his aunt and his dog," and in later life he climbed largely with guides and no comrades of his own. This somewhat dour man had no interest in the Caucasus, Himalayas, or the mountains of America, but concentrated on the Alps, not only climbing widely in them but also reading avidly all he could find in print about them, whether in German, French, Italian, or English.

Coolidge's encyclopedias are still the most complete books of their kind written about the Alps. His *Josias Simler et les origines de l'Alpinisme* is a monumental tome, bursting with factual information and written in French. For obvious reasons, however, we are more interested in his books in English, particularly *The Alps in Nature and History*, which in scholarly and critical fashion deals with topographic divisions, flora and fauna, the political history of the Alps, and modern ascents. Nowhere in English is there such an authoritative and thorough study of this huge subject. Coolidge had an eye for beauty, as we see frequently in his references, but his primary interests lay elsewhere. He definitely was not joking when he wrote to Douglas Freshfield, "It is notorious, my dear friend, that your accounts of your climb are *frightfully vague*; you care more for aesthetic impressions than accurate topography."[203]

Coolidge's earlier book, *Swiss Travel and Swiss Guide-Books*, lacks the broad interest and elasticity of style that we find in *The Alps in Nature and History*, where he rests his reader from time to time by vividly recounting legends, battles, or first ascents. Of the bouquetin, for instance, he tells us,

> Even so genuine a naturalist as the celebrated Conrad Gesner, writing in the middle of the sixteenth century, reproduces in all good faith the legend that the bouquetin, when it feels that the sands of its life are running low, betakes itself to some pinnacles of lofty loneliness, and there, hooking a horn to the summit, proceeds madly to twirl round, till at last the horn is worn through, and the animal is precipitated into the depths.[204]

About twenty years older than Coolidge was Clinton Dent, contributor to the *Alpine Journal*, author of *Above the Snow Line*, and later president of the Alpine Club. Dent's excellent sense of humor stood him in good stead in his Alpine wanderings as well as in his writings. Typical of his style is the opening sentence of an article in the *Alpine Journal*, which tells us, "Beginning an article with an apology is like beginning dinner with a bad oyster—it gives an unpleasant flavour to all that follows."[205] But Dent had no need to apologize either for his taste in mountains or for the flavor of his numerous articles on mountaineering subjects. His somewhat uneven style is vigorous and full of surprises, for his colorful sense of humor cannot remain hidden long. In the Caucasus he even christened his little donkey "Garlic," on the ground that "it was very strong and a very little of it went a very long way."[206] Despite such puns he could describe more serious moments effectively:

> "Come on," said voices from above. "Up you go," said a voice from below. I leaned as far back as I could, and felt for a hand-hold. There was none. Then right, then left—still none. So I smiled feebly, and said: "Wait a minute." Thereupon, of course, they pulled with a will, and struggling and kicking like a spider irritated with tobacco smoke, I topped the rock gracefully.[207]

Above the Snow Line is not so well written as some of Freshfield's work and will not be so admired today as it was formerly, but the book still holds the interest and gives a realistic account of climbing in the 1870s and '80s. The most striking chapters by this lovable author tell of the first ascent of the Dru, which Dent conquered on his *nineteenth* attempt.

Several years before Dent's success on the Aiguille du Dru, Englishmen had begun to reconnoiter the severe Norwegian mountains whose ice and snow and excellent rock afforded problems for the hardiest. As early as 1870 T.L.M. Browne, with his brother, had wandered through the valley of the Uledalstind where he found how "the keen peak of Simletind shot into the air thousands of feet over our heads, glittering with new-fallen snow, and sharp as the spear-head of a titan."[208] But Browne, though he described the Norwegian peaks well, did comparatively little to explore and climb them. This was left for another Englishman, William Cecil Slingsby, who was later affectionately known to Englishmen and Norwegians alike as the Father of Norwegian Mountaineering.

The career of this likable Englishman in Norway in many ways parallels the mountain experiences of his more accomplished contemporaries, such as Freshfield and Conway, who were now beginning to find the Alps too confining and were exploring newer and more personal areas in other parts of the world. Starting in 1872, Slingsby, who had already climbed in the Alps, made fifteen expeditions into a number of Norwegian mountain regions, doing pioneer climbing and exploration. He was a pleasant, genial man, modest and with great nerve and hardihood. On more than one occasion when his Norwegian companions refused to climb higher, he dared to go on alone to complete the ascent.

Slingsby is best known as the writer of the authoritative book on Norwegian mountains, *Norway the Northern Playground*. He tells of early explorations in the Horungtinder, Jotunheim, and other areas, winter and summer, and vividly describes the first ascents of Stedtind, Skagastolstind, known as the finest mountain in Norway, and other peaks. There are charming views of Norwegian farms and pleasant homes, as well as accounts of bear hunts and sports in the mountain valleys. Everywhere the happy, fearless Slingsby seems to have made friends, and nearly everywhere virgin gabbro or granite peaks fell before his determined onslaughts. The true mountaineer enjoys the whole story, particularly the first ascent of the magnificent, wedge-shaped Skagastolstind and the amazing descent of the dangerous Kjaendalsbrae Icefall. Although the author does not write with singular ability, his book has had modern editions and continues to read well today. Above all it gives a grim, realistic picture of that "terrible region of dark cliffs, sharp peaks, narrow ridges, and stony valleys, without one single blade of green grass."[209]

Slingsby also climbed in the Alps, where on one occasion he had a narrow escape when his rope was struck by lightning, and on another when he was forced to bivouac with his friend Mummery and two companions on a savage ice slope on the Aiguille du Plan. These and other adventures are described in the *Alpine Journal*, though generally without the benefit of Slingsby's excellent sketches.

More talented than Slingsby, however, and perhaps the finest British mountain artist, was lawyer Henry Willink, who drew, wandered, and climbed throughout the Alps. Willink writes fluently of the joys of sketching and the necessity of actually being a climber if one is to depict accurately the high mountain areas and the mountaineers who inhabit them. He loves to discuss worthy subjects for the artist, such as an "ice slope crossed by swarthy figures and alive with the jeweled showers of chips sparkling in the sun, as they fly skiddering down from the leader's axe"; or "Peter Kauffman's sun-dried head, of the hue and texture of pemmican, clothed in a black felt wide-awake tied over with a bright red handkerchief, peering through a deep blue sky gap in a dazzling snow cornice at the top of the Wetterhorn."[210] No one can fail to agree that fine mountain art would exist if more painters like Willink, men who know true mountain color values, would climb into the mountains instead of observing them from the valleys.

Willink's numerous articles abound in exact coloring and acute detail, as for example his *Snowdon at Christmas 1878*:

> Five minutes after taking our gloves off they were frozen hard; my beard and moustache were still with congealed breath and frozen snow which had got there from some tumble in the drift; our woolly clothes were tagged with little bobbins of ice which tinkled as we walked.[211]

Despite the wintry winds, he glows with pleasure at the ice filigree work, the soft contours of the slopes, and the strange color perspective, "the distant hills seeming to be of a warmer, duller white, with a tinge of red in it, which appears fainter and fainter in those nearer to us, until the highest pitch of light is reached in the blinding snow at our feet."[212]

Later, the scene grows wilder:

> The great hollow of Cwm Idwal is boiling with ragged clouds, which come tearing up as the fancy seizes them, to sweep overhead, and then whirl down again to the Devil's Kitchen, whence they have come. There is a mysterious lurid light in the mist; and through the gaps you catch glimpses of Snowdon with his supporters—how changed from yesterday—pallid and grim now. You can see the snow whisked up into driving whirlwinds along his ridges; and you know very well what those columns mean from the stinging of the icy particles against your face up here even under the lee of this big stone.[213]

Here we have all the colorful, breathless beauty of mountains in winter, with their sudden changes of light and mood. Such mountain vagaries were well known also to Frederic Harrison, though he was no artist, and were described by him after the turn of the century in his book of memories of early days in the mountains.[214] Harrison did not have Willink's artistic eye for objective detail, but he knew mountains and mountain men.

One of the most famous climbers of the period was Douglas Freshfield, whose career dated from his first visit to the Alps with his mother in 1854, at age nine, to his death in 1933. Freshfield had every opportunity to become interested in mountains, for his family had wealth, social position, and an appreciation of natural objects. His mother, Mrs. Henry Freshfield, admired the Alps and, encouraged by her son, in 1861 published *Alpine By-ways, by a Lady*, a story of mountain travels that had immediate influence on Alpine journeys of other English ladies. The following year appeared a companion volume, *A Summer Tour in the Grisons*, this time bearing her name as author.

Her son obviously had advantages from the start, and he made the most of them. He traveled and climbed eagerly in the Engadine, Tyrol, and northern Italy, as well as in the better-known climbing regions of France and Switzerland. Before many years had passed, this energetic and learned young geographer had made the classical climbs and begun to capture first ascents in widely distant areas. In 1868 he organized the first mountaineering expedition to the Caucasus, and succeeded in the first ascent of Mount Elbruz. Later he returned several times to the Caucasus, writing the definitive mountaineering book on the range in 1896. Other expeditions took him to Kangchenjunga in the Himalayas, to South Africa, Japan, and the Canadian Rockies. Everywhere he went, this charming, scholarly Englishman skillfully described the local people and their rocky fastnesses, producing innumerable articles and several books of both geographic and literary value. During his lifetime, Freshfield was president of the Alpine Club, as might be expected, and was editor of the *Alpine Journal* from 1872 to 1880.

His first publicly printed book, *Travels in the Central Caucasus and Bashan*, which appeared in 1869, gives a good account of the first ascents of Kasbek and Elbruz, where the author had a sensational experience with a crevasse. Although successful as a book of mountaineering and travel, this volume cannot compare with later literary efforts, such as *Italian Alps*, in which Freshfield describes moments of sensuous beauty on Italian summits:

> But the vision of those hours on a great peak stretches beyond what is actually before the eyes. At such moments even the dullest soul shares with inarticulate emotion the feelings which poets have put into words for all ages. Our pulses beat in tune with the great pulse of Life which is breathing round us. We lose ourselves and become part of the vast order into the visible presence of which we seem for a brief space to have been translated. On a lesser height, whence some town is seen like a great ant-heap with the black insects hurrying backwards and forwards across its lanes, the insignificance of the human race is often painfully prominent. But here, removed by leagues of snow and ice and a mile or two of sheer height from the rest of our race, no such thought oppresses us. Man is merged in nature, cities have become specks, provinces are spread out like fields, the eye ranges across a kingdom. . . .
>
> On its lofty standpoint the mind feels in harmony with the soul of the universe, and almost fancies itself to gain a glimpse of its workings.
>
> Seen from the valley the sublimity of the mountain precipice may be due to a sentiment at root akin to terror. Grandeur is there shown in its most overpowering—a Frenchman might say bru-

tal—form by some giant peak towering defiantly skywards, "remote, serene, and inaccessible," a chill colossus alien to human life. But on the peak we are conquerors; its terrors are left below and behind us. In our new scale of vision the Titans gathered in silent session round us are brothers. The masses which appeared from below "confusedly hurled" have become ordered. The valleys unfold their labyrinths.[215]

Freshfield's Victorian style is clearly shown in the above passage, with its inevitable sense of perspective and pleasant philosophy. In the same volume appear numerous illustrations capturing his keen eye. He likes all mountain country, whether the ridges are "capped by a most fantastic fence of dolomite splinters"[216] or are rounded and peaceful as in Lombardy, with lovely views up at Monte Rosa and down on the Piedmont plains: whence, "Through a Coan drapery of golden haze the great rivers could be seen coursing like veins over the bosom of fair Italy, open to where it was clasped round by the girdle of the far-off Apennine."[217]

Following *Italian Alps*, Freshfield's literary efforts for the next few years were confined to the *Alpine Journal*, *Geographical Journal*, and short articles in other publications. Meanwhile, he traveled widely and wrote numerous accounts of distant mountain ranges that he visited, like Suanetia, where "the wind from the Steppe suffuses the air with an impalpable haze, through which the great peaks glimmer like golden pillars of the dawn."[218]

In 1896 his monumental, two-volume *Exploration of the Caucasus* appeared. This beautifully printed and illustrated volume is also well written, and has for years been recognized as the unexcelled book on the region. It covers a tremendous area, adding to previous maps geographic material of great value. There is literary value as well, for instance in his description of reaching the summit of Tetnuld. On the top of Ukiu he gives us his feelings as he looks out across the snowy Caucasus, emotions inevitable to the sensitive man on a great mountain anywhere, whether in Alaska, New Zealand, or the Alps:

> I lingered long over the view; the sunlit snows were so beautiful, the mountain forms so sublime, that it was hard to leave them. Far beneath, the rivers sprang from their icy cradles, flashed in the depths of their forest-fringed ravines, or shone thin lines of silver, as they wandered out beyond the green foothills into the luminous

THE EXPLORATION OF
THE CAUCASUS

BY DOUGLAS W. FRESHFIELD

LATELY PRESIDENT OF THE ALPINE CLUB

FORMERLY HONORARY SECRETARY OF THE

ROYAL GEOGRAPHICAL SOCIETY

WITH ILLUSTRATIONS BY

VITTORIO SELLA

VOLUME I

EDWARD ARNOLD

LONDON AND NEW YORK

1896

Title page from Freshfield's most important book. The photo is by Vittorio Sella.

distances of the northern steppe. Close at hand, and far as the eye could reach, the great peaks of the Caucasus rose like "whiter islands" out of the untraversed sea of air. Before me, in its austere and stately splendour and perfect purity, was spread one of those great mountain landscapes in which the primitive powers of nature that were ages before, and shall be ages after, the face of men, seem to assert their independence of our brief consciousness, and at the same time to vindicate the permanence that underlies mutability. One felt for the moment uplifted: brought, as it were, spiritually, as well as materially, to the verge of some strange Promethean prospect. As in a starry night on a desert plain, but more forcibly from the utter strangeness of the spectacle, the mind at such seasons is carried away from the accidents of human life, and set face to face with the order of the Universe. It grows conscious of the throbbings of an imperfect sense or faculty by which it recognizes a spirit kindred to its own underlying Nature. The vision, it is true, soon fails; the veil loses its momentary semi-transparency. But the memory of the sensation remains distinct when much else is forgotten. How far are such experiences insight? how far idle phantasy? That is a matter in which philosophers must be left to differ, and poets to feel.[219]

The Exploration of the Caucasus is Freshfield's most important geographic work, but a few years later appeared *Round Kangchenjunga*, a large volume dealing with an expedition to the area surrounding the third highest mountain in the world. Other books followed, including collections of verse, a volume on Hannibal's travels through the Alps, and an excellent biography of De Saussure, but none of these has greater literary value than *Below the Snow Line*, which reprints some of Freshfield's best articles on wanderings in mountain lands. Here we have magnificent descriptions of flowers on the Gran Sasso, Alpine meadows rich with rhododendrons and anemones below the glittering summits of the Maritime Alps, and rich, ever-changing seascapes below classic Grecian summits. In Savoy he had a fine hour on the summit of the Pointe de Colloney:

That hour was perfect. There were clouds in the sky, but none touched even the highest earth. Only upon the brow of Mont Blanc the spirits of the air wound and unwound transparent rainbow-tinted scarves of vapour, visible for a moment and then again lost in the purple of noon. In the north a pillar-like cumulus stood over the summit of the Voirons. As I watched it two horizontal bars opened out, at one moment resembling the arms of a gigantic cross, at another the wings of some monstrous bird.

Across the upper sky the cloud processions moved peacefully with no audible sound of wind. The herds had already deserted the high pastures, and the face of the earth, but for some muffled sounds of falling waters, was noiseless about my "solitary hill." No living creature was visible in the vast horizon. I was alone with Mont Blanc.[220]

No wonder Freshfield assails Ruskin's famous statement: "that all of the strength and beauty the mountains have to reveal to us may be known by the cripple, the greybeard and the infant!"[221]

The unbiased reader will probably agree most emphatically with Freshfield after reading of his climbs through Greece and the Dinaric Alps, and of the soft, ethereal sunrise he saw from the summit of the poets' mountain, Mount Parnassus.

Freshfield's death in 1933 severed the last link between the golden age of Alpine mountaineering and the modern period of guideless ascents and expeditions to the highest peaks, but an American mountaineer nearly as old and as famous as Freshfield was still alive. This was Dr. William Hunter Workman (1847–1937) who with his wife had made many expeditions at the turn of the century. Dr. Workman, a Worcester, Massachusetts, surgeon, began his great expeditions to the Himalayas when he was fifty-two, and for the next twelve years he and his wife made mountaineering history. He was fifty-six when he made the then world's record climb by reaching a height of 23,394 feet. With his wife he wrote nine books, of which five, all beautifully illustrated, concern his high mountain expeditions.[222] Of these, *In the Ice-World of Himalaya* and *The Call of the Snowy Hispar* perhaps have most interest for the reader who is not primarily concerned with geographical surveys, meteorology, and physiology. The scientific value of Dr. and Mrs. Workman's books was fully acknowledged during their lifetimes. From a literary standpoint, their books, though well written, are not noteworthy.

Mr. and Mrs. Bullock Workman of Worcester, Massachusetts, began climbing in their 50s. They did six remarkable explorations into the Karakoram, wrote nine books, and set a world altitude record: 23,394 ft. From Workman, *Ice-bound Heights of the Mustagh*.

Another contemporary who outlived Douglas Freshfield was a Canadian, Arthur Coleman, professor of geology at the University of Toronto for many years and a president of the Alpine Club of Canada. His best-known work is his *Ice Ages, Recent and Ancient*, but we are more concerned with his less scientific writings, primarily *The Canadian Rockies, New and Old Trails*. In this book, with great freshness and charm he tells of a lifetime of pleasant climbing in the Canadian Rockies. His first peak, a small one along the railroad near Lake Louise, gave him an immediate stimulus:

> After twenty years of humdrum city life in the east, the assembly of mountains, lifting their heads serenely among the drifting clouds, gave one a poignant feeling of the difference between man's world and God's. Here was purity and dignity and measureless peace. Here one might think high thoughts. Below in the grim valley engines puffed, mule-teams strained at their loads, sweaty men delved in the muck, and man's work, looked at from above, did not seem desirable under its mantle of smoke.[223]

Professor Coleman's book describes with singular charm the days when climbing in the Canadian Rockies was young. The main problem then often was how to get to the base of the peak, not how to climb it, and adventures with moose and bears and turbulent streams were as much a part of the mountaineer's life as his step-cutting on steep ice. Perhaps the most vividly described moment in this excellent book comes when the climber's raft is overturned in Surprise Rapids and he and his companion are quickly swept four miles downstream. *The Canadian Rockies* is not a great book, but it has flavor. It makes us regret the author's failure in his spirited attempts on Mount Robson, though in his views of trappers and Native Americans, or of long twilight evenings with the resinous sap crackling in the campfire and the white-capped hills turning vermilion in the last light of the sun, he does not fail.

Some years before Professor Coleman's book appeared, Walter Dwight Wilcox, conqueror of Mount Temple, brought out his *Rockies of Canada*, which also gives fine pictures of the early days of Canadian mountaineering, though without the personal charm of the professor. Neither Wilcox nor Coleman, however, had as fluent a style as their English contemporary Francis Bourdillon, a poet of some ability and a climber who greatly loved the Alps. It is Bourdillon's prose rather than his verse that we wish to refer to here, for his familiar essays are well written and amusing. The following analysis of mountain lovers reminds one of Leslie Stephen:

> The love of mountains is, no doubt, in many persons an acquired habit—like smoking, or eating olives; in some it is even a simulated pleasure—again like smoking, or eating olives. But in the latter

case it is liable to break down under strain; as in the well-known story of the Frenchman in glacé boots and best kid gloves, toiling up the steep side of Ben Lomond, and at last exclaiming to his companion, "Aimez-vous les beautés de la nature? Moi, je les déteste!" But besides these persons we may distinguish at least four classes of mountain-lovers. First, there are those who like to gaze upon mountains at a safe distance, as from a comfortable hotel at Berne or Lucerne; or to play lawn tennis somewhere within forty miles of them, as at Villars or other places of that kind. Secondly, there is the numerous class of persons who have courage enough to go right up to them, without ever trusting themselves on their backs. This class composes the bulk of the holiday-makers who crowd the hotels of Grindelwald or Pontresina in the month of August; for them is the 20-centime-in-the-slot telescope focused on the peak of the Wetterhorn or the Cervin; for them is provided the cinematograph in the evening. The third class is of those who go in lifts and Funiculars and rack-and-pinion railways to the top of anything which can be ascended in this way. They enjoy the excellent table-d'hote at the top of Pilatus—and indeed it is—or was, worth going for—and stand muffled round with cloaks at the Eismeer station of the Jungfrau Bahn. The members of this class have a tendency to be stout and Teutonic; and their favourite air is Funicoli Funicola. The fourth class is that of the climbers, and includes many varieties male and female; from the would-be Tartarin, sandwiched between two strong guides, relieved when he gets to the top of his peak in safety, and still more devoutly thankful to find himself safely at the foot again; to the being of stalwart limbs to whom the mere exercise of a steep climb is delightful, the feel of a rope pure joy, the tinkle and slither of ice fragments under the axe the most exhilarating music.[224]

Bourdillon goes on to describe why he and other mountaineers love the mountains:

> One reason is never given openly, rather is disguised and hidden and never even allowed in suggestion, and I venture to think it is because it is really the inmost moving impulse in all true mountain-

lovers, a feeling so deep and so pure and so personal as to be almost sacred—too intimate for ordinary mention. That is the ideal joy that only mountains give—the unreasoned, uncovetous, unworldly love of them we know not why, we care not why, only because they are what they are; because they move us in some way which nothing else does; so that some moment in a smoke-grimed railway carriage, when in the pure morning air the far-off cloud of Mont Blanc suddenly hung above the mists as we rounded the curves beyond Vallorbes, or, still fairer, from the slopes near Neuchâtel, the whole Bernese range slept dreamlike in the lake at our feet, lives in our memories above a hundred more selfish, more poignant joys; and we feel that a world that can give such rapture must be a good world, a life capable of such feeling must be worth the living.*225*

Francis Bourdillon's thoughts, as we have just seen them expressed are personal feelings that would not be entirely subscribed to by all mountaineers, but they show the depth of emotion common to many climbers.

Slightly younger than Bourdillon was Alfred Denis Godley, Public Orator of Oxford University, classicist of distinction, and a lifelong lover of the Alps. His academic writings were scholarly but have not been as well remembered as his mountain essays and four volumes of humorous verse. The best of his writings were published after his death under the title of *Reliquiae by A.D. Godley.* Here are polished essays, never lacking in humor, never overstating the case, analyzing in a gentle and kindly way the foibles of tourists and mountaineers. His prose is pleasant, as is his humorous verse, of which an example from "Switzerland" follows:

> *In the steamy, stuffy Midlands, 'neath an English summer sky,*
> *When the holidays are nearing with the closing of July,*
> *And experienced Alpine stagers and impetuous recruits*
> *Are renewing with the season their continual disputes—*
> *Those inveterate disputes*
> *On the newest Alpine routes—*
> *And inspecting the conditions of their mountaineering boots.....*
> *They will lie beside the torrent, just as you were wont to do,*
> *With the woodland green around them and a snowfield shining*
> *   through:*

They will tread the higher pastures, where celestial breezes blow,
While the valley lies in shadow and the peaks are all aglow—
Where the airs of heaven blow
'Twixt the pine woods and the snow,
And the shades of evening deepen in the valley far below.[226]

This is very minor poetry, but the details are well selected and the whole has good spirit.

A decided contrast to Dr. Godley was his contemporary William Martin Conway, afterward Lord Conway of Allington—one of two Englishmen who received titles partly for their mountain exploits. Conway, a Cambridge graduate and later professor of art at Liverpool, like John Ruskin, wrote numerous books on art and the mountains. There, however, the resemblance ends, for Conway, though he wrote effectively, lacked Ruskin's literary exuberance, and unlike Ruskin was a great climber, becoming the foremost explorer-mountaineer of his day. Through much of his life Conway traveled in the mountains, but not like most of his contemporaries, who merely enjoyed the Alps, he trod not only the Alps "from end to end" but also the Himalayas, Spitsbergen, the great Andes, and the cloud-freighted peaks of misty Tierra del Fuego. Conway fulfilled his own definition of a mountain climber: One who "loves first and foremost to wander far and wide among the mountains, does not willingly sleep two consecutive nights in the same inn, hates centres, gets tired of a district, always wants to see what is on the other side of any range of hills, prefers passes to peaks but hates not getting to the top of anything he starts for, chooses the easiest and most normal route, likes to know the names of all the peaks in view, and cannot bear to see a group of peaks none of which he has climbed."[227]

Despite his exploring interest in many lands, Conway did much for the climbers in the Alps, editing a climber's guide in 1881 and bringing out his magnificent *The Alps from End to End* in 1895. The latter describes with considerable literary skill Conway's travels of the summer before from the Col de Tenda near the Mediterranean to Ankogl. During an extraordinary eighty-six-day period, accompanied by two Gurkhas and one or more guides, Conway made this fantastic journey, climbing twenty-one peaks and crossing thirty-nine passes on the way. The book, which shows how the different districts of

"The Vallot Hut. From Conway, *The Alps From End To End.*

the Alps are geographically integrated, praises the joys of mountain travel from one district to another. The whole is full of touches of local color, interesting incidents, and conversations that quickly silhouette the characters of the speakers.

The Alps from End to End gives us a profusion of lovely and dramatic scenes: green lichen–covered rocks in the Maritimes, silver moonlight on the Trelatête, frostbite on Monte Rosa, ice on the Gross Glockner. One dramatic chapter lists eye-witness accounts of the appalling Alpine landslide that in 1881 buried the village of Elm. Another describes how on the Hochfeiler, one of the Zillerthal peaks, Conway had rough weather:

> The wind struck us like a solid thing and we had to lean against it or be overthrown. It lulled for an instant and we advanced a few yards; then it struck us again and we gripped the mountain and doubted whether we could hold on. A far milder wind than this would suffice to sweep men from a narrow arete. It was not only strong, but freezing. It dissolved the heat out of us so rapidly that we could almost feel ourselves crystallising, like so many Lot's wives. We stood up to it for a minute or two, then rushed back into shelter and took stock of our extremities. My finger tips had lost all sensation. Amar Singh's toes had premonitions of returning frost-bite. It was enough. The Hochfeiler may be the easiest mountain of the Alps, but that day it would have killed us all. The upper hut, though scarcely a hundred yards off, was inaccessible.[228]

This inhospitable scene should be contrasted with the pleasant view he had had a few weeks earlier from the great Ruitor nèvè:

> The air was soft, a perfect silence reigned. Nothing in sight had an aspect of solidity; we seemed to be in a world of gossamer and fairy webs. Presently there came an indescribable movement and flickering above us, as though our bright chaos were taking form. Vague and changeful shapes trembled into view and disappeared. Low flowing light bands striped the white floor. Wisps of mist danced and eddied around. At last, to our bewildered delight, there spread before us in one long range the whole mass of Mont Blanc and the Grandes Jorasses, a vision of sparkling beauty beheld through a faint veil, which imperceptibly dissolved and disappeared.[229]

"The descent from the Hispar Pass" down the Biafo Glacier. From Conway, *Climbing and Exploration in the Karakoram Himalaya.*

Conway climbing among snow covered seracs and crevasses on Pioneer Peak in the Karakoram. From Conway, *Climbing and Exploration in the Karakoram Himalaya*.

Climbing in the Himalayas, another of Conway's records of mountain travel, is particularly interesting to those of us who, fifty years later, traversed much of the territory described. The exploration of the Baltoro Glacier is well outlined, together with some fine descriptions of K2 and the Golden Throne. As usual, with Conway's books, one appreciates the abnormal incidents of travel more than the daily developments, which at times he could profitably compress. On this expedition Conway reached a height of approximately 23,000 feet, thereby making a new altitude record.

Of Sir Martin's other books of mountain travel and recollections, four should be mentioned: *Climbing and Exploration in the Bolivian Andes*, *Aconcagua and Tierra del Fuego*, *The Alps*, and *Mountain Memories*. The first two are books of mountain travel similar to the last volume mentioned but with more travel than mountains, while *The Alps* is a collection of essays on glaciers, passes, Alpine pastures, and other mountain subjects.

Conway also climbed Aconcagua, the highest peak in South America, and tells us of the sunrise he saw high up on the peaks:

> Standing as we did on the shaded side of Aconcagua, and at no very

great distance from the summit, we saw its great cone of purple
shade reach out at the moment of sunrise to the remotest horizon,
more than two hundred miles distant—not, be it observed, a mere
carpet of shadow on the ground, but a solid prism of purple,
immersed in the glimmering flood of the crystalline sky, its outer
surface enriched with layers of rainbow-tinted colour. . . . With the
rising of the sun, the remotest point of the shadow slowly dropped
upon the ocean and travelled towards us, till it reached the Chilean
shore, hurried over the low hills, dipped into the Horcones Valley,
climbed the slope up which we had come, and finally reached our
feet. Then as we raised our eyes to the crags aloft, lo! the blinding
fires of the Sun God himself burning upon the crest and bringing
to us the fullness of day![230]

Some of Conway's best descriptions are concentrated in the fifth chapter of
The Alps, titled "The Moods of the Mountains," where he describes lovely summer sunsets and tempestuous storms:

The gathering squadrons of the sky grow dark and seem to hold
the just departed night in their bosoms. Their crests impend. They
assume terrific shapes. They acquire an aspect of solidity. They do
not so much seem to blot out as to destroy the mountains. . . . Each
member of our party is whitened over; icicles form on hair and
moustache, and the very aspect of men is changed to match the
wild surroundings. . . . How the winds tear the mists about. . . . The
new snow is soft like a liquid. It flows into the footprints and blots
them out. . . . Unpleasant is it? Well perhaps! but it is good to have
had such experiences. They develop a man's confidence, employ
his powers, and enrich his memory.[231]

And it enriches our experience, too, to read of the vicious storms that Sir
Martin has weathered in ranges throughout the globe. Varied struggles with
powerful and beautiful adversaries fill *Mountain Memories*, but for fine mountain thought one should read "Some Reminiscences and Reflections of an Old-
stager,"[232] in which he discusses objectively the mystic beauty of the mountains.

Sir Martin Conway—because of his mountaineering, geographical, and literary efforts—was the most famous explorer-mountaineer of his time. Many other skilled climbers and competent mountain writers were also present at about this period, such as Owen Jones, Mummery, and Norman Collie. Collie, a brilliant climber in distant lands, was for many years professor of organic chemistry at University College, London. Professionally, he was proud of his discovery of neon and his taking of the first X-ray pictures, but unprofessionally he may have been even prouder of his climbs in the Alps, Norway, the Canadian Rockies, and the Himalayas. In his chapter on the Alps in *Climbing on the Himalaya and Other Mountain Ranges* he tells us,

> Those who have learned to understand the language of the hills can appreciate the many-voiced calls of the mountains. . . . For my own part, they will always possess an attraction which I care neither to analyse nor to destroy. I shall go back there just as the swallow at the end of summer goes south, and if by an unfortunate combination of circumstances anything should happen to prevent me ever returning from that world of snow, my ghost, could it walk, would then at any rate be surrounded by nothing common nor unclean, which might perhaps not be so should it be compelled to wander amongst the tombstones of a London cemetery.[233]

The greatest rival of Conway in initiating major expeditions to exotic mountains was an Italian nobleman: H. R. H. Prince Luigi Amedeo di Savoia, Duke of the Abruzzi. He paid for his expeditions and always brought with him skilled Italian guides, a fine Italian writer named Filippo De Filippi, and the greatest mountain photographer the world had known. This was Vittorio Sella, whose photographs have stimulated admirers and climbers ever since. He was also a fine Alpinist, who, despite a heavy, awkward camera and fragile glass plates, climbed high to secure superb negatives. His work appears in accounts of the Duke's expeditions to Mount St. Elias, Alaska, in 1897, to Kangchenjunga, Sikkim, and Nepal in 1899, to the Ruwenzori, the Mountains of the Moon in central Africa, in 1906, and the Karakoram and Western Himalaya in 1909. Sella also went with Freshfield to the Caucasus in 1896 and his pictures of his home area, in the Swiss Alps, are among his best. The large format books about the Duke's expeditions were translated into English and republished in New York, London, or both.

H. R. H. Prince Luigi Amedeo di Savoia, Duke of the Abruzzi. Photograph by Vittorio Sella, from *The Ascent of Mount St. Elias.*

The Western Wall of K2 from Savoia Glacier. Photograph by Vittorio Sella, from *Karakoram and the Western Himalaya, 1909.*

Senecio Forest to the west of Freshfield Col, Savoia Peak in the background. Photograph by Vittorio Sella, from *Ruwenzori*.

Collie knew the Alps well, having climbed widely with Mummery, Slingsby, and Hastings. With these three companions he made the brilliant first ascent of the Dent du Requin at Chamonix in 1873. Two years later, with Mummery and Hastings, he made the first reconnaissance of Nanga Parbat, the expedition on which Mummery was lost. Collie grieved deeply for his friend and paid a warm tribute to him in his *Climbing on the Himalaya*. There we gather that Collie had no love for vast Asiatic peaks, though he rejoiced in mountains with an intense passion scarcely equaled by any of his contemporaries. To him "the dominant sensation in this strange land is that of fear and abhorrence. . . . Its rugged insolence, its brutal savagery, and its utter disregard of all the puny efforts of man, crushes out of the mind any idea that this spot belongs to an ordinary world."[234]

The Alps he preferred, even when he saw them from his bivouac on the Requin:

> Black peaks, arrow-headed, rose opposite, seamed here and there with faint lines of ice and snow. A solitary snowy cloud, like an avalanche of frozen light, blazed in the far-off blue. One by one the soft wreaths of the evening clouds faded into the night air, leaving cold grey ridges clear cut against the amber sky—ridges fantastic in their forms, full of writhing sinewy lines and fretted pinnacles; here and there narrow curved flakes, overhanging and smooth, carved by the lightning and the frost.[235]

Collie loved the Canadian Rockies and their unexplored mysterious solitudes, as he tells us in *Climbs and Explorations in the Canadian Rockies*, a book written in collaboration with H.E.M. Stutfield. These great peaks soothed his spirit, yet fired his love of the unexplored, with the result that he writes vividly about the semi-wilderness of the Canadian Rockies. Yet when he was an ancient mountaineer, Collie was drawn to the Coolins to spend his last days. Here, before he departed, he must have many times witnessed the changing light on the Corries, the driving storms and the writhing mists, all of which he had seen so often and described so well:

> When the wild Atlantic storms sweep across the mountains; when the streams gather in volume, and the bare rock faces are streaked with the foam of a thousand waterfalls; when the wind shrieks

Mt. Sir Donald in the Selkirk Range of Canadian Rockies. From Stutfield and Collie, *Climbs and Exploration in the Canadian Rockies.*

amongst the rock pinnacles, and sky, loch and hillside are all one dull grey, the Coolin can be savage and dreary indeed. Perhaps, though, the clouds towards evening may break; then the torn masses of vapour tearing in mad hunt along the ridges will be lit up by the rays of the sun slowly descending into the western sea. . . and as the light flashes from the black rocks, and the shadows deepen in the corries, the superb beauty, the melancholy, the mystery of these mountains of the Isle of Mist will be revealed. But the golden fury of the sunset will melt from off the mountains, the light that silvered the great slabs will slowly fail; from out the corries darkness heralding the black night will creep with stealthy tread, hiding all in gloom; then, last of all, beyond the darkly luminous, jagged, and fantastic outline of the coolin the glittering stars will flash from the clear sky, no wind will stir the great quiet, and only the far-off sound, born of the rhythmic murmur of the sea-waves beating on the rock-bound shore of lonely Scavaig, remains as a memory of the storm.[236]

Professor Collie, distinguished mountaineer that he was, still was not the most expert climber of his day, although Mummery frequently climbed with him. A.F. Mummery, Collie's companion on the Requin and on other Alpine climbs before their tragic expedition to Nanga Parbat in 1895, was at that time generally acknowledged to be the most skilled amateur climber. The avalanche that overwhelmed him was part of a calculated risk, for Mummery went to Nanga Parbat with open eyes. Like all true mountaineers, he recognized that "danger is the unavoidable concomitant of human life,"[237] and that life on a high mountain has its perils as does life in the boulevards of a great city or almost anywhere. Yet many hated to see him disappear in the strength of life, and of them few could express their regrets as acutely as Norman Collie:

> But although Mummery is no longer with us, though to those who knew him the loss is irreparable, though he never can lead and cheer us on up the "gaunt, bare slabs, the square, precipitous steps in the ridge, and the bulging ice of the gully," yet his memory will remain. . . . The pitiless mountains have claimed him—and—amongst the snow-laden glaciers of the mighty hill he rests. "The curves of the wind-moulded cornice, the delicate undulations of

the fissured snow," cover him, whilst the "grim precipices, the great brown rocks bending down into immeasurable space," and the snow peaks he loved so well, keep watch, and guard over the spot where he lies.*238*

Mummery was a great mountaineer and a surprisingly effective and delightful writer. He defends the rock climber from the calumnies of those who insist that he is a barbarian with no appreciation of the beauties of nature and shows by his accounts of many climbs that he has as fine an aesthetic understanding, humor, and sense of proportion as any climber of his day. To him, nevertheless, "the true mountaineer is a wanderer . . . a man who loves to be where no human being has been before, who delights in gripping rocks that have previously never felt the touch of human fingers."[239]

Mummery lived up to his own definition of a mountaineer from the time he first saw the crags of the Via Mala, at age fifteen, until his death on Nanga Parbat twenty-five years later. During this period his new routes and first ascents were astonishing. Among his climbs were first ascents in the Alps of the Grand Charmoz, the Grepon, the Grandes Jorasses, and the Dent du Requin, and during his two Caucasus campaigns, of Dych Tau and other peaks. His new routes, almost innumerable, include the Matterhorn by the Zmutt Ridge and the Täschhorn by the Teufelsgrat.

In a reflective moment he said, "To set one's utmost faculties, physical and mental, to fight some grim precipice, or force some gaunt, ice-clad gully, is work worthy of men; to toil up long slopes of screes behind a guide who can 'lie in bed and picture every step of the way up, with all places for hand and foot,' is work worthy of the fiberless contents of fashionable clothes, dumped with all their scents and ointments, starched linen and shiny boots, at Zermatt by the railway."[240]

Again and again, in the most exhilarating sense of the word, Mummery has proved himself a man. He was far from being a mere gymnast, however, for he was a true lover of the mountains in their varying moods and a writer of sustained ability. His essays, unlike those of many technically skilled climbers, were full of humor, and even when in great danger he was able to detect the incongruities of his position. Some of his humorous allusions are "dated," as for instance reference to "the contents of a certain bottle," but much of his humor is as fresh now as it was fifty years ago. The story of rugged Alexander

Burgener's superstitious fears of *Geister* and the true cause of his alarm will continue to be a favorite of climbers for many years. This peerless guide, Mummery's companion on so many great ascents, was not always the one being laughed at, however, as Mummery shows in describing their climb of the Charmoz:

> Everything went well for the first few feet, then the hold seemed to get insufficient, and a desperate effort to remedy this ended in my swinging free, unable to attach myself to either rocks or ice. A bearded face, with a broad grin, looks over the top of the gully, and cheerily asks, "Why don't you come on?"[241]

Contrast this joyful scene with the following predicament, which occurs on the Col du Lion:

> Suddenly the step-cutting ceases. "Der Teufel" is apostrophised in soul-cutting terms, and half the saints in the Romish calendar are charged, in the strongest language known to the German tongue, with the criminal neglect of their most obvious duties.
> Burgener's axe had broken!
> Midway in an ice couloir two thousand feet high a single axe alone stood between us and utter helplessness.[242]

Luckily, the single ax extricated them from their difficulty, though the reader has a bad moment too. As Mummery, however, has already told us,

> Yet each memory has its own peculiar charm, and the wild music of the hurricane is hardly a less delight than the glories of a perfect day. The idea which cleaves unto the orthodox mountaineer that a single ascent, on one day, in one year, enables that same mountaineer to know and realize how that peak looks on all other days, in all other years, suggests that he is still wallowing in the lowest bogs of Philistinism. It is true the crags and pinnacles are the same, but their charm and beauty lies in the ever changing light and shade, in the mists which wreath around them, in the huge cornices and pendent icicles, in all the varying circumstances of weather, season, and hour. Moreover, it is not merely that the actual vision impressed on the retina reflects every mood and change

of summer storm and sunshine; but the observer himself is hardly less inconstant. On one day he is dominated by the tingling horror of the precipice, the gaunt bareness of the stupendous cliffs, or the deadly rush of the rocks when some huge block breaks from its moorings and hurtles through the air—a fit emblem of resistless wrath. On yet another day he notices none of these things; lulled by the delicate tints of opal and azure, he revels in the vaporous softness of the Italian valleys, in the graceful sweep of the wind-drifted snow, or even in the tiny flowers wedged in the joints of the granite.[243]

Many other climbers, far different in personality and attitude toward the mountains, were also writing of their experiences during the years when Mummery was climbing. One of the most skillful rock climbers of this period was Norman-Neruda, who lost his life on the Funffingerspitze in the Dolomites. At the time of his death he had in manuscript form most of a book dealing with his climbs. This material, which his wife published the following year, together with a vivid account of their tragic last climb together, contains some fine accounts of joyful work on Dolomite rocks and Swiss snow. Unfortunately, the author did not live to put his writings into final form.[244]

Another skillful climber of wide experience who wrote well about the mountains was Captain J.P. Farrar, whose knowledge of the Alps was exceptional. Farrar for six years was the joint editor of the *Alpine Journal,* in which over a period of years he published many well-written articles, such as his description of a savage storm and a terribly exposed bivouac on the Bietschhorn.

Meanwhile, Mrs. Aubrey LeBlond and Gertrude Bell were setting feminine records in the Alps. Victorian conventions considerably increased the climbing difficulties of lady climbers, as shown by the story of Mrs. LeBlond's famous traverse of the Zinal Rothorn. She was nearly at Zinal before she remembered that she had left her skirt under a rock on the Trift Glacier, and had to go back over the mountain to Zermatt to get it. Well trousered as she was, she would not consider going into Zinal without a skirt, and preferred the long, difficult traverse over the mountain to a departure from convention. Mrs. LeBlond, who became the first president of the Ladies' Alpine Club, was well known as a writer. Her books include *High Alps in Winter, My Home in the Alps,* and *Story of an Alpine Winter*. All were popular in her day, but from a literary standpoint none is now worth notice.

Quantitatively, the writings of the redoubtable and thrice-married Mrs. LeBlond exceed those of the much younger Miss Gertrude Bell, whose literary output consists mostly of letters to her parents. The younger lady was a skillful climber and a graphic writer whose excellent observation and concrete detail give her letters vigor and reality. Probably her most famous account describes being caught in a blizzard on the Finsteraarhorn, when she was out for fifty-seven hours, all but nine of which were spent on the rope. Her experience is described in jerky fashion as if she is writing for her diary, but lightning makes the rocks fizz "like damp wood which is just beginning to burn,"[245] the glazed rocks, the avalanching snow, the sensational checking of "slips," the numb fingers trying to make a tent of her skirt and light a fire under it, and finally her falling asleep on the glacier despite the drenching rain. What a woman!

Among British climbers who were well known in the late nineteenth and early twentieth centuries we must mention Samuel Turner, E.A. Fitzgerald, and Owen Glynne Jones. The former was a self-centered climber who praised his own exploits in his books and wrote with only moderate proficiency, although *My Climbing Adventures in Four Continents* and *The Conquest of the New Zealand Alps* are both reputed to have sold well.

Turner's contemporary, a more or less solitary climber, was E.A. Fitzgerald, author of *Climbs in the New Zealand Alps* and *The Highest Andes*. Fitzgerald was less journalistic than Turner, but his writing cannot compare with Mummery's, for instance. Fitzgerald was not a particularly brilliant climber, yet we find him and his guide often "climbing cautiously up an almost vertical face of loose rock, clinging to it like flies"[246] or traveling on a glacier where "the peaceful moon seemed to enhance the horror of the tottering seracs and perilous crevasses among which we threaded our hazardous way."[247] Because of the highly colored adjectives used throughout *Climbs in the New Zealand Alps*, one is less impressed than one would otherwise be with what must have been a very serious accident on Mount Sefton:

> Suddenly, as I was coming up a steepish bit, while Zurbriggen waited for me a little way above, a large boulder that I touched with my right hand gave way with a great crash and fell, striking my chest. I had just been on the point of handing up the two ice-axes to

Zurbriggen, that he might place them in a cleft of rock a little higher up, and thus leave me both hands free for my climb. He was in
the act of stooping and stretching out his arm to take them from
my uplifted left hand, the slack rope between us lying coiled at his
feet, and I fell about eight feet, turning a complete somersault in
the air. Suddenly I felt the rope jerk, and I struck against the side of
the mountain with great force.[248]

His return to a safe position was hair-raising but the description is too long
to quote.

The Highest Andes likewise describes some exciting moments, but in general is less interesting than its predecessor. Both, however, compare favorably
with another well-known book of the period, Owen Glynne Jones's *Rock-
Climbing in the English Lake District*, which the average reader will find too
heavily larded with descriptions of route finding. Jones, who like Mummery
was eventually killed in the mountains, writes pleasantly but without the
humor or narrative ability of the conqueror of the Grépon. A friend of Jones,
George D. Abraham, a prolific writer and photographer, also did much of his
climbing in the British Isles. His books on mountaineering, however, range
from guidebooks like *British Mountain Climbs* to his *Complete Mountaineer*, a
thick volume on techniques of climbing. Among his other books, *Mountain
Adventures* and *On Alpine Heights and British Crags* are noteworthy, though
Abraham's style will be found heavy by the non-climber.

Harold Spender also wrote much about the mountains during this period,
his books including *In Praise of Switzerland*, a well-selected mountain anthology. Spender, however, is not a brilliant writer and his anthology is less successful than the collections of Arnold Lunn and R.L.G. Irving.

In many ways the most brilliant mountain writer of the period was C.E.
Montague, novelist, essayist, and for thirty-seven years an inveterate climber.
Montague undoubtedly will always be better known as writer than as mountaineer, but his record indicates that he should be discussed in this section.
Montague's novels and essays are full of references to mountains, which he
loved passionately. *The Right Place* has many excellent essays that show his love
for rugged country; they are skillfully written and depict the climber's point of
view. Of the Midlands and "black countries" he asks,

Who so base as live in Sheffield? . . . With all the delectable mountains of the world to feed on, what but some defect of nature or some taint of blood can make men willfully elect, like the elder Hamlet's misguided widow, to "batten on this moor"?:*249*

Montague's sense of topography is so excellent that we visualize at once his routes across jumbled ridges and valleys. "Along an English Road," an essay in the volume just mentioned, gives a particularly clear description of changing topography and geologic structure. As he says,

> Overland travel is all, you may say, mountaineering. For us no country is flat, not even Russia, not even Holland. Certainly some of the hills that diversify the whole earth are higher than others; those of the Lincolnshire fenland are as much lower than the Alps as the Alps are lower than the Himalaya. Still, it is only a question of higher or lower relief; there is always relief. For any patch of land, a continent or an eyot, to keep above water, its surface has to be shaped more or less like the back of a hippopotamus or a whale, with a spinal ridge somewhere or other; highest of all, and all sorts of ribby ridges and intercostal hollows dropping down from that spine to the water-line on each side. The sailors in Sinbad, who took the whale's back for an island, were not so far wrong, after all.*250*

When one crosses from Chamonix to Macugnaga, Montague tells us, the climber is like a fly walking about on the back of a bony horse, traversing the spine and crossing the ribs and the hollows between. This writer savors the gentle slopes of the English countryside, but he smacks his lips over the Alps. "Across the Pennine," another familiar essay, shows the delightful joys of Alpine passes, in contrast to the storm on an Alpine pass that he pictures in his war novel *Right off the Map*. Both scenes are accurate, but I agree with his dictum: "There was no bad wine in one's youth, and even today there is not such a thing as a bad mountain pass."[251]

Another novel, *The Morning's War*, has two chapters describing a severe climb in the Valais, while "Action," a short story, has an interesting theme but far-fetched plot. In "Action," Bell, the main character is a climber whom life has treated harshly, and who, feeling that he has lived long enough, decides to end his life in a gallant attempt to climb the overhang of a great ice slope. All goes as planned until he gets to the most difficult place and is about to give in. Just at this moment an ice axe falls past him, and spurred by hearing the Alpine distress signal and realizing that people are in danger close above him, he cuts up over the last ice bulge and is able to rescue two amateurs from what would have been sure death. Later he stands with one of them in the moonlight outside their mountain hut:

> Gowned in new snow and bejewelled with sparkles of light, the Weisshorn, the greatest great lady in Nature, looked as lovely to Bell as when the first sight of that pale supreme grace had taken his breath away in his youth. At the height where they stood the frost had silenced every trickle of water, leaving all space to be filled with subtler challenges to the ear. The air almost crackled with crispness: it was alive with the massed animation of millions of infinitesimal crystallizations. The Schalliberg Glacier, a little way to their right, had its own living whisper, the sum of the innumerable tiny creaks and fractures of its jostling molecules of ice. Up here, where the quiet of night was suffused with this audible stir of the forces fashioning the earth, it felt as if some murmurous joint voice of all existence were abroad and life itself were trying to make its high urging felt.[252]

The beauties of the Alpine night give Bell courage and he decides to begin his life again. "Action" is a serious story but Montague is happiest when he can give play to his sense of humor. "In Hanging Garden Gully," one of the essays in *Fiery Particles*, gives both rock climbing and humor full play. We find how the author, hating to climb alone, joins forces with a botanist, whose interest in stiff rock climbs is purely botanical. Their subsequent adventures—especially when the botanist sees a supposedly rare specimen on the other side of a smooth slab of stone hundreds of feet above the ground—are delightfully described, including the climbers' return minus a borrowed rope.

Montague's essays chuckle whimsically at the world, and his flexible style and varied subject matter lead on the reader. His passages about the mountains are usually gentle, not sensational, but they show common sense and a true estimate of the value of the hills. "To climb up rocks is like all the rest of your life, only simpler and safer," he philosophizes. "Each time that you get up a hard pitch you have succeeded in life. Besides, no one can say you have hurt him."[253]

Completely different from Montague's splendid essays are a quartet of American books on Mount McKinley: *The Shameless Diary of an Explorer, To the Top of the Continent; The Conquest of Mount McKinley;* and *The Ascent of Denali.* All but the second are excellent examples of American mountaineering literature in the early twentieth century.

Robert Dunn's *Shameless Diary of an Explorer* is written in a pungent, colorful, jerky style, of which the following is a fair example:

> There was McKinley. Falling mists defined a blur in mid-air; a white, feathery dome, tiny specks of rock and ridge lines developed, threw out the long, curved summit in breathless and suppressed proportion—sheer on its broad face, buttressed by tremendous white haunches to right and left, which quaked and quivered through the mist, mounting 20,300 feet, to the very zenith. Thank God that the speechless tundra was hidden![254]

Dunn's pithy descriptions contrast strikingly with Frederick Cook's lurid fictional account of how he climbed Mount McKinley, the highest mountain in North America. Cook's book *To the Top of the Continent* is now, however, a collector's item, for Cook, although he attempted Mount McKinley, was turned back near the base of the mountain, and his story of climbing the peak is based on an unhealthy imagination.

Cook's chicanery brought him immediate honors, but his deception was suspected by Belmore Browne, the leading American artist of mountain subjects. Browne discovered Cook's deceit on a subsequent expedition and exposed him in his *Conquest of Mount McKinley.* Cook's account was a complete falsification, as Browne's photographs, taken on his 1910 expedition, show. Cook's pictures of his companion standing on the summit of Mount McKinley were actually taken on a small rock nubbin 14,000 feet below the actual summit and several miles away. As far as Alpine records show, this is the only example of such falsification in mountain literature, although controversies have occasionally occurred as to whether certain points have been reached.

Browne's book rivals Clarence King's *Mountaineering in the Sierra Nevada* as the finest American work on mountaineering. As an observer, Browne is outstanding:

heads up the knife edge of the north arête, around a great spur, from cornice to cornice, cresting sheer cliffs over which there was a sickening drop of ten thousand feet, into the mystery of a lower arctic world, and then began the awful task of making a ladder for two thousand feet. With eternity but an easy step below every moment of this climb we went from hanging glacier to snow slopes, from blue grottoes to pink pinnacles, from security to insecurity, with the thundering rush of avalanches on both sides. If there ever was a more disheartening task it has not been my misfortune to be confronted with it.

slush!

We would have been glad enough to return and give up the task at this time but night was near and the little light that remained was blotted out by the gloom of a coming snowstorm. To return over the dangerous cornices in the dark was impossible. To camp anywhere within reach was equally impossible. For self-preservation we must move up out of the dangerous area. Keeping the rope tight we chipped steps as near the ridge as was possible and remained sheltered from the wind. One hundred steps and Barrille took the axe, then another one hundred steps and it was my turn. We could not see the slopes above for more than a hundred yards, and below everything was obscured by twisting clouds and drifting snows. It was black at seven o'clock. We dropped into the steps from sheer exhaustion. There is a limit

over an hour per hundred if in ice as stated.

impossible on a 60° slope (see P.217)

Cook doesn't know what a cornice really is evidently

A page from Cook's *To the Top of the Continent*, with margin notes by then president of the American Alpine Club Henry B. Schwaub. On the title page, where Cook is listed as president of the Explorer's Club, Schwaub has written "Expelled Dec. 24, 1905."

Our route led us along the foot of magnificent cliffs that towered straight above us, grim and majestic. Against the rocks pressed the stupendous ice-wall of the big glacier—its surface broken and crushed into countless crevasses and dazzling pinnacles. Sweeping down from cloudland we saw the first of the many hanging glaciers that, like frozen Niagaras, bring down the surplus ice harvests of the upper snow-fields. The almost unearthly grandeur of these walls would have made Doré throw down his brushes in despair, as they were more weird and awe-inspiring than even the pictures of his mind. As the setting sun lowered, great, pointed shadows, such as cathedrals or enchanted castles might cast, would zigzag across the cliffs, and creep in deep blue ribbons across the lower snow-fields. The lights changed constantly as one great peak after another shut off the sunlight, and, very slowly as the shadows joined, the great gorge took on the deep blue mantle of night; it was then that the twisted towers and broken masses of the seracs loomed like fantastic frozen forms through the dusk.[255]

The Conquest of Mount McKinley is written by a man of delightful personality, great determination, and unusual ability in many types of endeavor. The long campaign of Browne and Professor Parker to reach the summit of McKinley recalls Whymper's epic struggle to win the Matterhorn, only with Browne and Parker each attempt meant a major expedition with long-range planning and neither guides nor porters. Their third expedition with Merl Lavoy brought them to the foot of the summit horseshoe of Mount McKinley in good weather, and the first ascent appeared inevitable. By bad luck, however, as frequently happens on great single peaks, a severe storm struck the party as it was nearing the summit. Despite intense cold and bitter wind, they slowly moved higher, but as they "topped a small rise," the full velocity of the storm struck them. Browne writes, "The breath was driven from my body and I held to my axe with stooped shoulders to stand against the gale; I couldn't go ahead. As I brushed the frost from my glasses and squinted upward through the stinging snow I saw a sight that will haunt me to my dying day, *The slope above me was no longer steep!*"[256]

Driven back by the terrible gale, Browne, Parker, and LaVoy were never able to attempt the summit again. Actually, in good weather they could have

Belmore Browne, artist, and America's first exploratory mountaineer, shown here in later years teaching survival techniques to American troops in World War II.

strolled in a few minutes from their high point to the top. Ironically enough, years later, on a day when a lighted match would hardly flicker at the summit, I stood on the place Belmore Browne had striven so hard to reach. But before we leave Belmore Browne, mention must be made of the gigantic earthquake that struck Mount McKinley a few days after Browne's gallant final attempt to reach the summit. Had he been high on the mountain at the time, he probably would not have survived. As it was, Browne witnessed a famous seismological disturbance. He tells us:

> I remember that as I looked, the Alaskan Range melted into mist and that the mountains were bellowing, and that Aten was yelling something that I could not understand and that the valley above us turned white—and then the earth began to heave and roll, and I forgot everything but the desire to stay upright. In front of me was a boulder weighing about two hundred pounds. We had pulled it there with a sled and dog team to anchor our tent; it had sunk into the moss from its own weight, and as I watched, the boulder turned, broke loose from the earth, and moved several feet.
>
> Then came the crash of our falling caches, followed by another muffled crash as the front of our hill slid into the creek, and a lake near by boiled as if it was hot.
>
> The mossy surfaces of the hills were opening all about us, and as the surface opened the cracks filled with liquid mud, and then suddenly everything was still.[257]

The earthquake Browne saw did not seriously interfere with the return of his expedition, but it greatly hampered the attack on Mount McKinley by Hudson Stuck, Archdeacon of the Yukon, in the following year. The ridge that Browne's party had used in 1913 was so badly shattered by the earthquake that it was negotiable by Stuck's party only after three weeks of step-cutting. Stuck describes their successful attack on the ridge and on the summit itself in *The Ascent of Denali*. The archdeacon "had almost to be hauled up the last few feet, and fell unconscious for a moment on the floor of the little snow basin that occupies the top of the mountain."[258] Like Browne, he had conducted a masterly expedition, and, as the gods were with him, he won. When it came to literary honors, however, although Stuck's book is clear and vigorously written, Browne's *Conquest* takes the palms by a wide margin.

Browne's writing on mountain subjects was limited to one book and several articles, for World War I interrupted his climbing career, as it interfered with the plans of many British climbers. One of the latter, a man whose daring mountaineering campaigns ended when he lost a leg in the war, was Geoffrey Winthrop Young, perhaps the leading British climber in the years following Mummery's death, and the most brilliant modern British writer on the mountains.

Young's first ascents and new routes in the Alps amazed his contemporaries, even as his description of these climbs startles his readers today. Nowhere else among mountain writers has such technical proficiency and daring been possessed by a man of such literary talent. Young eschews ordinary words. Sometimes his imagery creates brilliant successes, though not always, but inevitably it stimulates the interest of the reader. His sense of suspense and the dramatic is excellent. In particular his descriptions of ascending the Täschhorn and the Grépon in *On High Hills* are classics of a volume that ranks high in English mountain literature.

Young dramatizes sensational moments most effectively and avoids the habit of many skilled climbers of describing the details of routes as if writing for a guidebook. Best of all he describes his own sensations, though it must be admitted that there are times when the forward momentum of an exciting narrative is too abruptly stopped by sudden discussion of his feelings. Still, as will be seen, Young's mountain background helps him produce verse and prose of definite high caliber.

Wind and Hill: Poems, Young's first book of verse, shows his great love of mountains and his skill in translating vastly differing moods into lines of verse. Among the notable poems are "Knight Errantry," "Looking Forward," and "On the Mountain," from the last of which the following lines are taken:

> *Together on the ice-glazed wall,*
> *Numbed by the slow snow-breath,*
> *Oft have we heard that instant pace*
> *And looked intent upon the face*
> *Of our rude comrade, Death;*
> *And our clear hearts have leapt to feel*
> *Muscle and will brace tense as steel*
> *To wrestle one more fall.*[259]

Five years later appeared more poems under the title *Freedom*, including the verses called "The Lonely Peak," "The Cragsman," and the lines that begin,

> *There is great easing of the heart,*
> *and cumulance of comfort on high hills.*[260]

In 1923, when Young's career as an active climber was over and he was more or less reconciled to his fate, he published *April and Rain*, another volume of polished verses singing of snowdrops and starry nights and cobwebs of snow high on rocky peaks. The last lines to be quoted are particularly touching:

> *I have not lost the magic of long days;*
> *I live them, dream them still.*
> *Still am I master of the starry ways,*
> *and freeman of the hill.*
> *Shattered my glass, ere half the sands had run—*
> *I hold the heights, I hold the heights I won.*[261]

Mountain Craft, a 590-page technical volume that Young edited and largely wrote, is still the most authoritative work in English on some technical phases of mountaineering. Like most books on technique, however, much of its information is dated. In addition to Young's sections there are chapters by Farrar, Arnold Lunn, George Finch, Sir Martin Conway, and others. The exposition throughout is of exceptionally high standard, as for instance in Young's preface to his chapter "Ice and Snow Craft."

Young's prose articles in the *Alpine Journal* and other magazines have color, artistry, and usually good suspense. For instance, we find him on the Weisshorn literally holding on with his teeth because one hand has been gashed and numbed by a falling rock, and we share a bivouac with him under a hollow boulder at the foot of the Géant icefall when he is blinded by lightning and roared at by a "choir of colossal thunderstorms."[262] What a contrast to the drowsy sunbath he describes taking a few years later on a grassy ledge of the Gspaltenhorn. There avalanches boomed down from the semicircle of peaks across the valley, while "over the Gamchi-Lücke, slung in a high white curve against the sky, long single clouds crept stealthily, clinging down the glacier fall and snuffing with their noses like great dragons across the ribs and hollows of the Morgenhorn. As they passed, the avalanches seemed to shrink from their noisy game, to begin again tentatively when they felt the cold muzzles and breath safely withdrawn."[263]

On High Hills, as has been said, is a mountaineering classic. This thick volume tells of Young's mountain experience from when he scrawled in his school hymnbook, "Shall I ever go to the Alps?" to his return to Switzerland a one-legged veteran, revered as one of the world's most distinguished mountaineers. This chain of brilliant climbing adventures where thrilling narratives are interspersed with moods of reverie gives great variety to material that less gifted writers would make repetitive and tiresome. Of all the books on mountain literature written in English, *On High Hills* probably shares with Leslie Stephen's *Playground of Europe* the distinction of being the most quotable.

Young's moods are accentuated by vivid phrasing. High on the Täschhorn, during a most sensational climb, he falls, but the rope is held by his comrades, standing on little nicks in the sheer cliff wall above him:

> When I spun outward, I looked down—no matter how many thousand feet to the dim, shifting lines of the glacier at the foot of the peak, hazy through snowfall; and I could see, well inside my feet, upon the dark face of the precipice the little blanched triangle of the recess and the duller white dot of J's face. . . . Then the arms gave out completely, so much at the end of their strength that they dropped lifeless. But the teeth of the upper jaw held on a broken spilliken and, with the strong succor of the rope, supported me for the seconds while the blood was running back into my arms.
>
> Wrestle by wrestle it went on. Every reserve of force seemed exhausted, but the impulse was now supplied by a flicker of hope. Until, at last, I felt my knee catch over a moulding on the edge, and I could sink forward for an instant's rest.[264]

On a severe climb like this, the mood can change quickly from despair to relief to foreboding.

> The first flare of blinding relief died down. The obscure future settled round again like a fog. The precipice receding into murky uncertainty above looked more than ever dark with discouragement for a vitality ebbing on the tide of reaction. The shadowy, humping figures above were silent; there was none of that heartening talk which greets us over a difficult edge, giving us assurance that the worst is past.[265]

Young was not the only one who fought for his life on the sheer rock wall of the Täschhorn. His companion Ryan, another famous climber, was in trouble, too:

> Very coolly, Ryan shouted a warning before he started off of the insufficient power left in his frozen hands. Some twenty feet up, the

rope tore him from his inadequate, snowy holds. He swung across above our heads and hung suspended in mid-air. The rope was fixed round his chest. In a minute it began to suffocate him. He shouted once or twice to the men above to hurry. Then a fainter call, "I'm done," and he dangled to all appearances unconscious on the rope.[266]

When Young faced death on the Täschhorn the experience was not new to him, although this strain must have been severe. For instance, there had been his fine climb up the Zmutt Ridge, his terrible experience with lightning on the Teufelsgrat, and his fall unroped into a huge crevasse on Les Écrins. On the Viereselgrat of the Dent Blanche, a cornice suddenly broke off along his line of march, leaving his "left foot projected foolishly over nothingness."[267] Among these accounts of great adventures are views of mountain beauty: icicles on the Ober Gabelhorn, a frosty sunrise when the Matterhorn was sheeted with "silver flutings of ice,"[268] and a starlit winter night on the Styehead Pass when he could see his shadow by starlight:

> The harmony of the white hills and of the silvery night was so overwhelming that it filled not only sight but all the senses; and whenever imagination would now revive it, the ear of memory first responds, and to a rhythm as of chanting the start, the snow, and the silence are reborn.[269]

Young's mountain experiences, most eloquently expressed when his diction is most simple, cover an extremely wide range. We find him holding George Mallory magnificently when this excellent climber suffered a forty-foot fall on the Unterbachhorn. Later he is cutting his way up a "Rosamond's Tower" of ice, the color of skimmed milk, below les Dames Anglaises, fearful that his step-cutting "would start an ice-quake and bring all the crazy castles of bubbled glass running over and above us in a general cataclysm."[270] What a contrast with his delicate "rock work" on the Grandes Jorasses, where he tells us,

> On another part, where I stood on a ledge with my face against a sheer smooth wall, I found that I was expected to absorb myself into myself like India-rubber, and wilt subtly downward until my fingers could grip the beading between my toes, and so lower myself again to arm's length.[271]

English climbers undoubtedly consider Young's valedictory address as president of the Alpine Club a particularly fine example of his writing, but the average reader probably prefers his magnificent story of the ascent of the Grépon from the Mer de Glacé.

> There may have been air-pockets over the smooth face of that all but perpendicular slab: there was certainly no other perceptible irregularity. I slipped with my knees, slithered with hands and elbows, and flopped like a fish against the haul of the tight, thin waist-line. Just below my futile boots the slab slid over into space. Above my head, it towered evilly—until in a high dark angle, between the outward leaning cliffs, it died away upon a sort of corner-bracket of hope. Out of this dark corner peered Brocherel's pallid face; while Josef's dark puttied legs dangled down beside him, the rest of him hidden behind a belaying splinter of rock.
>
> Exasperation was my only conscious feeling: a surprise of anger at the place being even worse than I had allowed for; irritation at my helplessness; vexation with Josef for attempting it, and vexation with my own vexation—for after all it was the best-worst way out of a cheerless position. Death may be as certain from above a hundred-foot drop; but imagination and the view down a three-thousand-foot wall can make a far more flustersome business of it! I might not pull myself up the rope with my hands— fatal temptation!—for that would prevent the men above from hauling it in, and so increase the risk with every foot I might gain. I could but scuffle, and try to spread myself adhesively, like butter—melting butter, on a tilted plate![272]

This brilliant climb—led by a guide whose favorite method of advance up sheer slabs was to set his iceaxe top in a nick in the rocks and pull himself up on the axe—completely exhausts the reader, for Young spares none of the sensations of the deadly struggle thousands of feet in the air, on a precipitous wall with only empty depth below.

Other climbers before the war grappled with the Grépon, the Jorasses, and other peaks described by Young, but none so magnificently dramatizes his struggles. There were great men, however, and some of them, like Thomas Longstaff, describe their mountaineering with great effect. For instance, in

Longstaff's "Six Months Wandering in the Himalaya,"[273] there is an amazingly graphic account of his being swept down 1,000 feet in an avalanche. Quite a different article, lighthearted and well written, is "An Eccentric Holiday,"[274] the story of climbs in the southern Alps of France. Equally modest is the fine account, also in the *Alpine Journal*, of his splendid first ascent of Trisul. At the summit (23,400 feet) he was fatigued, but his emotions are characteristic of the sensitive climber on any high peak in a mountain wilderness:

> Remote from the world, the sense of isolation was complete: the inhabited earth was at our feet, but we stood on a different planet, removed from it by undreamed-of spaces; and the turmoil of the elements around us intensified the indescribable majesty of that stupendous vision. Over the foot-hills to the south was piled a dense copper-coloured haze—a dust-storm from the plains, but to the west I seemed to be gazing into space itself across the scarp of the Himalaya, whose lines fell in long sweeping curves to the vast unbroken plains, lapping at their feet as did the ocean of a forgotten epoch.[275]

Longstaff's philosophical musings do not interfere with his top-notch climbing or his sense of humor, which sparkles. Thanks to him, we make the acquaintance of the Gurkha porter Karbir, whose stories of Tibet include one about men "whose ears are so large that they are able to sleep on one while they cover themselves over with the other."[276]

It seems especially fitting that Dr. Longstaff, who had contributed so much to Himalayan climbing and Himalayan literature, should take part in the first expedition to Mount Everest, the highest and certainly the best-known peak in the world today. The expedition of which he was a member took place in 1921 and its exploits were factually described by Colonel Howard-Bury in *Mount Everest, the Reconnaissance, 1921.* This exploratory party found a successful route to the mountain and closely examined its defenses, but, more important, stimulated what has become man's greatest duel with a mountain, and has directly or indirectly influenced the writing of dozens of books and hundreds of articles in many languages.

Following the reconnaissance of Mount Everest, then officially surveyed as 29,002 feet, the Alpine Club in London year after year at great expense sent out gallant expeditions, yet the mountain today still remains unconquered. These expeditions have brought new names both to mountain history and to mountain literature, for the stories of the repeated assaults on this giant peak reflect endurance, initiative, and courage of almost epic proportions. No epic has been written, it is true, but the attempts have stimulated shorter poems and had their influence on philosophers, psychologists, and theologians, who have striven vainly to analyze why the challenge of Everest has such a profound influence on men.

Norton, Somervell, Mallory, Finch, Odell, C.G. Bruce, Shipton, Smythe, Tilman, and many others have been frustrated in their courageous attempts to gain the summit, but they have won honor in defeat through both their actions and their written words. Of these men, A.C. Benson has said,

> We must not lightly or tamely question the right of men to risk their lives for great or glorious or chivalrous ends. Upon that right and upon those risks some of our highest freedoms and privileges have been founded.*277*

Certainly the men who have taken part in Everest expeditions knew the risks, accepted them, and have indulged in no mock heroics. Similarly, their writings are straightforward, sincere, and full of ideals and desires so deeply felt and so difficult to express that many pages suffer from too severe restraint. These books are not literature but they deal with material worthy of the finest pens. When the restraint relaxes, we have writing of intrinsic value.

General C.G. Bruce's *Assault on Mount Everest, 1922* has fine chapters by George Finch and George Mallory, while *The Fight for Everest: 1924*, the best-known climbing book of this generation, has stirring accounts by E.F. Norton and N.E. Odell. Before discussing individual writers, however, some of the numerous books subsequently written about Everest should be mentioned. These include J.B.L. Noel's *Story of Everest*, Hugh Ruttledge's trio of *Everest, 1933, Attack on Everest*, and *Everest, the Unfinished Adventure*, and Sir Francis Younghusband's *Epic of Mount Everest* and *Everest, the Challenge*.

All of these books concern themselves with George Mallory, the sensitive and inspired Cambridge lecturer who provided much of the stimulus for the first three Everest expeditions. His life was full of excitement, but his death was even more dramatic, for Mallory and a companion, Sandy Irvine, were last seen high on the slopes of Mount Everest and still going toward the summit. Theirs was to be the final attempt by the 1924 Everest expedition. Why he and

Irvine disappeared nobody knows, but the symbolic circumstances of their death was recognized immediately by writers the world over. [Editor's note: Mallory's body was found in 1999; he apparently had been killed in a fall. Irvine's body has yet to be located. The best biography of Mallory was written by David Robertson, Mallory's son-in-law, in 1969 and republished in 1999.]

Although Mallory's death brought his name to the attention of many who had never heard of him, he was already well known to the climbers in many countries. Several of his Alpine ascents were outstanding, while his record on the first three Everest expeditions was unequaled. More than this, Mallory had a dynamic if introspective personality that instantly kindled the imagination, a quality evident in his writing, as are his modesty, idealism, sense of chivalry, and great appreciation of beauty.

Mallory calmly appraised the terrible risks involved in attempting to climb Mount Everest in his section of *Mount Everest, the Reconnaissance, 1921*. His writing here, however, is more restrained and subdued than it is, for instance, in his *Alpine Journal* account of a new route on the Charmoz in 1919. In the latter, his love of rock-climbing stimulates the narrative and we sense the terrific duel between the climber's determination and the cumulative nerve-shattering effects produced by hours spent high on the wall of a precipice. With terrifying depths below us, we live through a deadly battle between fear and nerve that keeps the reader under real tension until the danger is over.

Mallory's language is restrained and serious. Witness his chapters in *The Assault on Mount Everest: 1922*, with their simple, unelaborated story of the highest point reached and of the slip on the return with Morshead; or observe how, like a true champion, he could praise his adversary, Everest, and even "puckishly" enjoy his own defeat:

> . . . when I call to mind the whole begoggled crowd moving with slow determination over the snow and up the mountain slopes and with such remarkable persistence bearing up the formidable loads, when after the lapse of months I envisage the whole prodigious evidences of this vast intention, how can I help rejoicing in the yet undimmed splendour, the undiminished glory, the unconquered supremacy of Mount Everest?[278]

Though Mallory's style is often jerky, his writing commands attention, for he has something to say. Perhaps most interesting to the psychologist or the student of mountain literature is his introspective article in the *Alpine Journal* called "Mont Blanc from the Col du Géant." His thoughts as he slowly gains the summit are typical of the man:

> A breeze cool and bracing seemed to gather force as they plodded up the long slopes, more gentle now as they approach the final goal. He felt the wind about him with its old strange music. His thoughts became less conspicuous, less continuous. Rather than thinking or feeling he was simply listening—listening for distant voices scarcely articulate. . . . The solemn dome resting on those marvelous buttresses, fine and firm above all its chasms of ice, its towers and crags; a place where desires point and aspirations end; very, very high and lovely, long-suffering and wise . . . *experience*, slowly and wonderfully filtered; at the last a purged remainder. . . . And what is that? What more than the infinite knowledge that it is all worthwhile—all one strives for? How to get the best of it all? One must conquer, achieve, get to the top; one must know the end to be convinced that one can win the end—to know there's no dream that mustn't be dared.
>
> . . . Is this the summit, crowning the day? How cool and quiet! We're not exultant; but delighted, joyful; soberly astonished. . . Have we vanquished an enemy? None but ourselves. Have we gained success? That word means nothing here. Have we won a kingdom? No and yes. We have achieved an ultimate satisfaction . . . fulfilled a destiny . . To struggle and to understand—never this last without the other; such is the law.[279]

Mallory's death has been the subject of much prose and some verse by authors who lament his passing, but Mallory, Norman-Neruda, Mummery, Hudson, and other climbers and writers who have died in the mountains knew the risks they were taking. That a man should risk death in the mountains, many writers will deny; in fact, so much has been written about this that I hope I may be excused for examining C.E. Montague's thoughts on the subject:

> If we all knew the dates of our deaths and could choose only the manner, who would take long over the choice? On the one side the stilled, unnatural room; the long, slow losing fight for breath; the

Mount Everest, photographed by T. Howard Somervell. See page 179 for details.

The three remarkable photographs of the north side of Everest on the preceding pages were taken in 1924 by British climber T. Howard Somervell just three days before the disappearance of Mallory and Irvine. On the back of each photograph Somervell made a few notes, some of which appear to be from a journal. Photo on page 176: "The last 2000 feet of Everest. Close to the place we had made camp no. 6 at 26700 feet. The general angle of upper Everest is not very steep but the outward edge of every rock makes climbing here dangerous, in case of a slip. Fresh snow is to be avoided here. Chalk cross [lower circle, center of photo] - from which photo [page177] was taken. X [in circle just below summit] highest point attained by [Lt. Col. E. F.] Norton 1924, same place by Smythe 1933. A [in circle on ridge at left] Place on ridge where Mallory and Irvine were last seen, 1924 (second step). B [in circle on ridge at left] Odell's version of the same (first step)." Photo on page 178: "The last 900 feet of Everest. We reached this point, panting and weary, at 2:30 in the afternoon. Only food for one meal, and one small drink of coffee. I was about 'done' here, and asked Norton to go on while I recovered from a frostbitten throat on this ledge of rocks; Norton is going on but he didn't get far before he too realised that it was hopeless to go further. Perhaps Mallory and Irvine, a day behind us would have better luck and get higher with oxygen than we had been able to do without it." Photos on pages 177 and 178 show Norton above Somervell. Photographs courtesy of the Somervell family.

lonely waiting, perhaps in a kind of ante-chamber to extinction, impenetrable by your friends; perhaps worse. On the other an Enoch's translation from the full height and heat of radiant vigor, effort and joy: an instant fall down two thousand feet of ice or rock wall into peace, or the restful collapse of all the muscles into the acquiescence of bodily exhaustion; and this in no smothering prison of curtains and lamplight, but with the sane and clean touch of sun and wind on you still.[280]

No climber intends to die in the mountains and few actually do. George Finch, the brilliant Everest climber and author of one of the best climbing books of our period, *The Making of a Mountaineer*, shows what skillful climbers can dare without getting hurt, but as will be seen he also shows the penalties as well. His book is well written and unembroidered, though its style is not outstanding. The most thrilling experiences he describes simply, whether he is bivouacking in winter on the Todi, cutting steps up the Brenva face of Mont Blanc, or being buried in an avalanche on the Eiger. Typical of his coolness, and unfortunately of some Alpine tragedies, is a tale of an accident on the Wetterhorn that he saw when only a youthful climber. His relation of it is far more real than Montague's generalizations about death, good as they are, though the style is less skillful and the point made is very different. At the time of the accident the writer was cutting steps down an icy gully, a route that the German party thought to be too dangerous:

> The Germans betrayed an inclination to take to the snow and ice-plastered rocks to the left, cutting a way down in the hard snow bed of the gully. The leading German, however, soon abandoned step-cutting and moved out on to the rocks where he and his companion sat down, one close behind the other. Throughout the climb they had appeared to find difficulty in managing the sixty feet of rope to which they were attached; seldom had it been taut from man to man, and now, as they rested, it lay in loose coils between them. Max and I carried on, cutting steps down the gully, and had passed below the level of the two Germans when I saw one of them stand up. He slipped. His legs shot out beneath him and he began to slide down over the slabs onto the hard snow slope below. He dropped his axe. I shouted a warning to his companion who was, however, too startled to take up the slack of the rope which was fast running out as the man at the other end slid on with increasing impetus. He had by now turned over on to his face, and was scraping frantically into the hard snow with his fingers in a desperate endeavor to save himself. At length the sixty feet of rope had run out; with a terrific jerk the second man was dragged from the rock and hurled through the air. Striking against a projecting crag, his left arm was wrenched from the shoulder and his chest crushed in. The body went on until the rope's length was spent. Again a jerk, and the first man, whose pace had slackened as his comrade was dragged from his seat, was in his turn hurled through the air—to smash his head in on the rocks below. It was a sickening spectacle. The bodies bounded over and over each other in wide curves until the edge of the first great precipice leading down to the Krinne Glacier hid them from our sight. . . . There was nothing to do but go steadily on, and, not yet realizing the condition of the party behind, Max and I turned our attention once more to step-cutting.[281]

The Making of a Mountaineer is distinguished neither for its literary style nor for its melodrama, but it is uniformly well written. More typical of Finch

The north face of the Dent d'Hérens, showing route
followed.

Back at the Schönbühl hut after the climb.

Facing page 210.

A page from Finch, *The Making of a Mountaineer*. In the lower photograph, left to right, are Peto, Forster, and Finch.

than the quotation above, however, is the author's enjoyment of a nap on the top of the Grépon:

> Memories of hours spent stretched out in half-somnolent ease on the great sun-kissed slabs of summits, in splendid isolation, with the blue vault of heaven above and the brown-green earth spread out below, are treasure beyond price, eternally one's own and never to be lost, inviolate to the onslaught of the getting, grabbing world.[282]

If more space were available, further attention would be paid to the writings of Norton, Somervell, and Odell, for these fine climbers all wrote well, though in general limiting their efforts to articles or chapters in books.[283] Similarly, J.B.L. Noel's *Story of Everest* should be mentioned, though Sir Francis Younghusband's books on Everest, written in his old age, beautifully composed and philosophically interesting, are worth much more attention. In *Everest: The Challenge*, for instance, he ponders,

> Remote from the distractions of common life, impressed by the immensities about us, by the magnitude of the mountains, the utter purity of their summits, and the mellow radiance of the stars, we ponder deeply on all we have read or heard about the inner nature and constitution of things—what is the Motive Power of the universe, what it is that ultimately drives the world, and what it is driving at.[284]

Everest, like mountains in general, affects writers in vastly different ways. Younghusband is moved by the beauty and wonder of the great peak, and the challenge it presents to men's sense of adventure. Leslie Stephen might have been similarly affected, but young climbers of the present generation are mostly concerned with technical problems. Providing a nicely adjusted balance between these extremes are Eric Shipton, F.S. Smythe, and H.W. Tilman, all former members of Everest expeditions, and still among the most famous mountaineers and mountain writers in the English-speaking world today. Strangely enough, each has written several books on the mountains and all are able if not brilliant writers.

Frank Smythe's is far and away the most impressive record, for he published some fifteen books, many more than the other two together. Smythe's books are

Photo A. I. I. Finck

Good, sound rock.

What more could a climber want? From Finch, *The Making of a Mountaineer.*

pleasant and well written, and some have special attractiveness and charm. Among them is a biography of Edward Whymper and such readable accounts of expeditions as *Kangchenjunga Adventure, Kamet Conquered,* and *Camp Six.* Less serious wanderings are the subjects of such books as *The Spirit of the Hills, Over Tyrolese Hills,* and *Mountaineering Holiday.* The quantity of Smythe's work is so great that it covers many of the mountains.

For instance, there are camps in lovely Alpine meadows contrasting with grim bivouacs on snow and ice. Avalanches appear, too, such as the big one on Kangchenjunga and the smaller ones that carried Smythe and Shipton down over a bergschrund on Kamet. Of Smythe's experiences, those on Everest are perhaps best known, but his good writing is not as sustained as that of Young, though his infinite variety of mood and broad experience give his writing diversity. He writes of a fall on Chamonix's Aiguille du Plan as follows:

For a moment or two I was too stunned and winded to realize what had happened. Then I found myself hanging on the rope while oscillating from side to side of the narrow and almost vertical ice chimney in which the groove ended, above the cavernous depths of the great crevasse. My companion had held, and the rope, despite the tremendous jerk, had held too.

But danger was not at an end. Had I let go of my ice-axe, or had it been snatched from my grasp, I do not know what would have happened, as I could not have hung there indefinitely, nor could Bell have lowered me on to firm ground, for there was nothing but the depths of the crevasse beneath me... Fortunately, however, I had retained my hold on the axe, and although winded, shaken, and almost exhausted, I managed to cut a nick in the ice into which I could get one foot and so take my weight off the rope, which seemed likely to cut me into two halves.[285]

Perhaps we have not done justice to Smythe, the most widely read writer of mountain travels of today, for he suffers in quotation, but we prefer the style of two of his companions on the last Everest expedition, Eric Shipton and H.W. Tilman. Each of these mountaineers has written three good books, but Shipton's style appears more fluent. *Nanda Devi, Blank on the Map,* and *Upon That Mountain* were written by Shipton's books so far, but it is to be hoped that others will follow. The first two describe mountain explorations in Garhwal and Chinese Turkestan, while the last is an autobiography in which he tells us:

In mountaineering... in my view, the attraction lies in the memory of those rare moments of intellectual ecstasy which occur perhaps on a mountain summit, perhaps on a glacier at dawn or in a lonely moonlit bivouac, and which appear to be the result of a happy coincidence in the rhythm of mind and scene. These moments of course are not peculiar to mountaineering; they may be realised on deserts, on the sea and elsewhere. Such exaltation of feeling is achieved more often, I imagine, and in more normal circumstances by the mind of the creative artist, but for ordinary folk it would seem that it is more readily found in close contact with nature.[286]

Throughout the book Shipton describes with great sensitivity rare moments on ridge, glacier, or summit. He writes with humility, poise, and good selection of detail.

H.W. Tilman, a less skillful stylist than Shipton and less expansive than Smythe, is especially enjoyable for his sense of humor. For instance, one fondly remembers his pawky observations on Alaska in *Nanda Devi* and his remarks about swirling mists in *When Men and Mountains Meet*. Of the summit snow slopes of Nanda Devi, highest mountain so far climbed, he can say:

> One foot would be lifted and driven hard into the snow and then, on attempting to rise on it, one simply sank down through the snow to the previous level. It was like trying to climb up cotton wool, and a good deal more exhausting, I imagine, than the treadmill. But, like the man on a walking tour in Ireland, who throughout a long day received the same reply of "Twenty Miles" to his repeated inquiries as to the distance he was from his destination, we could at any rate say, "Thank God, we were holding our own."[287]

Before leaving the recent books written about great Himalayan peaks, James Waller's *The Everlasting Hills* and F. Spencer Chapman's *Helvellyn to Himalaya* and *The Ascent of Chomolhari* should be mentioned. The latter particularly make pleasant reading. In the same grouping can be placed Burdsall and Emmons's *Men Against the Clouds* and Elizabeth Knowlton's *The Naked Mountain*.[288] Miss Knowlton writes effectively of an expedition to Nanga Parbat, but her style is not so crisp and enjoyable as that of Dorothy Pilley (Mrs. I.A. Richards) in her fine *Climbing Days*. Dorothy Pilley was probably the most capable woman writing on mountain scenes in her day, but her eminent position was later endangered by Janet Adam Smith (Mrs. Michael Roberts) with her charming *Mountain Holiday*. The writings of both these ladies can be pleasantly contrasted with the works of Mrs. LeBlond or the *Letters of Gertrude Bell* of the preceding generation.

Since the time of Mrs. LeBlond's famous traverse of the Zinal Rothorn, several distinguished writers on both sides of the Atlantic have dealt with early climbers. Of our own generation, Claire Engel and Charles Vallot are outstanding, but as they have written mainly in French, their critical work, valuable as it is, concerns us only indirectly, though their researches regarding English men of letters are excellent. J. Monroe Thorington, however, for many years editor of *The American Alpine Journal*, has proved almost as informative and indefatigable. Such books as *Where The Clouds Can Go, Mt. Blanc Sideshow,* and *The Glittering Mountains of Canada* have a crisp style lightened by dry humor, while scores of articles in the better Alpine journals attest to his abilities in research and his lucid style.

Another contemporary writer with antiquarian interests, one of the outstanding writers on mountain subjects today, is R.L.G. Irving, whose literary efforts include *The Romance of Mountaineering, The Mountain Way, Ten Great Mountains,* and *The Alps.* Irving writes well, and though his content is a little sugary, his style is excellent. *The Mountain Way,* probably the most complete mountain anthology in English, is marvelous, though it could be profitably condensed. *The Romance of Mountaineering* is a somewhat dated and very personal account of mountaineering, but the style is good and the book is the best of its kind. His other books also deserve attention. In *The Alps* he writes,

> The stillness, the absolute purity of the snowy floor, the lovely curves of the steepening walls that rise from it, the beauties that the winds and frosts have hung upon them, the golden light that plays among their corniced crests; to be with these is to be in the bosom of the Alps.[289]

Again, in *The Mountain Way* he tells us:

> There is abundant evidence that most men have been conscious at certain moments among high mountains of being in the presence of greatness, a greatness which is indefinable and elusive to approach, but which has a real influence, similar to that produced by greatness of character in men; what is mean appears meaner in their presence, and what is great is more apparent.[290]

These sentiments are undoubtedly approved by a friend of Irving, also a mountain writer of considerable literary ability, H.E.G. Tyndale, brilliant translator of German books on the mountains and present editor of the *Alpine Journal.* During Tyndale's years as editor, many excellent articles and several sound books on the mountains have appeared, among the latter *Days of Fresh Air* by L.S. Amery and *Approach to the Hills* by C.F. Meade. With these, though written earlier, may be coupled Sir Claud Schuster's delightful *Peaks and Pleasant Pastures* and *Men, Women and Mountains,* which like Schuster's witty articles in the *Alpine Journal* have been justifiably acclaimed.

Among other good writers on mountain subjects must be mentioned Michael Roberts, well-known poet and accomplished mountaineer, who declares,

> If climbing were nothing more than a brief escape from worry and responsibility it would be the same as any other sport, but the fact that we can talk of the poetry of mountaineering and keep near to the subject of great poetry shows that there is an element in climbing that is lacking in golf or motor racing.[291]

An author who appreciates this distinction, for he has spent most of his life in the mountains, is Arnold Lunn, distinguished writer in many fields and perhaps the most articulate "mountain philosopher" of this generation. Among his numerous books we must mention first his edition in 1912 of *Oxford Mountaineering Essays*, with its fine pieces by Julian Huxley and H.E.G. Tyndale, as well as his own. Then there is the fine book of reminiscences, *The Mountains of Youth*, with its days of sparkling beauty contrasting with the grim moment of his terrible fall on Table Mountain in Wales. Lunn's style reminds one of Geoffrey Winthrop Young, whom Lunn obviously admires, but it has less nervousness and more moderate figures of speech. Lunn does not rise to the descriptive heights of Young, but his writing wears well, and his philosophical musings are outstanding.

In writing of illegitimate risks in climbing he says,

> The full flavour of such moments is appreciated only by the solitary climber. He may, perhaps, be straining for a handhold just beyond his reach. If he is prudent he will readjust his plans, rather than risk his safety by straining too far. He will allow the usual margin for recovery. But prudence sometimes deserts him. The summit is near; the retreat is difficult and perhaps dangerous. He makes a final effort, perhaps shifts a vital foothold; his fingers dart upwards, and just fail to close on a ledge of safety. Very slowly they slide backwards a fraction of an inch, and suddenly he realizes that he has lost his balance. Perhaps he falls; perhaps the fates are kind and permit him to recover his balance through an agonizing struggle, which is none the less severe because, from the nature of the case, it is a matter of infinitely small adjustments, and infinitely

delicate rearrangements of muscles hard as iron with the strain. The fight for life is carried out on a battlefield measured in centimeters, and in a space of time measured in fractions of a second. Perhaps his recovery is incomplete; he may fail to find his old handhold or foothold. He may find himself crucified against the rock, unable to move up and unable to move down. His knees shake and beat a horrible tattoo against the cliff; they threaten to dislodge him; he becomes desperate, and very cautiously moves his fingers, sliding them slowly in search of a new hold. He discovers something which may just serve to balance on until he can reach a higher and firmer handhold. Almost anything is preferable to the suspense.

Now comes the supreme effort. Forehead, eyebrows, chin and feet are all enlisted in the battle where friction and gravity are contending for his life. For a moment he wavers, and just as the depths below threaten to suck his body back into their vortex, his balance rights itself, and he grips a cranny which the careless gods of wind and sun made in the beginning of years . . . pulls himself into safety, and is rewarded by that exquisite reflection of safety following terror, which is even more intense than the relief which follows the cessation of agonizing pain.[292]

This view of dangerous rock climbing is very real, as is a picture of dangerous icy slabs in *Mountain Jubilee*, an admirable collection of essays on mountain subjects:

Little puffs of snow volleyed off the crest of the pass, and the wind, still feeble and undecided, took on a new note of querulous shrillness. The clouds broke and a crepitating staccato of hailstones pattered down on such iceglazed slabs as protruded through the snow. And then the temperature fell sharply and soft clinging snowflakes began to fall.

. . . We had no crampons. During an awkward traverse a stone shot out of the mist and cut our rope in two. I worked back across the icy slabs and looped up the broken strands.[293]

More trouble! Why is it, then, that climbers knowingly expose themselves to storm and danger or to the chance of a terrible fall such as Finch witnessed from the Wetterhorn? Lunn gives his answer:

> There is no sport which illustrates more perfectly the ascetic prin-
> ciple that happiness must be paid for by pain, and that the degree
> of happiness is in proportion to the price paid. Few sports offer
> their devotees a wider range of disagreeable moments. The agony
> of the half-slip when one is leading on an exposed climb, the des-
> perate struggle to regain balance . . . are the price which the crags-
> man pays, not only for the exquisite relief of safety after peril, but
> also for the quasi-mystical happiness of those moments when his
> mind has established complete dominion over his body.[294]

Douce, sober people accustomed to living colorless lives without moments of great joy, of passion, terror or woe, cannot be expected to understand the wild joy of the mountaineer in a successful adventure of difficulty or danger where his fear has been vanquished by honest skill and nerve. A victory over a passive enemy is a victory to be scorned, but a conquest over a relentless mountain obstacle, with no quarter asked or given, is a source of intense delight to the climber. Neither man nor woman who has dueled with nature on the high peaks can thereafter rejoice as fully in the tamer pleasures and syn-thetic amusements of city life. But joy in the struggle is only part of the moun-taineer's benison, for some moments among the peaks are so beautiful they are painful, and something inside seems to throb at the overpowering goodness of nature. Emotions at such times are almost impossible to phrase.

Unnumbered mountain travelers in many lands have known such moments, but if one asked them whether they chose to climb in order to gain these interludes, they might shake their heads. Yes and no. Partly for such expe-riences, but also for a variety of other reasons, on which few of them would agree. One may be the companionship of close friends in a joint enterprise. Perhaps it is sufficient that the mountains have emotionally and articulately stirred them, and led some to reveal intense feelings latent in most of us but rarely disclosed.

"Our livestock on Bolchuo Col, at 17,021 feet. From Workman, *Ice-Bound Heights of the Mustagh.*

Conclusion

FROM THE WRITINGS that have been discussed, it is obvious that mountains have stimulated articulately in various ways countless people of widely differing backgrounds and interests. The diversity of the inspiration is obvious, for the stimulus that Young found in the Grépon, or Shelley on Mont Blanc, was not like the emotions Coleridge describes, for instance, in a letter to Thomas Wedgwood:

> I never find myself alone, within the embracement of rocks and hills, a traveler up an Alpine road, but my spirit careers, drives and eddies, like a leaf in autumn; a wild activity of thoughts, imaginations, feelings and impulses of motion rises up within me; a sort of bottom wind, that blows to no point of the compass, comes from I know not whence, but agitates the whole of me.[295]

Similarly Eric Shipton can write of "rare moments of intellectual ecstasy . . . the result of a happy coincidence in the rhythm of mind and scene";[296] and Peter Lunn can tell of ski racing:

> When the racer is ski-ing well there come moments when he knows that his mind has won, and for a few brief seconds he has complete control over his body. Such moments are rare, but it is for them that men endure the physical discomforts attendant upon all ascetic sports, for they then experience a happiness, almost an ecstasy, which has nothing in common with pleasure or enjoyment as these terms are normally understood. . . .
>
> It is this spiritual, perhaps almost mystical, thrill . . . which causes men to encounter gladly the dangers and hardships of mountaineering.[297]

191

"Rare moments" of the type that Peter Lunn describes are possible only to the one who receives intense delight from the complete control of his mind over his body. It is a type of ecstasy that Tennyson and Byron were never able to feel in the mountains, though in the valleys they also experienced "rare moments" that emotionally moved them. We have only to examine the feelings of Shelley, Ruskin, Hunt, or Belloc on their first vision of the Alps to feel the surge within them and to realize that the stimulus to these men, though different, was not less great than that which gave Shipton or Peter Lunn feelings of ecstasy. Coleridge, too, in the letter just quoted, appears to be moved in a similar way, but to be less able to direct his actions.

Many writers on mountaineering have been more prosaic or reticent and have not mentioned feelings of this sort; others have been unable to describe them. In fact, the bulk of mountain literature is not inspired. But the more sensitive mountaineers, like the more sensitive literary people who roamed the valleys, felt more deeply and described what they felt. Men of letters naturally describe more effectively than amateurs what they see; and what a climber might describe as "ice pinnacles" becomes to Shelley "spires of radiant crystal, covered with a network of frosted silver."[298] The same is naturally true with the descriptions of Symonds, Meredith, Ruskin, and others. What is frequently not realized, however, is that the stimuli of great emotion caused by beauty or danger or the complete contrast of life in the mountains so worked on non-professional writers that men like Gossett, Tyndall, and Mummery developed unsuspected talents, became more articulate, and produced well-written material marked by a sense of awe, respect, or humility. This material perhaps caused Clifton Fadiman to comment not long ago that mountaineering is "the only sport that has produced not merely a literature but literature."[299]

Certainly it is clear that both literary men and mountaineers have been stimulated by the mountains, though in different ways. For instance, the struggles against the Matterhorn and Everest have inspired certain types of people. Science has led on others like De Saussure, Forbes, and Tyndall. City dwellers, particularly in their first visits to the mountains, like Hunt and Charles Lamb, frequently have been greatly moved, while those living in the mountains for their health, like Stevenson and Llewelyn Powys, often perceived in them beauties unsuspected by the casual traveler.

The stimulus of adventure has not produced the best writing by mountaineers. Many of the expedition books are fair and much of the "adventure" writing by Freshfield, Mummery, and particularly Young is good, but of the physical and mental stimulants to good writing, beauty perhaps has been the greatest. Beauty, of course, has animated countless men in the mountains, though what was beauty to Marti was not necessarily beauty to Conway, and few have gone as far as Ruskin, who describes mountains romantically as "great cathedrals of the earth, with their gates of rock, pavements of cloud, choirs of stream and stone, altars of snow."[300] One wonders whether Ruskin would have shared Mummery's appreciation of "the great brown slabs bending over into immeasurable space, the lines and curves of the wind-moulded cornice, the delicate undulations of the fissured snow . . ."[301] What Hearn thought would be beautiful on Fujiyama turned out to be ugly when he reached it, of course, while the true beauties he had never suspected.

Mountains have made many writers optimistic about life. Bourdillon, for example, writes of "the ideal joy that only mountains give" and declares that "a world that can give such rapture must be a good world, a life capable of such feeling must be worth living."[302] Similarly, Shelley states cryptically,

Thou hast a voice, Great Mountain, to repeal
Large codes of fraud and woe; not understood
By all, but which the wise, and great, and good
Interpret, or make felt, or deeply feel.[303]

Freshfield, too, expresses corresponding thoughts on the summit of Ukiu and Clarence King on Mount Whitney, while Irving contents himself with remarking "that most men have been conscious at certain moments among high mountains of being in the presence of greatness which is indefinable and elusive to approach, but which has a real influence, similar to that produced by greatness of character in men."[304] In each of these utterances there is something obscure and mysterious, expressed more simply perhaps by Leslie Stephen, who says of the mountains:

Their voice is mystic . . . but to me at least it speaks in tones at once more tender and more awe-inspiring than that of any mortal teacher.[305]

This spiritual uplift, a sort of pantheism perhaps that great mountains make men feel, occasionally leads to the idea that there is actually religion in the mountains. Biblical writers and the ancient Greeks, of course, thought the high places holy, and even today we find General Smuts declaring in a speech on Table Mountain in South Africa:

> The Mountain is not merely something externally sublime. . . . It stands for us as the ladder of life. Nay, more; it is the ladder of the soul, and in a curious way the source of religion. . . . We may truly say that the highest religion is the Religion of the Mountain.[306]

Even Leslie Stephen says,

> If I were to invent a new idolatry (rather a needless task) I should prostrate myself, not before beast, or ocean, or sun, but before one of those gigantic masses to which, in spite of all reason, it is impossible not to attribute some shadowy personality.[307]

These somewhat extravagant statements clash with the more materialistic analysis of Arnold Lunn, who critically asks in *Mountain Jubilee*, "Are mountains cathedrals among which we worship or idols which we worship?"[308] He adds a more moderate explanation of the mystic utterances of mountain writers, for he says, "the mountaineer . . . has chosen the ascetic way to understanding, and among the hills, as elsewhere, asceticism is the key to the higher forms of mystical experience."[309] He then continues to discuss brilliantly the singular relationship of happiness and pain.

Lunn's exposition on this subject does not agree with the mysticism that Mark Twain, Stephen, and John Buchan felt existed in mountains. Hunt's vision of the Alps as "very earthly, yet standing between earth and heaven"[310] is also esoteric, yet more moderate than Meredith's sentiment that the Alps "have the whiteness, the silence, the beauty and mystery of thoughts, seldom unveiled within us, but which conquer Earth when once they are."[311] Belloc even goes so far as to say, "the great Alps, seen thus, link one in some way to one's immortality . . . from the height of Weissenstein I saw, as it were, my religion."[312] These are impassioned utterances that asceticism on the part of the writer could hardly intensify, indeed might even obscure, for physical discomforts tend to distract the mind from the sublime.

It is clear that the poetical intoxication with which the mountains imbue any writer depends as much on the man himself as on any external happening. The vision that amazed Belloc might not have moved a companion, while the battle with the Grépon slabs that Young so incisively describes would not have so inspired a more phlegmatic climber. For as Shipton suggests, "rare moments of intellectual ecstasy" depend on the "happy rhythm of mind and scene"—of time, place, and person.

Mountains, like the sea, stimulate most imaginative people, giving Meredith, for instance, solace from trouble, Shelley occult beauty, and Mummery and Young the pull of adventure. Though the stimulus is varied, the effect is beneficial. Mountains have inspired not only authors and poets, but also amateurs whose writing shows that for brief intervals, at least, they are moved by strong surges of inspiration.

Endnotes

1 Stephen, Leslie, The Playground of Europe, London, 1894. p. 15

2 Coolidge, W.A.B., *Josias Simler et les origines de l'Alpinisme.* Grenoble, 1904. Pieces Annexes, p. 243

3 Ibid.

4 Wordsworth, William, *Poetical Works of William Wordsworth.* London, 1896. IV, p. 61 (The Sea and the Mountains, Each a Mighty Voice.)

5 *Alpine Journal,* XXII, p. 270

6 Lunn, Arnold, *The Englishman in the Alps.* London, 1913. p. 9

7 Gribble, Francis, *The Early Mountaineers.* London, 1899. p21

8 Ibid, p. 23

9 Ibid, p. 16

10 Ibid, p. 33

11 Gos, Charles, *Alpinisme anecdotique.* Paris, 1934. p. 43

12 Gribble, Francis, *The Early Mountaineers.* London, 1899. p. 52

13 Ibid, p. 57

14 British travelers in the Tepli region of the Caucasus in 1935 reported a strong local belief in the existence of the Tatzelwurm, a glacial serpent, one of which is said to inhabit each glacier in the vicinity. Medieval dragons obviously are not extinct, though they have changed their range.

15 Churchyard, Thomas, *The Worthiness of Wales.* London, 1776. p. 108

16 Shakespeare, William, *Complete Works of Shakespeare,* edited by G.L. Kittredge. New York, 1936. Sonnet 33, p. 1498

17 Evelyn, John, *The Diary of John Evelyn.* Akron, 1901. I, p. 229

18 Ibid, p. 233. *Horrid* at this time meant "rough."

19 Freshfield, Douglas W., *Life of Horace Benédict de Saussure.* London, 1920. p. 28

20 Walpole, Horace, *A Selection of Letters of Horace Walpole,* edited by W.S. Lewis. New York, 1926. p. 9

21 Freshfield, Douglas W., *Life of Horace Benédict de Saussure.* London, 1920. p. 28

22 Gribble, Francis, *The Early Mountaineers.* London, 1899. p. 96

23 Radcliffe, Mrs. Ann, *The Novels of Mrs. Ann Radcliffe.* London, 1824. pp. 171–173

24 Ibid, p. 173

25 Radcliffe, Mrs. Ann, *The Mysteries of Udolpho.* New York, 1931. p. 169

26 Radcliffe, Mrs. Ann, *the Novels of Mrs. Ann Radcliffe*. London, 1824. p. 183

27 Irving, R.L.G., *The Mountain Way*, New York, 1938. p. 619 (Goethe, J. W. von, *Travels in Switzerland.*)

28 Ibid, p. 620

29 *Alpine Journal* XXI, pp. 271–272

30 Cowper, William, *The Correspondence of William Cowper*; Thomas Wright, ed.. London, 1904. IV, p. 266

31 Thomson, James. *The Poetical Works of James Thomson*. Boston, 1863. p. 154

32 Wordsworth, William, *The Poetical Works of William Wordsworth*. Edinburgh, 1896. p. 59

33 Ibid, p. 59

34 Ibid, p. 302

35 Ibid, p. 53

36 De Selincourt, Ernest, *Dorothy Wordsworth*. Oxford, 1933. p. 328

37 Cottle, Joseph, *Reminiscences of S.T. Coleridge and R. Southey*. New York, 1847. p. 334

38 Ibid, p. 336

39 Byron, G.G., *The Poetical Works of Lord Byron*; H.J.C. Grierson, ed. New York, 1924. p. 205

40 Ibid, p. 213

41 Ibid, p. 230

42 Keats, John, *The Complete Poetical Works and Letters of John Keats*. Boston, 1899. p. 123

43 Brett-Smith, H.F.B., *Peacock's Memoirs of Shelley*. London, 1909. p. 114

44 Shelley, P.B., *The Poetical Works of Percy Bysshe Shelley*. London, 1882. "Mont Blanc: Lines Written in the Vale of Chamouni" I, p. 75

45 Ibid, p. 77

46 Shelley, P.B., *The Lyrics and Minor Poems of Percy Bysshe Shelley*, J. Skipsey ed. New York, 1912. p. 286

47 Ibid, p. 64

48 Shelley, P.B., *The Poetical Works of Percy Bysshe Shelley*. London, 1882. "Prometheus Unbound" I, pp. 186–191

49 Young, G.W., *On High Hills*. New York, 1926. Foreword

50 Smith, Albert, *The Story of Mont Blanc*, London, 1860. p. 38

51 Fellows, Charles, *Narrative of an Ascent to the Summit of Mont Blanc*. London, 1827. p. 22

52 Ibid, p. 32

53 Auldjo, John, *Narrative of an Ascent to the Summit of Mont Blanc*. London, 1828.
    p. 13

54 Ibid, p. 20

55 For more detail on early-nineteenth-century climbers in the Alps, see Coolidge,
    W.A.B., *The Alps in Nature and History*. New York, 1908. pp. 199–238

56 Forbes, James D., *Travels through the Alps of Savoy*. Edinburgh, 1843. p. 14

57 *Alpine Journal*. LIV, p. 379

58 Forbes, James D., *Travels through the Alps of Savoy*. Edinburgh, 1843. p. 82

59 Forbes, James D., *The Tour of Mont Blanc and of Monte Rosa*. Edinburgh, 1855.
    XXXIX

60 Thorington, J. Monroe, *Mont Blanc Sideshow*. Philadelphia, 1934.

61 Among the provisions Smith took with him were the following: sixty bottles of vin
    ordinaire, thirty-four bottles of other wines and cognac, ten small cheeses, twenty
    loaves, four legs of mutton, four shoulders of mutton, six pieces of veal, eleven
    large fowls, and thirty-five small fowl.

62 Smith, Albert, *Mont Blanc*. London, 1860. p. 260

63 Wills, Alfred, *Wanderings Among the High Alps*. London, 1858. p. 266

64 Ibid. p. 285

65 Hinchliff, Thomas W., *Summer Months among the Alps*. London, 1857. p.297

66 Hinchliff, Thomas W., *From Zermatt to the Val d'Anniviers by the Trift Pass*, from
    Peaks, Passes and Glaciers; John Ball, ed. London, 1859. pp. 141–143

67 Ormsby, J., *Ascent of the Grivola*, in *Peaks, Passes and Glaciers*, E.H. Blakeney, ed.
    London, 1926. p. 251

68 *Alpine Journal* I, p. 2

69 *Alpine Journal* I, pp. 290–293

70 Ibid, p. 38

71 Moore, A.W., *The Alps in 1864*, A.B.W. Kennedy, ed. Edinburgh, 1902. p. 243

72 *Alpine Journal* IV, p. 309

73 *Alpine Journal* I, p. 222

74 *Alpine Journal* V, p. 286

75 Tyndall, John, *Hours of Exercise in the Alps*. New York, 1873. p. 72

76 Ibid, p. 332

77 Ibid, p. 79

78 Ibid, p. 190

79 Ibid, p. 95

80 Whymper, Edward, *Scrambles Amongst the Alps in the Years 1860–69*. London, 1893.
    p. 107

81 Ibid, p. 74

82 Ibid, pp. 377-379

83 *Alpine Journal* LIV, p. 103

84 Scott, Walter, *Count Robert of Paris*. New York, 1894. p. 296

85 Whymper, Edward, *Scrambles Amongst the Alps in the Years 1860–69*. London, 1893.
      p. 384–387

86 *Peaks, Passes and Glaciers*, John Ball, ed. London, 1859. p. 96

87 Ibid, p. 122

88 *Alpine Journal* LV, p. 60

89 *Peaks, Passes and Glaciers*, by John Ball,. London, 1859. p. 134

90 *Alpine Journal* V, p. 265

91 *Peaks, Passes and Glaciers*, John Ball, ed. London, 1859. p. 400

92 *Alpine Journal* II, p. 175

93 Stephen, Leslie, *The Playground of Europe*. Blackwell, 1936. p. 153

94 Tuckett, F.F., *A Pioneer in the High Alps*, W.A.B. Coolidge, ed. London, 1920.
      pp. 353–355

95 Ibid, pp. 356–357

96 Stephen, Leslie, *The Playground of Europe*. Blackwell, 1936. p. 14

97 *Canadian Alpine Journal* XII, p. 140

98 Stephen, Leslie, *The Playground of Europe*. Blackwell, 1936. p. 53

99 Ibid, p. 73

100 Ibid,.p. 181

101 Buchan, John, *Scottish Mountaineering Club Journal*. April 1939

102 Stephen, Leslie, *the Playground of Europe*. Blackwell, 1936. p. 19

103 Ibid, p. 114

104 Ibid, p. 74

105 Ibid,. p. 197

106 Ibid. 212

107 Ibid,.p. 190

108 Douglas, James, *Theodore Watts-Dunton*. New York, 1906. p. 411

109 Shelley, P.B., *The Poetical Works of Percy Bysshe Shelley*. London, 1882. "Prometheus
      Unbound" I, p. 191

110 *Alpine Journal* LIV, p.181

111 Lamb, Charles, *The Letters of Charles Lamb*. New York, 1917. p. 201

112 Carlyle, Thomas, *Sartor Resartus*. New York, 1896. p. 123

113 Moore, Thomas, *The Poetical Works of Thomas Moore*. New York, 1916. p. 551

114 Elliott, Ebenezer, *The Poetical Works of Ebenezer Elliott*. London, 1876. I, p. 410

115 Blackie, J.S., *Lays of the Highlands and Islands*. London, 1888. p. 117

116 Tennyson, Alfred, *Works of Alfred Tennyson*. London, 1891. "The Daisy," p. 233

117 Ibid, "The Lotus-Eaters," p. 54

118 Ibid, "Oenone," p. 40

119 Ibid, "The Princess," Part Seventh. p. 213

120 Browning, Robert, *The Poems and Plays of Robert Browning*. New York 1934. "A Grammarian's Funeral," p. 172

121 Browning, Robert. Ibid, "*The Englishman in Italy*," p. 120

122 Arnold, Matthew. *Poems*. New York, 1883. "Parting," p. 3

123 Rossetti, D.G., *Poems and Translations by Dante Gabriel Rossetti*. London, 1901. p. 123

124 Morris, William, *The Collected Works of William Morris*. New York, 1911. "Sigurd the Volsung," p. 120

125 Dobell, Sydney, *Poetical Works of Sydney Dobell*. London, 1875. II, p. 158

126 Watts-Dunton, Theodore, *The Coming of Love and Other Poems*. New York, 1898. p. 75

127 Ibid, p. 78

128 Kingsley, Charles, *Life and Works of Charles Kingsley*. London, 1903. XVI, p. 209

129 Butler, A.G., from *The Englishman in the Alps*, Arnold Lunn, ed. London, 1913. p. 261

130 Forster, John, *The Life of Charles Dickens*. New York, 1899. I, p. 465

131 Dickens, Charles, and Collins, Wilkie, *No Thoroughfare*. Philadelphia, 1849. p. 55

132 Cooke, H.E., "Whymper Again," *Alpine Journal* LIII, p. 363

133 Borrow, George, *Lavengro*. New York, 1906. p. 57

134 Borrow, George, *Wild Wales*. London, 1888. p. 96

135 Borrow, George, *Lavengro*. London, 1926. p. 187

136 Ruskin, John, *Praeterita*. New York, 1886. I, p. 154

137 Ruskin, John, *Modern Painters*. London, 1910. IV, p. 365

138 Ruskin, John, *Praeterita*, New York, 1987. II, p. 179

139 Ruskin, John, *Modern Painters*. London, 1910. IV, p. 371

140 Ruskin, John, *Sesame and Lilies*, New York, 1887. p. 58

141 Ibid, *Preface*, xxxvii

142 Ruskin, John, *Praeterita*, Boston, 1922. p. 98

143 Ruskin, John, *Praeterita*, Orpington, Kent. Vol. III, p. 3

144 Ruskin, John, *Modern Painters*. London, 1910. IV, p. 252

145 Hunt, Leigh, *Autobiography*. Oxford, 1928, p. 369

146 Meredith, George, *Letters*, ed. by his son. New York, 1912. p. 33

147 Meredith, George, *The Egoist*. New York, 1921. p. 10

148 Meredith, George, *The Adventures of Harry Richmond*. London, 1914. p. 649

149 Meredith, George, *Beauchamp's Career*. New York, 1921. p. 67

150 Meredith, George, *Vittoria*. New York, 1918. p. 1

151 Smith, Alexander, *A Summer in Skye*. New York, 1866. p. 118

152 Ibid, p. 255

153 Butler, Samuel, *Erewhon*. New York, 1917. p. 5

154 Bryce, James, *Transcaucasia and Ararat*. London, 1878. p. 278

155 Symonds, John Addington, *Our Life in the Swiss Highlands*. London, 1892. p. 127

156 Ibid, p. 287

157 Symonds, John Addington, *Sketches and Studies in Italy and Greece*. London, 1874.
    p. 292

158 Ibid, p. 296

159 Ibid, p. 302

160 Ibid, p. 303

161 Symonds, J.A., *Sketches and Studies in Southern Europe*. New York, 1880. p. 269

162 Stevenson, Robert Louis, *Essays of Travel*. New York, 1923. p. 246

163 Ibid, p. 249

164 Ibid, p. 232

165 Hearn, Lafcadio, *Exotics and Retrospectives*. Boston, 1907. p. 3

166 Ibid, p. 6

167 Ibid, p. 14

168 Ibid, p. 26

169 Ibid,. p. 31

170 Ibid, p. 35

171 Tomlinson, H.M. *Tidemarks*. London, 1924. p. 213

172 Ibid, p. 215

173 Ibid, p. 217

174 Kipling, Rudyard, *Kim*. New York, 1939. p. 305

175 Ibid, p. 306

176 Kipling, Rudyard, *From Sea to Sea*. New York, 1899. II, p. 102

177 Doyle, Arthur Conan, *The Memoirs of Sherlock Holmes*. Leipzig, 1894. p. 244

178 Conrad, Joseph, *A Personal Record*. New York, 1917. p. 78

179 Mason, A.E.W., *Running Water*. New York, 1907. p. 91

180 Buchan, John, *Mountain Meadow*. Boston, 1941, p. 109

181 Buchan, John, *Mr. Standfast*. New York, 1919. p. 105

182 Belloc, Hilaire, *The Path to Rome*. New York, 1902. p. 177

183 Ruskin, John, *Praeterita*. Boston, 1922. p. 97

184 For a study and bibliography of books of mountaineering fiction, see "The Climber in Fiction" by Edward Cushing and J.M. Thorington in the *American Alpine Journal*, 1942. p. 444

185 Masefield, John, *Poems*. New York, 1931, "The Dauber," p. 269

186 De La Mare, Walter, *Poems 1901 to 1918*. London, 1920. p. 152

187 Longfellow, H.W., *Poetical Works*. Boston, 1881. p. 254

188 Longfellow, H.W., *Hyperion*. London, 1853. p. 195

189 Whittier, J.G., *The Complete Poetical Works of John Greenleaf Whittier*. Boston, 1894. p. 156

190 Thoreau, Henry D., *The Maine Woods*. Boston, 1864. p. 63

191 Muir, John, *The Mountains of California*. New York, 1911. p. 5

192 Muir, John, *The Yosemite*. New York, 1912. p. 8

193 Mark Twain, *A Tramp Abroad*. New York, 1907. II, p. 142

194 Ibid, p. 109

195 Ibid, p. 126

196 Ibid, p. 137

197 Ibid, p. 101

198 Montague, C.E., *Action and Other Stories*. New York, 1929. p. 8

199 Adams, Henry, and King, Clarence, *Mountaineering in the Sierra Nevada;* Francis P. Farquhar, ed. New York, 1935. p. 19

200 Ibid, p. 304

201 Ibid, p. 41

202 Grove, Crauford, *The Frosty Caucasus*. London, 1875. p. 236

203 *Alpine Journal*. XXXVIII, p. 285

204 Coolidge, W.A.B., *The Alps in Nature and History*. New York, 1908. p. 49

205 *Alpine Journal*. VI, p. 268

206 *Alpine Journal*. XIII, p. 227

207 Dent, Clinton, *Above the Snow Line*. London, 1885. p. 212

208 *Alpine Journal*. V, p. 162

209 Slingsby, William Cecil, *Norway, the Northern Playground*. Edinburgh, 1904. p. 1

210 *Alpine Journal*. XII, p. 365

211 Ibid, XVI, p. 38

212 Ibid.

213 Ibid, p. 41

214 Harrison, Frederic, *My Alpine Jubilee*. London, 1908. p. ___

215 Freshfield, Douglas W., *Italian Alps*. London, 1875. p. 215

216 Ibid, p. 312

217 Ibid, p. 187

218 *Alpine Journal*. XIII, p. 507

219 Freshfield, Douglas W., *The Exploration of the Caucasus*. New York, 1896. II, p. 19

220 Freshfield, Douglas W., *Below the Snow Line*. New York, 1923. p. 211

221 Ibid, p. 223

222 *In the Ice-World of Himalaya*. London, 1900; *Ice-Bound Heights of the Mustagh*. New York, 1908; *Peaks and Glaciers of Nun Kun*. New York, 1909; *The Call of the Snowy Hispar*. London, 1910; *Two Summers in the Ice Wilds of the Eastern Karakoram*. New York, 1917.

223 Coleman, A.P., *The Canadian Rockies, New and Old Trails*. New York, 1911. p. 23

224 *Alpine Journal*. XXIV, p. 148

225 Ibid, p. 160

226 Godley, A.D., *Fifty Poems* London, 1927. p. 77

227 *Alpine Journal*. XXVI, p. 249

228 Conway, Sir William Martin, *The Alps from End to End*. Westminster, 1895. p. 301

229 Ibid, p. 93

230 Conway, Sir Martin, *Aconcagua and Tierra del Fuego*. New York, 1902. p. 91

231 Conway, Sir Martin, *The Alps*. London, 1910. p. 115

232 *Alpine Journal*. XXXI, p. 157

233 Collie, J. Norman, *Climbing on the Himalaya and Other Mountain Ranges*. Edinburgh, 1902. p. 184

234 Ibid, p. 131

235 *Alpine Journal*. XVII, p. 14

236 Collie, J. Norman, *Climbing on the Himalaya and Other Mountain Ranges*. Edinburgh, 1902. p. 223. Shortly before Collie's climb of the Dent Du Requin, he with Greoge Mummery had climbed the Grépon, "known as the most difficult climb in the Alps." In fact, he climbed it a second time with Slingsby and a Miss Briston "who showed the representtives of the Alpine Club the way steep rocks should be climbed." This statement led Mummery to write in *My Climbs in the Alps and Caucsaus*, "It has frequently been noticed that all mountains appear to be doomed to pass through three stages: An inaccessible peak—The most difficult in the Alps—An easy day for a lady."

237 *Alpine Journal.* XVII, p. 567

238 Collie, J. Norman, *Climbing on the Himalaya and Other Mountain Ranges.* Edinburgh, 1902. p. 134

239 Mummery, A.F., *My Climbs in the Alps and the Caucasus.* New York, 1908. p. 328

240 Ibid, p. 328

241 Ibid, p. 103

242 Ibid, p. 56

243 Ibid, p. 4

244 Norman-Neruda's famous guide, Christian Klucker, vividly recalls many of these same climbs in his *Erinnerungen Eines Bergfuhrer,* a book that has been translated into English.

245 Bell, Gertrude, *The Letters of Gertrude Bell.* London, 1930. p. 124

246 Fitzgerald, E.A., *Climbs in the New Zealand Alps.* New York, 1896. p. 204

247 Ibid, p. 199

248 Ibid, p. 206

249 Montague, C.E., *The Right Place.* Toronto, 1924, p. 162

250 Ibid, p. 122

251 Ibid, p. 142

252 Montague, C.E., *Action and Other Stories.* New York, 1929. p. 32

253 Montague, C.E., *Fiery Particles.* Toronto, 1929. p. 135

254 Dunn, Robert, *The Shameless Diary of an Explorer.* New York, 1907. p. 155

255 Browne, Belmore, *The Conquest of Mount McKinley.* New York, 1913. p. 125

256 Ibid, p. 344

257 Ibid, p. 356

258 Stuck, Hudson, *The Ascent of Denali.* New York, 1914. p. 99

259 Young, G.W., *Wind and Hill, Poems.* London, 1909. p. 88

260 Young, G.W., *Freedom.* London, 1914. p. 8

261 Young, G.W., *April and Rain.* London, 1923. p. 44

262 *Alpine Journal.* XXIV, p. 478

263 Ibid. XXX, p. 98

264 Young, G.W., *On High Hills.* London, 1927. p. 290

265 Ibid, p. 292

266 Ibid, p. 288

267 Ibid. p. 78

268 Ibid. p. 217

269 Ibid, p. 24

270 Ibid. p. 244

271 Ibid, p. 268

272 Ibid, p. 332

273 *Alpine Journal.* XXIII, p. 221

274 Ibid, XXI, p. 377

275 Ibid, XXIV, p. 120

276 Ibid, p. 122

277 *Alpine Journal.* XXXVI, p. 276

278 Bruce, C.G., et. al., *The Assault on Mount Everest: 1922.* New York, 1923. Mallory,
     p. 154

279 *Alpine Journal.* XXXII, p. 162

280 Montague, C.E., *The Right Place.* Toronto, 1924. p. 154

281 Finch, G.E., *The Making of a Mountaineer.* London, 1924. p. 43

282 Ibid, p. 260

283 Somervell's *After Everest* (London, 1936) is well written but deals more with medi-
     cine than with mountains.

284 Younghusband, Francis, *Everest: The Challenge.* New York, 1936. p. 229

285 Smythe, F.S., *Adventures of a Mountaineer.* London, 1940. p. 78

286 Shipton, E.E., *Upon That Mountain.* London, 1945. p. 30

287 Tilman, H.W., *The Ascent of Nanda Devi.* New York, 1937. p. 193

288 Burdsall, Emmons, and Miss Knowlton are Americans, the others English.

289 Irving, R.L.G., *The Alps.* London, 1939. p. 11

290 Irving, R.L.G., *The Mountain Way.* London, 1938. p. 365

291 *Alpine Journal* LII, p. 32

292 Lunn, Arnold, *The Mountains of Youth.* London, 1925. p. 186

293 Lunn, Arnold, *Mountain Jubilee.* London, 1943. p. 56

294 Ibid, p. 81

295 Cottle, J., *Reminiscences of S.T. Coleridge and R. Southey.* New York, 1847. p. 336

296 Shipton, E.E. *Upon That Mountain.* London, 1945. p. 30

297 Lunn, Peter, *High-Speed Skiing.* Brattleboro, 1935. p. 125. [Peter Lunn is the son of
     Arnold Lunn.]

298 Brett-Smith, H.F.B., *Peacock's Memoirs of Shelley.* London, 1909. p. 116

299 *American Alpine Journal.* IV, p. 447

300 Ruskin, John, *Modern Painters.* London, 1910. IV, p. 156

301 Mummery, A.F., *My Climbs in the Alps and Caucasus.* New York, 1908. p. 360

302 *Alpine Journal.* XXIV, p. 160

303 Shelley, P.B., *The Poetical Works of Percy Bysshe Shelley*. London, 1882. p. I, 75

304 Freshfield, Douglas W., *The Exploration of the Caucasus*. New York, 1896. II, p. 19

305 Stephen, Leslie, *The Playground of Europe*. Oxford, 1936. p. 197

306 *Alpine Journal* XXXV, p. 93

307 Stephen, Leslie, *The Playground of Europe*. Oxford, 1936. p. 197

308 Lunn, Arnold, *Mountain Jubilee*. London, 1943. p. 75

309 Ibid, p. 78

310 Hunt, Leigh, *Autobiography*. Oxford, 1928. p. 369

311 Meredith, George, *Letters*, edited by his son. New York, 1912. p. 33

312 Belloc, Hilaire, *The Path to Rome*. New York, 1902. p. 177

Bibliography

Abraham, A. P. *Rock-climbing in Skye*. New York, 1908

Abraham, G. D. *The Complete Mountaineer*. London, 1907

Abraham, G. D. *Modern Mountaineering*. London, 1932

Abraham, G. D. *On Alpine Heights and British Crags*. New York, 1916

Amedeo Di Savoia, H. R. H. Prince Luigi, Duke of the Abruzzi. *The Ascent of Mount St. Elias*, Westminster, 1900

Amery, L. C. M. S. *Days of Fresh Air*. London, 1939

Arnold, Matthew. *Poems*. New York, 1883

Auden, W. H. *The Collected Poetry of W. H. Auden*. New York, 1945

Auden, W. H. and Isherwood, Christopher, *The Ascent of F6*. New York, 1937

Auldjo, John. *Narrative of an Ascent to the Summit of Mont Blanc*. London, 1828

Austin, Alfred. *Prince Lucifer*. London, 1887

Bade, W. F. *Life and Letters of John Muir*. New York, 1924

Baker, E. A., and Ross, F. E. *The Voice of the Mountains*. London, 1905

Ball, John. editor of *Peaks, Passes and Glaciers*. London, 1859

Barry, Martin. *Ascent to the Summit of Mont Blanc in 1834*, London, 1836.

Bates, Ralph. *Sirocco and Other Stories*. New York, 1939

Bell, Gertrude. *The Letters of Gertrude Bell*. London, 1930

Belloc, Hilaire. *The Pyrenees*. London, 1909

Bent, A. H. *A Bibliography of the White Mountains*. Boston, 1911

Blackie, J. S. *Lays of the Highland and Islands*. London, 1888

Blakeney, E. H. editor of *Peaks, Passes and Glaciers*. London 1926

Bonney, T. M. *Alpine Regions of Switzerland and the Neighboring Countries.* Cambridge (England) 1868

Bonney, T. G. *The Building of the Alps*. London, 1912

Borrow, George. *Lavengro*. New York, 1906

Borrow, George. *Wild Wales*. London, 1926

Brett-Smith, H. F. B. *Peacock's Memoirs of Shelley*. London, 1909

Brown, T. G. *Brenva*. London, 1944

Browne, Belmore. *The Conquest of Mount McKinley*. New York, 1913

Browning, Robert. *Dramatic Lyrics, Dramatic Romances*. New York, 1898

Browning, Robert. *The Poems and Plays of Robert Browning*. New York, 1934

Bruce, C. G., and others. *The Assault on Mount Everest, 1922*. London, 1923

Bryce, James. *Memories of Travel*. New York, 1923

Bryce, James. *South America*. New York, 1912

Bryce, James. *Transcaucasia and Ararat*. London, 1878

Buchan, John. *The Last Secrets*. New York, 1923

Buchan, John. *Mountain Meadows*. Boston, 1941

Buchan, John. *Mr. Standfast*. New York, 1919

Buchan, John. *The Three Hostages*. New York, 1924

Burdsall, R. L., and Emmons, A. B., 3rd. *Men Against the Clouds*. New York, 1935

Burpee, L. J. *Among the Canadian Alps*. London, 1914

Burroughs, John. *Time and Change*. Boston, 1912

Butler, Samuel. *Alps and Sanctuaries of Piedmont*. London, 1882

Butler, Samuel. *Erewhon*. New York, 1917

Byron, G. G. *The Poetical Works of Lord Byron*, edited by H. J. C. Grierson, New York, 1924

Carlyle, Thomas. *Sartor Resartus*. New York, 1896

Chapman, F. S. *Helvellyn to Himalaya*. London, 1940

Clemens, S. G. (Mark Twain) *A Tramp Abroad*. New York, 1903

Coleman, A. P. *The Canadian Rockies, New and Old Trails*. New York, 1911

Collie, J. N., *Climbing on the Himalaya and other Mountain Ranges*. Edinburgh, 1902

Conrad, Joseph. *A Personal Record*. New York, 1917

Conway, Sir W. M. *Aconcagua and Tierra Del Fuego*. New York, 1902

Conway, Sir W. M. *The Alps*. London, 1910

Conway, Sir W. M. *The Alps from End to End*. Westminster, 1895

Conway, Sir W. M. *The Bolivian Andes*. New York, 1901

Conway, Sir W. M. *Climbing and Exploration in the Karakarom-Himalayas*. London, 1894

Conway, Sir W. M. *Mountain Memories*. New York, 1920

Cook, F. A. *To the Top of the Continent*. New York, 1908

Coolidge, W. A. B. *Alpine Studies*. New York, 1912

Coolidge, W. A. B. *The Alps in Nature and History.* New York, 1908

Coolidge, W. A. B. *Josias Simler et les Origines de L'Alpinisme.* Grenoble, 1904

Cottle, Joseph. *Reminiscences of S. T. Coleridge and R. Southey.* New York, 1847

Cowper, William. *The Correspondence of William Cowper,* edited by Thomas Wright. London, 1904

Cunningham, C. D., and Abney, W. de W. *The Pioneers of the Alps.* Boston, 1888

Daunt, Achilles. *Crag, Glacier and Avalanche.* London, 1894

De Beer, G. R. *Alps and Men.* London, 1932

De Beer, G. R. *Early Travellers in the Alps.* London, 1930

De Filippi, Filippo. *Karakoram and Western Himalaya, 1909, An Account of the Expedition of H.R.H. Prince Luigi Amedeo of Savoy, Duke of the Abruzzi,* New York, 1912

De Filippi, Filippo. *Ruwenzori, An Account of the Expedition of H.R.H. Prince Luigi Amedeo of Savoy, Duke of the Abruzzi,* New York, 1908

de la Mare, Walter. *Poems 1901 to 1918.* London, 1920

Dent, Clinton. *Above the Snow Line.* London, 1885

De Quincey, Thomas. *Collected Writings.* Edinburgh, 1889

De Saussure, Horace Benedict. *Voyages Dans Les Alpes.* Neuchatel, 1804

De Selincourt, Ernest. *Dorothy Wordsworth.* Oxford, 1933

Dickens, Charles, and Collins, Wilkie. *No Thoroughfare.* Philadelphia, 1849

Dobell, Sydney. *Poetical Works of Sydney Dobell.* London, 1875

Douglas, James. *Theodore Watts-Dunton.* New York, 1906

Doyle, A. C. *The Memoirs of Sherlock Holmes.* Leipzig, 1894

Dunn, Robert. *The Shameless Diary of an Explorer.* New York, 1907

Edwards, A. B. *Untrodden Peaks and Unfrequented Valleys.* London, 1890

Elliott, Ebenezer. *The Poetical Works of Ebenezer Elliott.* London, 1876

Engel, C. E. *Byron et Shelley en Suisse et en Savoie Mai - Octobre 1816.* Chambery, 1930

Engel, C. E. *La Litterature Alpestre en France et en Angleterre aux XVIIIe et XIXe Siecles.* Chambery, 1930

Engel, C. E., and Vallot, Charles. *Ces Monts Affreux.* Paris, 1934

Engel, C. E., and Vallot, Charles. *Ces Monts Sublimes.* Paris, 1936

Evelyn, John. *The Diary of John Evelyn.* Akron, 1901

Fellows, Charles. *Narrative of an Ascent to the Summit of Mont Blanc.* London, 1827

Finch, G. E. *The Making of a Mountaineer.* London, 1924

Fitzgerald, E. A. *The Highest Andes.* New York, 1899

Fitzgerald, E. A. *Climbs in the New Zealand Alps.* New York, 1896

Forbes, James D. *The Tour of Mont Blanc and of Monte Rosa.* Edinburgh, 1855

Forbes, James D. *Travels through the Alps of Savoy.* Edinburgh, 1903

Forster, John. *The Life of Charles Dickens.* New York, 1899

Freeman, L. R. *On the Roof of the Rockies.* New York, 1925

Fremont, J. C. *Report of the Exploring Expedition to the Rocky Mountains in the Year 1842.* Washington, 1845

Freshfield, D. W. *Below the Snow Line.* New York, 1923

Freshfield, D. W. *The Exploration of the Caucasus,* two vols. New York, 1896

Freshfield, D. W. *Hannibal Once More.* London, 1923

Freshfield, D. W. *Italian Alps.* London, 1875

Freshfield, D. W. *Life of Horace Benedict de Saussure.* London, 1920

Freshfield, D. W. *Round Kangchenjunga.* London, 1903

Freshfield, D. W. *Travels in the Central Caucasus and Bashan.* London, 1896

Freshfield, Mrs. Henry. *A Summer Tour in the Grisons.* London, 1862

Gesner, Konrad. *On the Admiration of Mountains,* edited by J. Monroe Thorington. San Francisco, 1937

Girdlestone, A. G. *The High Alps Without Guides.* London, 1870

Godley, A. D. *Fifty Poems.* London, 1927

Godley, A. D. *Reliquiae by A. D. Godley,* edited by C. R. L. Fletcher. London, 1926

Goldsmith, Oliver. *The Works of Oliver Goldsmith.* New York, 1908

Gos, Charles. *Alpinisme Anecdotique.* Paris, 1934

Grand-Carteret. John, *La Montagne a Travers les Ages.* Grenoble, 1904

Gribble, Francis. *The Early Mountaineers.* London, 1899

Gribble, Francis. *The Story of Alpine Climbing.* London, 1904

Grove, Crauford. *The Frosty Caucasus.* London, 1875

Haggard, H. R. *King Solomon's Mines.* New York, 1921

Halliburton, Richard. *The Royal Road to Romance.* Indianapolis, 1925

Harrison, Frederic. *My Alpine Jubilee.* London, 1908

Hawthorne, Nathaniel. *Tales of the White Hills.* Boston, 1908

Hearn, Lafcadio. *Exotics and Retrospectives.* Boston, 1907

Hewlett, Maurice. *The Letters of Maurice Hewlett,* edited by Laurence Binyon. London, 1926

Hilton, James. *Good-bye, Mr. Chips.* Boston, 1934

Hinchliff, T. W. *Summer Months among the Alps.* London, 1857

Hinchliff, T. W. *From Zermatt to the Val d'Anniviers*, London, 1857

Hosmer, J. K. editor of *History of the Expedition of Captains Lewis and Clark, 1804-5-6.* Chicago, 1902

Howard-Bury, C. K. *Mount Everest, the Reconnaissance, 1921.* London, 1922

Hudson, Charles, and Kennedy, E. S. *Where There's a Will There's a Way.* London, 1856

Hunt, Leigh. *Autobiography.* Oxford, 1928

Irving, R. L. G. *The Alps.* London, 1939

Irving, R. L. G. *The Mountain Way.* New York, 1938

Irving, R. L. G. *The Romance of Mountaineering.* London, 1935

Irving, R. L. G., *Ten Great Mountans.* London, 1940

Irving, Washington. *Captain Bonneville.* London, 1837

Jacobs, Thornwell, editor. *The Oglethorpe Book of Georgia Verse.* Oglethorpe, 1930

Jeffers, Le Roy. *The Call of the Mountains.* New York, 1922

Jones, O. G. *Rock-Climbing in the English Lake District.* New York, 1897

Keats, John. *The Complete Poetical Works and Letters of John Keats.* Boston, 1899

Kennedy, E. S. editor of *Peaks, Passes and Glaciers.* London, 1862

King, Clarence. *Mountaineering in the Sierra Nevada*, edited by F. P. Farquhar. New York, 1935

Kingsley, Charles. *Life and Works of Charles Kingsley.* London, 1903

Kipling, Rudyard. *From Sea to Sea.* New York, 1899

Kipling, Rudyard. *Kim.* New York, 1901

Knowlton, Elizabeth. *The Naked Mountain.* New York, 1933

Lamb, Charles. *The Letters of Charles Lamb.* New York, 1917

Le Blond, Mrs. Aubrey. *Adventures on the Roof of the World.* London, 1904

Le Blond, Mrs. Aubrey. *The High Alps in Winter.* London, 1883

Le Blond, Mrs. Aubrey. *The Story of an Alpine Winter.* London, 1907

Le Conte, Joseph. *A Journal of Ramblings Through the High Sierra.* San Francisco, 1930

Longfellow, H. W. *Hyperion.* Boston, 1868

Longfellow, H. W. *The Poetical Works of Henry Wadsworth Longfellow.* Boston, 1885

Lowell, J. R. *Poems.* Cambridge, 1843

Lunn, Arnold. *The Englishman in the Alps.* London, 1913

Lunn, Arnold. *The Exploration of the Alps.* New York, 1914

Lunn, Arnold. *Mountain Jubilee*. London, 1943

Lunn, Arnold. *The Mountains of Youth*. Oxford, 1925

Lunn, Arnold. editor of *Oxford Mountaineering Essays*. London, 1912

Lunn, Arnold. *Switzerland*. London, 1928

Lunn, Peter. *High-Speed Skiing*. Brattleboro, VT, 1936

MacIntyre, Neil. *Attack on Everest*. London, 1936

Masefield, John. *Poems*. New York, 1931

Mason, A. E. W. *Running Water*. New York, 1907

Mathews, C. E. *The Annals of Mont Blanc*. London, 1900

McSpadden, J. W. *The Alps as Seen by the Poets*. New York, 1912

Meade, C. F. *Approach to the Hills*. New York, 1940

Meredith, George. *The Adventures of Harry Richmond*. London, 1914

Meredith, George. *Beauchamp's Career*. New York, 1921

Meredith, George. *The Egoist*. New York, 1923

Meredith, George. *Letters*, edited by his son. New York, 1912

Meredith, George. *Vittoria*. New York, 1918

Montague, C. E. *Action and other stories*. New York, 1929

Montague, C. E. *Fiery Particles*. Toronto, 1929

Montague, C. E. *The Right Place*. Toronto, 1924

Moore, A. W. *The Alps in 1864*, edited by A. B. W. Kennedy. Edinburgh, 1902

Moore, Thomas. *The Poetical Works of Thomas Moore*. New York, 1916

Morris, William. *The Collected Works of William Morris*. New York, 1911

Muir, John. *The Mountains of California*. New York, 1911

Muir, John. *The Yosemite*. New York, 1912

Muller, Edwin Jr. *They Climbed the Alps*. New York, 1930

Mumm, A. L. *Five Months in the Himalaya*. New York, 1909

Mummery, A. F. *My Climbs in the Alps and the Caucasus*. New York, 1908

Musgrove, E. R. *The White Hills in Poetry*. New York, 1912

Norman-Neruda, L. *Climbs of Norman-Neruda*. London, 1899

Norton, E. F. and others. *The Fight for Everest: 1924*. New York, 1925

Noel, J. B. L. *The Story of Everest*. Boston, 1927

Outram, James. *In the Heart of the Canadian Rockies*. New York, 1905

Palmer, Howard. *Mountaineering and Exploration in the Selkirks*. New York, 1914

Pascoe, J. D. *Unclimbed New Zealand*. London, 1939

Peacocke, T. A. H.,*Mountaineering*. London, 1941

Peck, A. S. *High Mountain Climbing in Peru and Bolivia*. London, 1912

Pilley, Dorothy. *Climbing Days*. New York, 1935

Powys, Dlewelyn. *Skin for Skin*. New York, 1925

Pye, David. *George Leigh Mallory*. London, 1927

Radcliffe, Mrs. Ann. *The Mysteries of Udolpho*. New York, 1931

Radcliffe, Mrs. Ann. *The Novels of Mrs. Ann Radcliffe*. London, 1824

Rexroth, Kenneth. *The Phoenix and the Tortoise*. Norfolk, CT, 1944

Richardson, Samuel. *The History of Sir Charles Grandison*. London, 1824

Robbins, L. H. *Mountains and Men*. New York, 1931

Rogers, Samuel. *The Complete Poetical Works of Samuel Rogers*. Boston, 1854

Rossetti, D. G. *Poems and Translations by Dante Gabriel Rossetti*. London, 1909

Ruskin, John. *Modern Painters*, Vol. IV. London, 1901

Ruskin, John. *Praeterita*. New York, 1887

Ruskin, John. *Sesame and Lilies*. New York, 1887

Ruttledge, Hugh. *Attack on Everest*. New York, 1935

Ruttledge, Hugh. *Everest, 1933*. London, 1934

Ruttledge, Hugh. *Everest: the Unfinished Adventure*. London, 1937

Schuster, Sir Claud. *Men, Women and Mountains*. London, 1931

Schuster, Sir Claud. *Peaks and Pleasant Pastures*. Oxford, 1911

Scott, Walter. *Count Robert of Paris*. New York, 1894

Scott, Sir Walter. *Works*. Boston, 1912

Shairp, J. C. *Glen Desseray and Other Poems*. London, 1888

Shakespeare, William. *Complete Works of Shakespeare*, edited by G. L. Kittredge. New York, 1936

Shelley, P. B. *The Lyrics and Minor Poems of Percy Bysshe Shelley*, edited by J. Skipsey. New York, 1912

Shelley, P. B. *The Poetical Works of Percy Bysshe Shelley*. London, 1882

Shipton, E. E. *Blank on the Map*. London, 1938

Shipton, E. E. *Nanda Devi*. London, 1936

Shipton, E. E. *Upon That Mountain*. London, 1945

Slingsby, W. C., *Norway the Northern Playground*. Edinburgh, 1904

Smith, Albert. *Mont Blanc*. London, 1860

Smith, Alexander. *A Summer in Skye*. New York, 1866

Smith, Janet Adams. *Mountain Holidays*. London, 1946

Smythe, Frank. *The Adventures of a Mountaineer*. London, 1940

Smythe, F. S. *An Alpine Journey*. London, 1934

Smythe, F. S. *Camp Six*. London, 1937

Smythe, F. S. *Edward Whymper*. London, 1940

Smythe, F. S. *Kamet Conquered*. London, 1932

Smythe, F. S. *The Kangchenjunga Adventure*. London, 1930

Smythe, F. S. *The Mountain Vision*. London, 1942

Smythe, F. S. *Mountaineering Holiday*. London, 1940

Smythe, F. S. *Over Tyrolese Hills*. London, 1936

Smythe, F. S. *The Spirit of the Hills*. London, 1935

Somervell, T. H.. *After Everest*. London, 1936

Spender, Harold. *In Praise of Switzerland*. London, 1912

Spencer, Sydney, and others. *Mountaineering*. Philadelphia, 1934

Stead, Richard. *Adventures on the High Mountains*. Philadelphia, 1908

Stephen, Leslie. *The Playground of Europe*. London, 1894

Stevenson, R. L. *Essays of Travel*. New York, 1894

Stuck, Hudson. *The Ascent of Denali*. New York, 1914

Stutfield, H. E., and Collie, J. N. *Climbs and Explorations in the Canadian Rockies.*
    New York, 1903

Symonds, J. A. *Our Life in the Swiss Highlands*. London, 1892

Symonds, J. A. *Sketches and Studies in Italy and Greece*. London, 1874

Symonds, J. A. *Sketches and Studies in Southern Europe*. New York, 1880

Synge, P. M. *Mountains of the Moon*. London, 1937

Tennyson, Alfred. *Works of Alfred Tennyson*. London, 1891

Thomson, James. *The Poetical Works of James Thomson*. Boston, 1863

Thoreau, H. D. *The Maine Woods*. Boston, 1864

Thorington, J. Monroe. *The Glittering Mountains of Canada*. Philadelphia, 1925

Thorington, J. Monroe, editor and part author. *Where the Clouds Can Go*. New
    York, 1935

Tilman, H. W. *The Ascent of Nanda Devi*. New York, 1937

Tilman, H. W. *Snow on the Equator*. London, 1937

Tilman, H. W. *When Men and Mountains Meet*. Cambridge (England), 1946

Tomlinson, H. M. *Tidemarks*. London, 1924

Tuckett, F. F. *A Pioneer in the High Alps*, edited by W. A. B. Coolidge. London,
    1920

Turner, Samuel. *The Conquest of the New Zealand Alps*. London, 1922

Tyler, J. E. *The Alpine Passes*. Oxford, 1930

Tyndall, John. *Hours of Exercise in the Alps*. New York, 1873

Tyndall, John. *Mountaineering in 1861*. London, 1862

Tyndall, John. *The Glaciers of the Alps.* New York, 1896

Ullman, J. R. *High Conquest.* New York, 1941

Ullman, J. R. *The White Tower.* New York, 1945

Waller, James. *The Everlasting Hills.* London, 1939

Walpole, Horace. *A Selection of the Letters of Horace Walpole,* edited by W. S. Lewis. New York, 1926

Watts-Dunton, Theodore. *The Coming of Love and Other Poems.* New York, 1898

Weston, Walter. *Mountaineering and Exploration in the Japanese Alps.* London, 1896

Weygandt, Cornelius. *The White Hills.* New York, 1934

Whiteside, M. B. *The Eternal Quest and Other Poems.* London, 1925

Whittier, J. G. *Poetical Works of John Greenleaf Whittier.* Boston, 1895

Whymper, Edward. *Scrambles Amongst the Alps in the Years 1860-69.* London, 1893

Whymper, Edward. *Travels Amongst the Great Andes of the Equator.* New York, 1892

Wilcox, W. D. *The Rockies of Canada.* New York, 1900

Wills, Alfred. *'The Eagle's Nest' in the Valley of Sixt.* London, 1860

———. *Wanderings Among the High Alps. London, 1858*

Wordsworth, William. *Poetical Works of William Wordsworth.* London, 1860

Workman, Mrs. F. B. and W. H. *The Call of the Snowy Hispar.* London, 1910

Workman, Mrs. F. B., and W. H. *Ice-Bound Heights of the Mustagh.* New York, 1908

Workman, Mrs. F. B. and W. H. *In the Ice World of Himalaya.* London, 1900

Workman, Mrs. F. B. and W. H. *Peaks and Glaciers of Nun Kun.* New York, 1909

Workman, Mrs. F. B. and W. H. *Two Summers in the Ice-Wilds of Eastern KaraKoram.* New York, 1917

Young, G. W. *April and Rain.* London, 1923

Young, G. W. *Collected Poems of Geoffrey Winthrop Young.* London, 1936

Young, G. W. *Freedom.* London, 1914

Young, G. W. *Mountain Craft.* London, 1920

Young, G. W. *On High Hills.* New York, 1926

Young, G. W. *Wind and Hill: Poems.* London, 1909

Younghusband, F. E. *The Epic of Mount Everest.* New York, 1926

Younghusband, F. E. *Everest: The Challenge.* New York, 1936

Younghusband, Francis. *The Heart of a Continent.* London, 1937

PERIODICALS

Various issues of the following publications:

Alpine Journal: the journal of the Alpine Club (London)

American Alpine Journal: the journal of the American Alpine Club

Appalachia: the journal of the Appalachian Mountain Club

Canadian Alpine Journal: the journal of the Canadian Alpine Club

Scottish Mountaineering Club Journal: the journal of the Scottish Mountaineering Club

Sierra Club Bulletin: the journal of the Sierra Club (San Francisco)

Index

"Above and Below" (Lowell), 121
Above the Snow Line (Dent), 129-130
Abraham, George D., 159
accidents, 43-47, 45p
Aconcagua, 146-147
Aconcagua and Tierra del Fuego (Conway), 146-147
"Across the Pennine" (Montague), 160
"Action" (Montague), 161
Adams, Henry, 126-127
Adventures of Harry Richmond (Meredith), 100-101
Aeggishhorn, 52
Africa, 133, 148, 194
Agassiz,, 30, 96
Aiguille d'Argentiere, 11, 96, 114, 115
Aiguille de Dru, 130, 131
Aiguille du Plan, 183-184
Aiguille Verte, 59
Alaska, ix, 148, 162, 166, 184, 185
Aldrich, Thomas Bailey, 121
Aletschorn, 49
All the Year Round (magazine), 94
"Along and English Road" (Montague), 160
Alpine By-ways, by a Lady (Freshfield), 132
Alpine Club, 13, 31, 37, 39-40, 42, 85, 86, 87, 91, 94, 96, 97, 104, 114, 115, 126, 129, 133, 171, 172
Alpine Club of Canada, 138
Alpine Journal, xiv, 37, 38, 40, 41-48, 51, 68, 104, 126, 128, 129, 131, 133, 134, 157, 168, 172, 174, 175, 186
"An Alpine Picture" (Aldrich), 121
Alpine Regions of Switzerland and the Neighboring Countries (Bonney), 66-67
"The Alpine Wreath" (Symonds), 105
Alps, 9, 23-78, 148. See also Mont Blanc
Alps (Conway), 146, 147
Alps (Irving), 186
Alps and Sanctuaries (Butler), 103
Alps from End to End (Conway), 142-144, 143p
Alps in 1864 (Moore), 48-49, 60
Alps in Nature and History (Coolidge), 128-129
"The Alps in Winter" (Stephen), 77
"The Ambitious Guest" (Hawthorne), 121
American Alpine Club, xi, 163p
American Alpine Journal, 42, 185
Amery, L.S., 186
"Among the Hills" (Whittier), 120
Andermatten, Franz, 57p
Andes, 104, 142
Annals of Mont Blanc (Mathews), 66
Apennine, 134
Apennine (Byron), 18
Appalachia (AMC journal), 42
Appalachian Mountain Club, 42
Approach to the Hills (Meade), 186
April and Rain (Young), 167-168
Arnold, Matthew, 87-88
Ascent of Chomolhari (Chapman), 185
Ascent of Denali (Stuck), 162, 166
Ascent of F-6 (Auden and Isherwood), 118
Assault on Mount Everest (Bruce), 173

Assault on Mount Everest: 1922
  (Mallory), 174
Astor, John Jacob, 119
"Atlanta in Calydon" (Swinburne), 89
Attack on Everest (Ruttledge), 173
Auden, W.H., 118
Auldjo, John, 25-28, 26p, 27p, 32, 35,
  37, 71, 77
Austin, Alfred, 90
Autobiography (Hunt), 99-100
avalanche, 43-47, 93, 105, 154, 172,
  179, 183

"Balder" (Dobell), 89
Ball, John, 40, 60, 67
Balmat, Jacques, 24, 37
Balmat, Michal, 78p
Baltoro Glacier, 146
Bates, Ralph, 117
"Bather's Pool" (Clough), 87
"The Baths of Santa Catarina"
  (Stephen), 74
Beauchamp's Career (Meredith), 101-
  102
Beaufoy, Mark, 24-25
Beckford, William, 11
Bel Alp, 96
Bell, Gertrude, 157-158
Belloc, Hilaire, xiv, 100, 116-117, 192,
  194
Below the Snow Line (Freshfield), 136
"Ben Grieg" (Stuart), 83-84
Ben Nevis, 18
Bennen, Johann Joseph, 45p, 47, 50p,
  53
Benson, A.C., 173
Biafo Glacier, 145p
Bible, 2-3
Bietschhorn, 157
Blaikie, Thomas, 11
Blaitiere, 99
Blank on the Map (Shipton), 184-185

"Bodensee" (Symonds), 105
Bolchuo Col, 190p
Bonney, T.M., 66-67, 77
Borrow, George, 94-95
Bourdillon, Francis, 139-141, 193
Brenner Pass, 11
Brenva face, 179
Brenva Ridge, 49, 114
"The Bridal of Pennacook" (Whittier),
  120
British Isles, 160-161
Brocken, 87
Browne, Belmore, 162-166, 165p
Browne, T.L.M., 130
Browne, Thomas, 9
Browning, Elizabeth Barrett, 87
Browning, Robert, 86-87
Bruce, C.G., 173
Brun, Frederica, 16
Bryant, William Cullen, 121
Bryce, James, 104
Buchan, John, xiv, 72, 115-116, 118,
  194
Buchanan, Robert, 89
Buet, 96
Building of the Alps (Bonney), 66
Burdsall, R.L., 185
Bury, Howard, 172
Butler, A.G., 91, 92
Butler, Samuel, 103-104
"Bye-Day in the Alps" (Stephen), 74, 77
Byrd, Admiral, ix
Byron, G.G., 13, 17-18, 75, 79, 192

California, 126-127
The Call of the Snowy Hispar
  (Workman), 137
Camp Six (Smythe), 183
Canadian Alpine Journal, 42
Canadian Rockies, 133, 139, 148, 152,
  153p

The Canadian Rockies, New and Old Trails (Coleman), 138-139
Carlyle, Thomas, 81-82
Carrel, Jean-Antoine, 56, 59
Catskill Mountains, 119
Caucasus, 49, 128, 133, 134-136, 135p, 148, 155
Chamonix, 11, 23, 24, 33, 35, 87, 92, 96, 98, 123, 183-184
Channing, William Ellery, 119
Chapman, F. Spencer, 185
Charles VIII, King of France, 5
Charmoz, 174
"Cheyenne Mountain" (Jackson), 121
Childe Harold (Byron), 18
Churchyard, Thomas, 1, 9
Climbing and Exploration in the Bolivian Andes (Conway), 146
Climbing and Exploration in the Karakoram Himalaya (Conway), 145p, 146, 146p
Climbing Days (Pilley), 185
Climbing on the Himalaya and Other Mountain Ranges (Collie), 148, 152
Climbs and Explorations in the Canadian Rockies (Collie), 152
Climbs in the New Zealand Alps (Fitzgerald), 158-159
Clough, Arthur Hugh, 85, 87
Col de Collon, 30
Col de la Faucille, 96
Col d'Herens, 30
Col du Lion, 156
Coleman, Arthur, 138-139
Coleridge, Samuel Taylor, 13, 16-17, 79, 192
Collie, Norman, 148, 152-154
Collins, Wilkie, 93
Complete Mountaineer (Abraham), 159
The Conquest of Granada (Irving), 119
The Conquest of Mount McKinley (Browne), 162-166, 165p

The Conquest of the New Zealand Alps (Turner), 158-159
Conrad, Joseph, 114
Conway, William Martin, 125, 130, 142-148, 168, 193
Cook, Frederick, 162, 163
Cooke, H.E., 93
Coolidge, W.A.B., 128, 129
Coolins, 116, 152
"Coriskin" (Scott), 82
Corries, 152
Courmayeur, 114
Couttet, Joseph, 78p
Cowper, William, 13
"The Cragsman" (Young), 167
"The Crocus and the Soldanella" (Symonds), 105
Croz, Jean, 57
Croz, Michael, 60, 61p
Crudities (Coryat), 9
Cuchullins, 102

D'Angeville, Henriette, 28-29, 29p
Da Vinci, Leonardo, 5
The Dauber (Masefield), 118
Davies, J.L., 66
Davos, 107
"Davos Revisited" (Symonds), 105
Days of Fresh Air (Amery), 186
De Alpibus Commentarius (Simler), 7
De Bremble, John, 3-5
De Filippi, Filippo, 148-151, 149p, 150p, 151p
De La Mare, Walter, 118
De Quincey, Thomas, 87
De Saussure, Horace Benedict, 23-24, 29, 31, 49, 136, 192
De Vere, Aubrey, 84
death, 175, 179-180
Delphi, 3
Dent Blanche, 47-48, 52, 170
Dent d'Herens, 49, 181p

Dent du Chat, 84
Dent du Requin, 152, 155
Dent, Clinton, 128, 129-130
Derwentwater, 95
Descriptive Sketches (Wordsworth), 15
Di Savoia, Luigi Amedeo, 148-151,
    149p, 150p, 151p
Dickens, Charles, 92-93, 94, 95
Dinaric Alps, 137
Dobell, Sydney, 89
Dolomites, 84, 157
Dom, 52
Dombey and Son (Dickens), 92
Dompjulian de Beaupre, 5
Doughty, C.M., 117
Douglas, Francis, 57, 61, 62
Douglas, Norman, 117
Doyle, Arthur Conan, 113-114
dragons, xii, 5
Dru, 130
Dunn, Robert, 162
Dutch East Indies, 111
Dych Tau, 155

'*The Eagle's Nest*' in the Valley of Sixt
    (Wills), 37
The Early Mountaineers (Gribble), xii,
    8p
earthquake, 165-166
Les Ecrins, 170
Egoist (Meredith), 100
Eigar, 68, 179
Eigerjoch, 71
Elbruz, 49, 128, 133
Eliot, George, 89
Eliot, T.S., 118
Elliot, Ebenezer, 83
Emerson, Ralph Waldo, 119
Empedocles, 3
"Enceladus" (Longfellow), 119
Engel, Claire, 185
England, 159-160, 161

"The Englishman in Italy" (Browning,
    R.), 86-87
"Enthralled" (Thaxter), 119
Epic of Mount Everest (Younghusband),
    173
Erewhon (Butler), 103-104
Essays of Travel (Stevenson), 107-109
Evelyn, John, 9
Everest, 1933 (Ruttledge), 173
Everest, the Challenge (Younghusband),
    173, 182
Everest, the Unfinished Adventure
    (Ruttledge), 173
The Everlasting Hills (Waller), 185
"Excelsior" (Wordsworth), 119
The Excursion (Wordsworth), 14-16, 95
Exotics and Retrospectives (Hearn), 109-
    111
Exploration of the Caucasus
    (Freshfield), 134-136, 135p
Explorer's Club, 163p

Fadiman, Clifton, 192
Farrar, J.P., 157, 168
Fellows, Charles, 25p, 25-26, 77
Fiery Particles (Montague), 161
The Fight for Everest: 1924 (Norton),
    173
Finch, George, 168, 173, 179-182, 181p,
    189
Finsteraarhorn, 107, 158
Finsteraarjoch, 49
Fitzgerald, E.A., 158-159
The Five Red Herrings (Sayers), 117
Forbes, James D., 29-31, 40, 77, 96, 192
Fors Clavigera (Ruskin), 30
Forster, John, 92, 181p
43rd Division (Bates), 117
The Four Feathers (Mason), 114
France, 4, 6, 172
"Franconia from Pemigewasset"
    (Whittier), 120

Freedom (Young), 167
Freshfield Col, 151p
Freshfield, Douglas, 49, 73, 125, 129, 130, 132-137, 193
Freshfield, Mrs. Henry, 132
Friar's Crag, 95
From Sea to Sea (Kipling), 113
Frosty Caucasus (Grove), 128
Fujiyama, 109-111, 112, 193
Funffingerspitze, 157
Furka Pass, 114, 120

Garwhal, 112, 184
Gauli Glacier, 51
Gayle, Newton, 117
Geant icefall, 168
Geographical Journal, 134
George, H.B., 41-42, 67
Gesner, Conrad, 6-9, 8p, 12, 22, 129
Girdlestone, Arthur, 127-128
The Glaciers of the Alps (Tyndall), 51
The Glittering Mountains of Canada (Thorington), 186
Godley, Alfred Denis, 141-142
Goethe, Johann Wolfgang von, 12-13, 21
Golden Throne, 146
Goldsmith, Oliver, 13
Good-bye Mr. Chips (Hilton), 117
Gorner Glacier, 123
Gorner Grat, 124
Gossett, Philip, 43-47, 45p, 192
Gran Sasso, 136
Grand Charmoz, 155, 156
Grand Combin, 52
Grandes Jorasses, 155, 170
Grands Mulets, 37
Gray, Thomas, xiii, 10
Great St. Bernard Pass, 3-5
"The Great Stone Face" (Hawthorne), 121
Greece, 3, 116, 137

Grenoble, 84
Grepon, 155, 167, 171, 182, 191, 194
Gribble, Francis, xii, 8p
Grice, L.O., ix-x
Gross Glockner, 144
Grove, Crauford, 128
Gspaltenhorn, 168

Hadow, Douglas, 57, 60
Hadrian, 3
Hall, W.E., 49
Hardy, J.F., 40
Harrison, Frederic, 132
Haut-de-Cry, 43-47, 45p
Hawthorne, Nathaniel, 121
Hazlitt, William, 103
He Who Ascends to Mountain-Tops (Byron), 17-18
Hearn, Lafcadio, xiv, 109-111, 112, 114, 193
Helvellyn, 18, 82, 96
Helvellyn to Himalaya (Chapman), 185
Hemanns, Mrs., 119
Hewlitt, Maurice, 116
High Alps in Winter (LeBlond), 157
The High Alps without Guides (Girdlestone), 127-128
The Highest Andes (Fitzgerald), 158
Hills and the Sea (Belloc), 117
"The Hill Summit" (Rossetti), 88-89
Hilton, James, 117
Himalayan Journal, 42
Himalayas, 112-113, 114, 133, 137, 142, 148, 172, 185. *See also* Mount Everest
Hinchliff, T.W., 37-39, 40, 60, 65, 123
Hispar Pass, 145p
Hochfeiler, 144
Hogg, Thomas Jefferson, 79-80, 82
Holmes, Oliver Wendell, 119
Homer, 3
Hornli ridge, 57
Horungtinder, 130

Hours of Exercise in the Alps (Tyndall), 51

Houston, Charles, xi

Houston, Nellie, xi

Houston, Oscar, xi

Howells, William Dean, 126

Hudson, Charles, 24, 31, 33, 35, 56, 57, 60, 175

Hunt, Leigh, 99-100, 192, 194

Huxley, Julian, 187

Hymn Before Sunrise in the Vale of Chamouni (Coleridge), 16-17

Hyperion (Longfellow), 120

Ice Ages, Recent and Ancient (Coleman), 138

Ice-Bound Heights of the Mustagh (Workman), 190p

Iceland, 104

"In Hanging Garden Gully" (Montague), 161

In Praise of Switzerland (Spender), 159

"In the Alps" (Rogers), 82

"In the Heart of Things" (Browning, R.), 87

In the Ice-World of Himalaya (Workman), 137

Interlaken, 35

Irvine, Sandy, 173-179

Irving, R.L.G., 159, 186, 193

Irving, Washington, 119

Isherwood, Christopher, 118

"I Stood at Sunrise on an Alpine Height" (Symonds), 105

Italian Alps (Freshfield), 133, 134

Jackson, Helen Hunt, 121

Japan, 109-111, 133

Jones, Owen Glynne, 148, 158, 159

Josias Simler et les origines de l'Alpinisme (Coolidge), 128-129

Jotunheim, 130

Journal of a Tour on the Continent (Wordsworth, D.), 16

Jungfrau, 52

Jungfraujoch, 71-72

K2, 146, 150p

Kamet, 183

Kamet Conquered (Smythe), 183

Kandersteg, 35

Kangchenjunga, 133, 148, 183

Kangchenjunga Adventure (Smythe), 183

Karakoram, 148

Karbir (Gurkha porter), 172

Kasbek, 133

Keats, John, 18

Kennedy, E.S., 24, 31, 33, 35, 39, 40, 60

Kennedy, Thomas, 47-48

Kim (Kipling), 112-113

King, Clarence, 121, 126-127, 162, 193

King, Starr, 121

Kingsley, Charles, 90

Kipling, Rudyard, 111, 112-113, 114

Kjaendalsbrae Icefall, 131

"Knight Errantry" (Young), 167

Knowlton, Elizabeth, 185

"Ktaadn" (Thoreau), 121-122

Ladies' Alpine Club, 157

"Lady of the Lake" (Scott), 82

Lake Louise, 139

Lamb, Charles, 80-81, 100, 192

landslides, 144

Larcom, Lucy, 119

Lauener, Ulrich, 57p

Lauterbrunnen, 35

"Lauterbrunnen" (Rogers), 82

Lavengro (Borrow), 94

Lavoy, Merl, 164

"The Lay of the Last Minstrel" (Scott), 82

LeBlond, Mrs. Aubrey, 157-158, 185

Letters of Gertrude Bell (Bell), 185
"The Lonely Peak" (Young), 167
Longfellow, Henry Wadsworth, 119-120
Longstaff, Thomas, 171-172
"Looking Forward" (Young), 167
"Lord of the Isles" (Scott), 82
Lost Horizon (Hilton), 117
"The Lotus-Eaters" (Tennyson), 84-85
Lowell, James Russell, 121
Lunn, Arnold, 159, 168, 187-189, 194
Lunn, Peter, 191-192

Maguignaz, J.J., 57p
The Maine Woods (Thoreau), 121-122
The Making of a Mountaineer (Finch), 179-182, 181p
Mallory, George, 170, 173-179
Mandeville, John, 9
Manfred (Byron), 17-18
Marti, Benoit, 1-2, 22, 128, 193
Masefield, John, 118
Mason, A.E.W., xiv, 114-115, 118
Masque of Pandora (Longfellow), 119-120
Mathews, William, 39, 40, 65, 66
Matterhorn, 42, 49, 51, 53-65, 90-91, 94, 97, 99, 155, 164, 170, 192
Meade, C.F., 186
Memories of Travel (Bryce), 104
Men Against the Clouds (Burdsall and Emmons), 185
Men, Women and Mountains (Schuster), 186
Mer de Glace, 11, 93, 171
Meredith, George, xiv, 100-102, 104, 114, 192, 194, 195
"Midnight on Helm Crag" (North), 84
Mischabelhorner, 106
Modern Painters (Ruskin), 96, 98
"Monadnock from Afar" (Emerson), 119

"Monadnock from Wachusett" (Whittier), 120
Mont Aiguille, 5
Mont Blanc, 12-13, 15, 16-17, 18, 19-20, 23-78, 83, 92, 120, 179, 191
Mt. Blanc Sideshow (Thorington), 186
Mont Cenis Pass, 10-11
Mont Cervin, 107
Mont Inaccessible, 5
Mont Ventoux, 4
Montague, C.E., xiv, 125, 159-161, 175, 179
Monte Generoso, 105, 106
Monte Rosa, 5, 84, 86, 106, 134, 144
Monte Viso, 107
"The Moore of Rannoch" (Schairp), 84
Moore, A.W., 48-49, 60, 128
Moore, John, 11
Moore, Thomas, 82-83, 84
Morgenhorn, 168
The Morning's War (Montague), 160-161
Morris, William, 89
"Mount Agiochook" (Whittier), 120
Mount Ararat, 104
Mount Carmel, 2
Mount Chimborazo, 63
Mount Cotocachi, 64p
Mount Crillon, 76-77
Mount Etna, 3
Mount Everest, 5, 128, 172-174, 176p, 177p, 178p, 179, 182, 192
Mount Everest, the Reconnaissance (Howard-Bury), 172, 174
Mount George, 39
Mount Haemus, 3
Mount Jaman, 88
Mount Katahdin, 121-122
Mount McKinley, 162-166
Mount Monadnock, 119, 120
Mount Moriah, 2
Mount Olympus, 3

Mount Parnassus, 3, 137
Mount Pilatus, 6
Mount Robson, 139
Mount Sefton, 158-159
Mount Shasta, 127
Mount Sinai, 2
Mount Sir Donald, 153p
Mount St. Elias, 148
Mount Temple, 139
Mount Tidore, 111
Mount Tyndall, 127
Mount Whitney, 127, 193
Mountain Adventures (Abraham), 159
Mountain Craft (Young), 168
"The Mountain Gloom" (Ruskin), 98-99
"The Mountain Glory" (Ruskin), 96-97, 99
Mountain Holiday (Smith), 185
Mountain Jubilee (Lunn), 188, 194
"The Mountain Language" (De Vere), 84
Mountain Meadow (Buchan), 115
Mountain Memories (Conway), 146, 147
The Mountain Way (Irving), 186
"Mountaineer and Poet" (Browning, E.), 87
Mountaineering Holiday (Smythe), 183
Mountaineering in the Sierra Nevada (King), 126-127, 162
"The Mountains" (Taylor), 121
The Mountains of California (Muir), 122
Mountains of the Moon, 148
The Mountains of Youth (Lunn), 187
Mr. Standfast (Buchan), 115-116
Muir, John, 122-123
Mummery, A.F., 125, 131, 148, 152, 154-157, 158, 175, 192, 193, 195
My Climbing Adventures in Four Continents (Turner), 158

My First Summer in the Sierra (Muir), 122
My Home in the Alps (LeBlond), 157
The Mysteries of Udolpho (Radcliffe), 11-12

The Naked Mountain (Knowlton), 185
Nanda Devi, 184, 185
Nanda Devi (Shipton), 184
Nanga Parbat, 152, 154, 155, 185
"Natura Benigna" (Watts-Dutton), 89, 90
"Natura Maligna" (Watts-Dutton), 89-90
"Nearing the Snow-Line" (Holmes), 119
Nepal, 148
New Hampshire, 119, 120, 121
"New Year's Eve in the Alps" (Watts-Dutton), 89
New Zealand, 103-104, 158-159
Niesen, 1, 128
"Night Upon the Schwartzhorn" (Symonds), 105
No Thoroughfare (Dickens and Collins), 93
Noel, J.B.L., 173, 182
Norman-Neruda, L., 157, 175
North, Christopher, 84
Norton, E.F., 173, 179, 182
Norway, 130, 131, 148
Norway the Northern Playground (Slingsby), 130

"Obermann" (Arnold), 88
"Obermann Once More" (Arnold), 88
Odell, N.E., 173, 179, 182
"Oenone" (Tennyson), 85
Oldenhorn, 29
On Alpine Heights and British Crags (Abraham), 159
On High Hills (Young), 167, 168-170

"On the Mountain" (Young), 167
Ormsby, J., 40-41
Our Life in the Swiss Highland (Symonds), 105-106
Over Tyrolese Hills (Smythe), 183
Oxford Mountaineering Essays (Lunn), 187

Paccard, Doctor, 24
"Palinodia" (Kingsley), 90
Pantagruel (Rabelais), 5
Pascoe, John, 103
"The Pass of Ampezzo" (Jackson), 121
Passage of Fenetre de Saleinaz (Wills), 37
The Path to Rome (Belloc), 117
Peacock, Thomas Love, 19, 79, 117
Peaks and Pleasant Pastures (Schuster), 186
Peaks, Passes and Glaciers (Kennedy, ed.), xiv, 37, 38, 40, 53, 66
Pendlebury brothers, 67
Perrn, Peter, 57p
A Personal Record (Conrad), 114
Peter III, King of Aragon, 5
Petrarch, 5, 6
Philip of Macedon, 3
Pic Canigou, 5
Pic du Midi, 84
Pic Tyndall, 49
Pictures from Italy (Dickens), 93
Pilley, Dorothy, 185
Pioneer Peak, 146p
Playground of Europe (Stephen), 70-77, 169
Pointe de Colloney, 136-137
Ponte des Ecrins, 59
Pontius Pilate, 6-7
Pontresina, 84
Powys, Llewelyn, 192
Praeterita (Ruskin), 95-96
The Prelude (Wordsworth), 15

Pre-Raphaelites, 88-89
Prince Lucifer (Austin), 90
"The Princess" (Tennyson), 85
Prometheus Unbound (Shelley), 19-22
Pseudodoxia Epidemica (Browne), 9
Pyrennes, 5
The Pyrenees (Belloc), 117

Rabelais, Francois, 5
Radcliffe, Ann, 11-12
Rakaia Mountains, 103-104
Rakaia River, 103
Ramsay, A.C., 66
Reichenbach Falls, 113
Reliquiae by A.D. Godley (Godley), 141
Requin, 154
Rexroth, Kenneth, 121
"Rhymes on the Road" (Moore), 83
Richards, Mrs. I.A., 185
Richardson, Samuel, 11
Riffelberg, 123
Right off the Map (Montague), 160
Roberts, Michael, 187
Roberts, Mrs. Michael, 185
Robertson, David, 174
Roche Melon, 68
Rock-Climbing in the English Lake District (Jones), 159
Rockies of Canada (Wilcox), 139
Rocky Mountains, 119, 122
The Rocky Mountains or the Adventures of Captain Bonneville (Irving), 119
Rogers, Samuel, 82, 84
The Romance of Mountaineering (Irving), 186
The Romance of the Forest (Radcliffe), 11-12
A Romance of Wastdale (Mason), 114
The Romany Rye (Borrow), 94
Rossetti, Dante Gabriel, 88-89
Round Kangchenjunga (Freshfield), 136
Rousseau, Jean-Jacques, 12, 13, 24

Royal Society, 7, 9

"Rugby Chapel" (Arnold), 87-88

Running Water (Mason), 114-115

Ruskin, John, xiv, 30, 73, 85, 95-99, 100, 117, 142, 192, 193

Ruttledge, Hugh, 173

Ruwenzori, 148

Saas-Fee, 35

St. Bernard, 80

St. Elias Mountains, ix

St. Gotthard, 80, 120

Saleinaz, 47

"Sanct Margen" (Eliot), 89

Savoia Glacier, 150p

Savoia Peak, 151p

Sayers, Dorothy, 117

Scafell, 96

Scheuchzer, Johann Jacob, 7

"Schihallion" (Shairp), 84

Schlag-Lawine, 105

Schreckhorn, 72, 82

Schuster, Claud, 186

Schwaub, Henry B., 163p

Scotland, 11, 18, 82

Scott, Walter, 13, 75, 82, 102, 116

Scottish-Mountaineering Club Journal, 72

Scrambles Amongst the Alps (Whymper), 53-65, 55p, 57p, 61p, 64p

Selkirk Range, 153p

Sella, Vittorio, 148-151, 149p, 150p, 151p

Senecio Forest, 151p

Sesame and Lilies (Ruskin), 97-98

Shairp, John Campbell, 84

Shakespeare, William, 9

Shameless Diary of an Explorer (Dunn), 162

Shelley, Percy B., 14, 18-22, 75, 79, 80, 82, 100, 117, 191, 192, 193, 195

Shipton, Eric, 173, 182, 183, 184-185, 191, 192, 195

Sierra Club Bulletin, 42

Sierras, 121, 122-123, 126-127

"Sigurd the Volsung" (Morris), 89

Sikkim, 148

Simler, Josias, 7

Simletind, 130

Simplon Pass, 9, 14, 80, 93, 96

Sinister Crag (Gayle), 117

Siple, Paul, ix-xi

Sir Charles Grandison (Richardson), 11

"Six Months Wandering in the Himalaya" (Longstaff), 172

Skagastolstind, 130, 131

Sketches and Studies in Italy and Greece (Symonds), 105, 106-107

Skiddaw, 18, 80-81

Slingsby, William Cecil, 128, 130-131, 152

Smith, Albert Richard, 31-35 32p, 34p, 37, 49, 71, 98

Smith, Alexander, 102-103

Smith, Janet Adam, 185

Smuts, General, 194

Smythe, Frank S., 173, 179, 182-184, 183p

Snowdon, 14, 94-95, 119

Snowdon at Christmas 1878 (Willink), 131-132

Somervell, T. Howard, 173, 176p, 177p, 178p, 179, 182

South Africa, 133, 194

South America, 63, 104, 146-147

South America (Bryce), 104

Spender, Harold, 159

The Spirit of the Hills (Smythe), 183

Spitsbergen, 142

Staub-Lawine, 105

Stedtind, 130

Stephen, Leslie, xiii, xiv, 31, 40, 43, 67-77, 82, 94, 98, 99, 100, 104, 125, 126,

139, 169, 182, 193, 194
Stevenson, Robert Louis, xiv, 107-109, 111, 192
Stockhorn, 30
Story of an Alpine Winter (LeBlond), 157-158
Story of Everest (Noel), 173, 182
Story of Mont Blanc (Smith), 32-33, 34p
Stuart, John, 83-84
Stuck, Hudson, 166
Stutfield, H.E.M., 152
Styehead Pass, 170
"Summer by the Lakeside" (Whittier), 120
Summer Months (Hinchliff), 37-38
A Summer Tour in the Grisons (Freshfield), 132
"Sunset on the Bearcamp" (Whittier), 120
Swift, Jonathan, 104
Swinburne, Algernon Charles, 89
Swiss Travel and Swiss Guide-Books (Coolidge), 129
"Switzerland" (Arnold), 88
"Switzerland" (Godley), 141-142
Symonds, John Addington, 104-107, 118, 192

Table Mountain, 187, 194
Taker, John, 103
Tartarin sur les Alpes (Daudet), 123
Taschhorn, 155, 167, 169, 170
Tatra, 104
Taugwalder, Peter, 57, 57p
Taylor, Bayard, 121
Teedon, Samuel, 13
Ten Great Mountains (Irving), 186
Tennyson, Alfred, 84-86, 192
"The Terrace at Berne" (Arnold), 88
Teufelsgrat, 155, 170
Thaxter, Celia, 119

Theodule Pass, 3
Thoreau, Henry David, 118, 121-122
Thorington, J. Monroe, 185-186
Thrale, Mrs., 11
The Three Hostages (Buchan), 115
Tibet, 172
Tidemarks (Tomlinson), 111-112
Tierra del Fuego, 142
Tilman, H.W., 173, 182, 184, 185
Titlis, 87
"To a Pine-Tree on Mt. Katahdin" (Lowell), 121
"To the River Arve" (Bryant), 121
To the Top of the Continent (Cook), 162, 163
Todi, 179
Tomlinson, H.M., 111-112
Tour of Mont Blanc (Forbes), 30-31
Tramontane Club, 39-40
A Tramp Abroad (Twain), 123
Transcaucasia and Ararat (Bryce), 104
Travels Amongst the Great Andes of the Equator (Whymper), 63, 65
Travels in Alaska (Muir), 122
Travels in Switzerland (Goethe), 12-13
Travels in the Central Caucasus and Bashan (Freshfield), 133
Travels Through the Alps of Savoy (Forbes), 29-30
Trelaporte, 30
Trelatete, 144
Trift Glacier, 157
Trift Pass, 38-39, 65
Trisul, 172
"The Trossachs" (Scott), 82
Tuckett, F.F., 40, 56, 67-70
Turkestan, 184
Turner, Samuel, 158-159
Twain, Mark, xiv, 118, 123-124, 194
"The Two Homes" (Taylor), 121
"Two on a Mountain" (Browning, R.), 86

Tyndale, H.E.G., 186, 187
Tyndall, John, xiv, 30, 31, 37, 40, 49-53, 50p, 54, 56, 59, 63, 73, 74, 77, 94, 96, 98, 125, 192

Ukiu, 134, 193
Uledalstind, 130
Unclimbed New Zealand (Pascoe), 103
Unterbachhorn, 170
Upon That Mountain (Shipton), 184-185

Vadianus of St. Gall, 6
Val Anzasca, 84
Valais pyramid, 57
Vallot, Charles, 185
Viereselgrat, 170
Vittoria (Meredith), 101, 102
"The Voice and the Peak" (Tennyson), 85
Von Haller, Albrecht, 23
Voyage dans les Alpes (De Saussure), 24

Wales, 187
Waller, James, 185
Walpole, Horace, xiii, 9-11
Wanderings Among the High Alps (Wills), 35-38
Watts-Dutton, Theodore, 79, 89-90
Wedgwood, Thomas, 17, 191
Weissenstein, 116, 194
Weisshorn, 49, 51, 52, 53, 54, 90, 168
Wengern Alp, 74-75
West, Richard, 10
Western Himalaya, 148
Westmoreland, 82
Wetterhorn, 35, 131, 179, 189
When Men and Mountains Meet (Tilman), 185
Where the Clouds Can Go (Thorington), 186

Where There's Will There's a Way: Ascent of Mont Blanc (Hudson and Kennedy), 33, 35
Whitcombe Pass, 103
White Mountains, 119, 120, 121
Whiteside, Mary Brent, 121
Whittier, John Greenleaf, 118, 120-121
Whymper, Edward. xiv, 31, 40, 53-65, 55p, 71, 77, 94, 125, 164, 183
Wilcox, Walter Dwight, 139
Wild Wales (Borrow), 94
"William Tell" (Bryant), 121
Willink, Henry, 131-132
Wills, Alfred, xiv, 31, 35-38, 47, 60, 65
Win-Hill (Elliot), 83
Wind and Hill: Poems (Young), 167
Windham, William, 11, 23
women mountaineers, 11-12, 28-29, 29p, 157-158, 185
Wordsworth, Dorothy, 16
Wordsworth, William, 3, 13, 14-16, 75, 79, 95
Workman, William Hunter, 137, 138p, 190p

Yellowstone Canyon, 113
Yosemite, 123
The Yosemite (Muir), 122
Young, Geoffrey Winthrop, xiv, 59, 99, 125, 166-171, 183, 187, 191, 193, 194, 195
Younghusband, Francis, 173, 182
Yukon Territory, ix

Zermatt, 35, 56, 57, 87, 123, 155
Zillerthal, 144
Zinal Rothorn, 157, 185
Zmutt Ridge, 155, 170

About the Author

For nearly 70 years, Robert H. Bates has been recognized for his ability as a mountain climber and for his contributions to the sport of mountaineering. He pioneered climbs in Alaska and the Himalayas, and designed and tested cold weather clothing and equipment for the Army during World War II. He made two serious attempts to climb K2, the second of which has become one of the most remarkable stories in the annals of mountaineering. He is a co-author and editor of two books on his K2 climbs and, in 1994, wrote his mountaineering and traveling autobiography, *The Love of Mountains is Best*. He is a past president and honorary life member of the American Alpine Club, has lectured about mountaineering throughout the United States and Europe, and was the first director of the Peace Corps in Nepal. He is graduate of Phillips Exeter Academy, Harvard, and the University of Pennsylvania. For nearly four decades he was an instructor of English at Phillips Exeter Academy, where in 2000 he was honored with the establishment of the Bates-Russell Distinguished Faculty Professorship. He and his wife Gail live in Exeter, New Hampshire.